HAY FESTIVAL
CONVERSATIONS

Hay Festival Conversations

THIRTY CONVERSATIONS
FOR THIRTY YEARS

edited by

Ellah Wakatama Allfrey *&* Mary Chesshyre

with an introduction by
Peter Florence

HAY FESTIVAL PRESS 2017

Published May 2017 by Hay Festival Press
The Drill Hall, 25 Lion Street
Hay HR3 5AD UK
www.hayfestival.org

HAY FESTIVAL
imagine the world

ISBN 978-0-9547168-9-9

Publication of this anthology has been made possible with the
generous support of The Elmley Foundation

Typography & 12/14.4 Arno setting
by Five Seasons Press, Hereford HR1 2QH
Printed and bound by SRP Ltd, Exeter EX2 7LW

The inside of the cover reproduces a handmade marbled paper
by Victoria Hall at hand-decorated-papers.com

Linear B syllabograms (page 144)
courtesy of Curtis Clark
California State Polytechnic University

*Dedicated with thanks
to Norman Florence and Rhoda Lewis
for their vision and inspiration,
and around whose kitchen table
Hay Festival was created thirty years ago.*

*Thanks to all the writers and thinkers
who have contributed to this anthology,
and to conversations across the world
over the past thirty years.*

CONTENTS

INTRODUCTION

Toni Morrison's voice ranges over two or three octaves. She plays with dynamics and pace, she confides and declares, she speaks with a rhetorical magnificence that almost demands a full musical score. The transcription of her conversations isn't a record of the time she spent onstage in Hay; but it does convey a sense of her eloquence, and the way in which this Nobel Prize-winning novelist tells stories and articulates truths that we all recognize. Literature offers that extraordinary gift of being able to see the world from someone else's perspective. This interview allows us the beginnings of an understanding of how creativity works.

Hay Festival was dreamed up around my parents' kitchen table, and it has evolved over the past thirty years as a development of those family discussions about books and how to talk about them. The sessions are based on the premise of deep appreciation of the interviewees and a desire to hear them share insight into their work. The versions in this book have rendered the cadence and originality of conversation, they've caught the spontaneity of phrasing and idiom that characterizes people who play fluently with language, facilitated by chairs who host their guests with grace and subtle skill. The speakers talk to an audience who come to the festival from all over the world. They're young and old, well-read, and fired by curiosity and a willingness to engage with new ideas. They're a great crowd.

Let me give you a physical context: Hay is a market town in the Black Mountains on the eastern reaches of the Brecon Beacons National Park in Wales. It has 1600 people and twenty-four bookshops. The landscape is awesomely beautiful. The River Wye and Offa's Dyke, the border between England and Wales, kiss the town. Our medieval castle was built in one night by a giantess called Moll Walbee. Hay is twinned with Timbuktu, Macondo and Middlemarch.

The Festival started in the garden of the Kilvert pub and now sits on a twenty-acre tented campus at the west end of the town. It's also adventured across the world in Hay Festivals on five continents – from Dhaka in Bangladesh to Arequipa in Peru, from Beirut in Lebanon to Querétaro in Mexico, and from Aarhus in Denmark to Nairobi in Kenya. There are conversations collected here from our festivals in Cartagena de Indias, Colombia and the Alhambra in Spain, and you can find the original audio and video versions of these and thousands more sessions through the Hay Player platform on our website.

Thanks to everyone who made these conversations happen in real time, to the vast coalition of wranglers and dreamers, of stewards and volunteers, of experts and students. Thanks to Mary Chesshyre for her elegant close work on the texts, and to Ellah Wakatama Allfrey for her editorial flair. Thanks most of all, of course, to the Hay speakers who have shared their wisdom and mischief with such generosity and genius.

The writers featured in this collection are free-thinkers, people who imagine the world. The scientists and activists are instrumental in changing it. In an age of promises and reaction, of volatility and certainty, of identity and borders these people offer inquiry, thought and empathy; they tell truths, they embrace plurality and they range across time and space. They are all inspiring, enlightening and often very funny.

Welcome to Hay.

Peter Florence
Festival Director

Tahmima Anam
with George Alagiah
Hay-on-Wye 2016

GEORGE ALAGIAH: For those of us of a certain age, our first acquaintance with Bangladesh was probably way back in 1971. Madison Square Garden: George Harrison and the concert for Bangladesh. At the time, we were invited to feel sorry for this country and its people, and unfortunately, for a lot of us, like a record getting stuck, our perception of Bangladesh got stuck there too. It didn't move on.

Our guest today has changed that. She's put Bangladesh on the map. And we're going to be talking about her new novel, *The Bones of Grace*, the culmination of what has been described as the 'Bengal Trilogy'. Where the first two books were preoccupied with the violent birth of a nation, and the way it was poised between that birth and a complex, problematic future, *The Bones of Grace* brings this trilogy right up to date. It is the story of one of that nation's daughters as she struggles to find meaning in her life.

Tahmima, you've said that, when you first thought about writing this trilogy, you had a vision of an epic tale, a sort of Asian *War and Peace* perhaps. But, when it came down to sitting at the laptop, something different came out. What happened?

TAHMIMA ANAM: I was going to write a novel about a war, and I thought it would have great battle scenes, and it would be this epic, muscular narrative, a grand narrative. In fact, what I ended up being more interested in is how ordinary people survive war and what happens to them, especially women, on an everyday basis. Who gets left behind? So, that first novel is a book about a woman whose children are revolutionaries. Every day she's thinking: Are they ever going to come back to me? I took that theme and I ended up writing with a larger backdrop of historical and political events. I became interested in the small details of everyday life because that is how we live through large historical events: we live them every day.

As you said, this new book – it's a story of one woman, and she is trying to deal with some of her confusions about who she is. The confusion stems from several places: she's an adopted daughter of two revolutionaries who tell her she's adopted when she's nine, and then never speak of it again, and, because she's afraid talking about it will wound them, she really doesn't know 'who she is'. And she also has a complicated relationship to her homeland.

GA: I wasn't aware enough of Bangladesh's history. It was a brutal civil war. Why did you want to write a book specifically about your country's history?

TA: I grew up outside Bangladesh. My dad used to work for the UN, and we moved all over the world. But I grew up on these stories, and I found it all fascinating, something that I wish I had been a part of. Because being part of that war made my parents so sure who they were. Their moral certainties were very clear: this is where we come from; this is where we belong. Yet they were carting me all over the world, and I didn't 'belong' in the way they did. Writing these books was a way for me to own a piece of that history on my own terms.

GA: Your central character is Zubaida. It struck me, reading *The Bones of Grace*, that this is someone in a psychological no man's land, a geographical no man's land. I wonder if you could talk a little about being caught between those two places?

TA: Zubaida calls herself an 'in-between species' because she feels she is kind of neither here nor there, and that is partly because she doesn't know who her parents are. But it's also because she feels different loyalties to different places, and that confusion and ambivalence is captured in whom to love – her childhood sweetheart, whom she's fated to be with – his name is Rashid – or this other man that she meets. They have an instant connection, but she can't really believe in that connection because he's a stranger, and he makes her feel that, if she gives up the person that she's been fated to be with, she will lose all the other connections, the ones to her family and home.

GA: So here's a woman caught between these two loves. There are also a lot of other people caught between two places. And there's also a whale. Now you're going to have to explain this . . . there's a whale, called Diana.

TA: The thing about being a writer is you can take all the quirky things that are interesting to you and put them in books, and, if you try hard enough, you can weave them in to make it as though they were meant to be there. So I became fascinated with this story of a whale. As a species, whales actually evolved from land mammals that looked a little bit like dogs, and then slowly, over time, about fifty million years ago, they went into the sea. There's an in-between species called the *ambulocetus* – 'the walking whale' – that both walked and swam. So, although they were mammals, they behaved like amphibians. Zubaida is obsessed with this whale. She's a palaeontologist, and throughout the novel she is looking for the bones of the whale, and trying and failing to find them. It's a metaphor for her looking to find herself

– in the fossils of a creature that walked and swam at the same time.

It's also a way for her not to answer the question she really wants to ask, which is: Who am I? So, instead of trying to find her own origins, she's trying to find the origins of the whale, and it's a kind of displacement for her. It's really not until she goes on that journey to discover her own origins that she can own who she is as a person, with all of her dualities.

She goes home, and there's this great homecoming. Everyone's been waiting for her, including the sweetheart whom she's supposed to marry. She does end up marrying him, but she feels like a fish out of water; it's as if she had never really felt at home there after all. I think she is symbolic of a lot of us – it's so rare now for people to be born, and live, and die, in one place. We have loyalties to all these other places, whether it's because of travel or love or relationships. Zubaida leaves her heart behind in the places where she goes to study, or to be with her beloved, so she ends up not fitting in when she comes back, and she's deeply disturbed by that.

GA: I was interested in that, because it's similar in both our histories. I certainly felt when I went back to Sri Lanka – in my case after twenty years – that there was a kind of umbilical connection. But you're saying for Zubaida it doesn't exist.

TA: It's not that it doesn't exist. I think she says in the book that she feels a connection, but it's in particular experiences: she loves the smell of paperbacks in the monsoon, and the whirring of the ceiling fan, and her grandmother's parathas. She does feel that umbilical connection, but not that deep sense of belonging that her parents feel.

I think it also has a little bit to do with class. The people who adopt her are very privileged, but she knows she must have been adopted from a very poor family. And she looks around – she's driving in her air-conditioned car through the city – she looks around the streets, and she thinks: Any of these people could have been my mother. She sees herself in the faces of others.

GA: Zubaida's parents are freedom fighters, revolutionaries; they helped to create Bangladesh out of East Pakistan. You called the first book in the trilogy, that covers that period of conflict, *A Golden Age*. But it was a brutal war. Millions of people were killed.

TA: I called it that because I grew up listening to the stories about war, and, when I decided to write the novel, I talked to lots of people about what they had done in that war. Their stories were tragic – people in their family had been killed by the army; they had seen terrible things. But they also had this sense of purpose . . . they were born without a country, and then they made a country. And they always look back on that time with great nostalgia. Not perfect nostalgia, but with this belief: We really did something. We changed the world. That's such a magnetic story.

They also talked about love. So many people told me they fell in love during the war because the barriers between men and women broke down at that time. They were allowed to mix more freely. They were calling each other 'Comrade', so that really felt like a *moment* . . . where they were fighting in a war, where they were falling in love: it felt golden.

GA: *The Good Muslim* was the second book of the trilogy, about the same family, and in that story there's conflict between a sister and her brother who has turned to extremism. You've said that, as much as the West is frightened of extremism, people in the Muslim world are much more frightened. What are they frightened of?

TA: There are these little courts in America where they're

trying to pass laws saying Sharia law will never be admitted in Texas, worrying about something which is never going to happen. That's just a way of people addressing their fear. But, in Bangladesh, we have political parties on the religious right that really want to bring in Islamic law as part of the judicial law. They never get voted into power, because that's not what people want. People may be devout, they may have their prejudices against the outside world, but they still want to hold fast to their civil rights and their secular beliefs. I was just trying to say that, for a possibly very devout country of Muslim citizens, having religious law is in fact something the majority of people do not want.

GA: When you write in this new book about the relationship between Elijah and Zubaida, it's a relationship that is soft, caring and beautiful. Yet, when you describe Zubaida's relationship with Rashid, it's more about people getting up and having a fag in the middle of the night. Very pedestrian. Were you trying to tell us something about arranged marriages – that you don't think they work?

TA: Well, no. I think arranged marriages do work for a lot of people. What I was trying to say was not, in this love triangle, that the Asian relationship was somehow less *romantic* than the interracial relationship. It was that the relationship that had been presented to Zubaida as the one that should seem most natural was the one that felt deeply unnatural, and that sometimes it's very contradictory: we can fall in love with people who have nothing in common with us. Zubaida feels this deep connection with someone, and I wanted him to be as different from her as possible. She says she visits his home, and she looks at pictures of people on the wall and thinks: You can trace your history back generations and I don't even know who my mother was. And yet I feel we were born to be together.

Margaret Atwood

with David Aaronovitch

Hay-on-Wye 2003

DAVID AARONOVITCH: Margaret, your new book, *Oryx and Crake*, is described as a dystopia. So that makes it your second dystopia. Some people have suggested that it's greedy for anybody to have two dystopias, so, at some point, we'll be exploring the question: If Margaret were forced to choose between her dystopias, which one would she settle for, and which one ought we to be most worried about, and why?

But the first question I want to ask is why *this* dystopia? As you say, you've got a guy on a beach. It's after practically the whole human race has been wiped out.

MARGARET ATWOOD: The name of the book is *Oryx and Crake*, the narrator is a man throughout, and this man started life as a boy called Jimmy, and then he became an adolescent boy called Jimmy, and then a young man called Jimmy. But when we meet him he has renamed himself Snowman, after the Abominable Snowman – an animal or human that may or may not exist, which is how he has come to think of himself. In the first part of the book he's living in a tree; he's wearing a bed-sheet, and he only has a couple of other possessions: he has a watch that doesn't work and a pair of sunglasses with only one lens. And there are no other people around.

There are some people in the book who are *sort of* like people – they *look* like people, except they're better-looking. They have, however, been modified. Some of the modifications, I think, would be quite good. For instance, they have built-in mosquito repellent, which I'm all for. And they have

built-in sunblock, and, not only are they completely veg-
etarian, but their digestive systems have been redesigned to
accommodate leaves, uncooked leaves. They have also solved
the problem of intermittent monogamy and sexual jealousy.
Which means they will never write Shakespeare, because
they're only periodically sexual, and these periods are sig-
nalled by clear colour changes in their bodies, which I think
would be a great advantage. No more 'No means Yes'. Everything is very clear – parts of you either turn blue or they don't.

Anyway, poor Snowman Jimmy is all alone people-wise,
because these other humanoids in his vicinity can't really
understand him emotionally. And they certainly have no
idea of what he's recently been through. They're innocent of
the past.

DA: He's living beside these creative people who have some
of the characteristics that you referred to earlier, and one or
two more that you didn't quite mention. But they've come to
this through the action of a human being, which is a result
of a series of other acts – by corporations or groups of other
human beings – that involve messing around with food,
messing around with medicine, messing around with technology. And they have come to this point, and the action of it
is a few decades in the future?

MA: I would say Jimmy is now [in 2003] aged four; I think
he's already been born. I think I may have been a bit generous
with time – that is, I think the timeline might be a bit more
speeded-up than that.

DA: So this is something that you say could credibly happen.

MA: It's a speculative fiction. It's not outer space. It's not
another planet. It's planet earth. It's like *The Handmaid's
Tale*, in that I didn't put into it anything that human beings

have not done already, or aren't doing right now, or aren't thinking about doing right now. Or any tendencies that are not already with us.

DA: But, even so, you chose this combination of tendencies. Why these ones?

MA: These are the ones that are actually with us right now. We're on a path that leads to a convergence of various elements. First of all, human population is expected to peak at ten billion in the year 2050. Second, we're running out of stuff; we're running out of stuff to eat, just for starters. We've done away with ninety per cent of fish stocks over the past ten years: we've only got ten per cent left of what used to be in the sea. And thirdly, and parallel to that, we've just opened the biggest toy box in the world, which is the one containing the components of living things, including the components of human beings themselves. We can now combine them in just about any way we want to. We haven't quite done that yet, but we're working busily away at it.

DA: OK. So, here's a series of tendencies that come together, as you say: the shortage of natural resources, plus our ability to manipulate. One thing you could say is that, in both of these cases, what has happened in the book is the worst thing that could happen.

MA: Oh, no. Some of the things that have been done are actually pretty good: mosquito repellent would be a plus! It's not an anti-science book. Science is a human tool like all other human tools. However, it is human beings who decide what to use those tools for. So, we have a lot of this technological potential for the future. But the tendency today is that it's become completely commercialized. Things are being made that the people making them hope other people will want to buy. And the market is manipulated in other ways as well. For example, so many diseases have been cured that people are getting a bit worried that the market for drugs may plummet. What would you do in that case, if you were a drug company?

DA: Manufacture an illness.

MA: Manufacture an illness? It didn't take you long to think of that.

DA: I've read the book.

MA: And we've seen what the tobacco companies did with the research, their own research, that said you might get cancer from smoking. They suppressed it, as we know. And we also know that various companies have done the same about their own drugs. When the profit motive is so important, there is a great temptation to do those things.

DA: Although some people might think that killing your target market is not so bright.

MA: Well, you don't want to kill your target market before you've extracted all of their money from them. So the thing to do would be to kill them slowly.

DA: But apart from the mosquito repellent, which I think is probably the most optimistic idea, the rest of the book is actually highly negative.

MA: I love to be proved wrong. Nothing would delight me more.

DA: Let's take an example. There's very little choice for

anybody. In fact, choice has nearly disappeared. So everybody gets to eat or drink almost exactly the same things?

MA: Not entirely. In the book, society has gone even further in the direction that ours is going in now, in that very smart, necessary people live inside compounds, where they get the best of everything and have lots of security. It's hard to get in; it's also hard to get out. They're just in there, complete with their golf courses, and restaurants, and movie theatres, and houses and everything else you might need. I don't know whether you know about gated communities in the States. Well, these compounds are sort of like that, only more so, so those people have *certain* kinds of choice. People on the outside, who live in the pleeblands, have other kinds of choices. The pleeblands are a wide, open district, not very safe, but you can buy lots of different things. What you have a hard time acquiring are things like beef. But there are quite a few soy products in the future coming your way.

DA: However, the Jimmy who's in the tree is only slightly worse off in a way than the Jimmy who's in the compound.

MA: Oh, I'd say he's much worse off. Have you ever lived in a tree?

DA: Only for a few days. And it was quite a big tree. But what I meant was that his life before the disaster was pretty awful. It's circumscribed by the very few things that you can get to eat, so by the monopolies, by companies like Happicuppa. It's difficult to get out of the compounds they're in because of the security. He just sits at home.

MA: Remember, he grew up this way. If *you* were plucked out of your present existence and put in there, *you'd* probably find it quite difficult. But children? Whatever they grow up in is normal to them until they get to the age of reflection. They just think: This is what life is like. So it's actually not so bad. Jimmy's certainly very secure; there's lots of security. It would be bad for *you*. But it's not actually that bad for him, because that's what he's used to.

DA: As far as I know, Jimmy is your first male narrator?

MA: There are other ones that have parts of books. But he's the first one that's got a whole book all to himself.

DA: Why did you do that?

MA: Because it was in there. Because it would be quite a different story if it were a female narrator. It just wouldn't be the same thing at all.

DA: Why?

MA: How many adolescent girls do you know who would spend that many hours playing video games? Of the kind that Jimmy and his friend Crake play for hours on end? They'll play them sometimes, but not usually to that extent. That's just for starters. We could get into it at some length. But it does tend to be that most utopias and dystopias have actually been written by men. And it does seem to be more of their tendency to do blueprints of the world. Of the kind that rearrange the world. Or to play video games in which you rearrange the world. Or in fact to rearrange the world in reality. Redraw the map of the Middle East, and that kind of thing. That doesn't tend to be women masterminds doing it, as a rule. Any of those big-picture, playing-with-the-world kinds of things.

DA: Now, going back to that first question. You've written

two dystopias, and some people would say that if you've written two dystopias you must be a science fiction writer. You say: I don't like science fiction.

MA: No, no, no. I never said that. I read lots of it. I just can't write it.

DA: Really? Then you call it speculative fiction?

MA: No. I think George Orwell's *Nineteen Eighty-Four* is speculative fiction. *Brave New World*: speculative fiction. H G Wells's *War of the Worlds*: science fiction. Smart squids in canisters shot from Mars: definitely science fiction.

DA: But Orwell famously only had one. And you've had two. Does having written *Oryx and Crake* make you think *The Handmaid's Tale* is less true than it was?

MA: If we're really, really lucky we'll get a combination of the two. There is a book by Yevgeny Zamyatin, called *We*, which was written in 1924 by a Russian person in the early stages of the revolution, and he wasn't allowed to publish it, needless to say. But it is a combination of those two kinds of things. It's got the Big Brother plus the Brave New World everybody-must-be-happy sort of thing. I think it would actually be very hard to get, in the same country, *The Handmaid's Tale* and *Oryx and Crake*. *Oryx and Crake* is more global. What goes on in *The Handmaid's Tale* is actually confined to what used to be the United States. And England, for instance, in that book, is free of it, you'll be happy to know. Because England already did all of that; it did it under Oliver Cromwell, and so delightful did they find the experience that they've never wanted to do it again. In fact, in *The Handmaid's Tale*, England is the country of choice where escaped women want to go. It was country-specific. And *Oryx and Crake* is dealing with tendencies that are *global* rather than country-specific or allied to national politics. So it's global, and allied to what's going on with the *earth*, right now.

Jimmy Carter

with *Philippe Sands*

Hay-on-Wye 2008

ALAN RUSBRIDGER: This is going to be a very brief introduction: if you want the full version of Jimmy Carter's life, he's written twenty-four books' worth of it.

His public life on the international stage splits into two parts. And I thought, watching him this afternoon at a little school here in Hay, giving his press conference about Israel–Palestine: Here are some clues. I thought that there was something about his humour and grace, something about his plain speaking, his ability to explain a highly complex subject like Israel–Palestine in terms that people could understand. I was struck by his fearlessness: he doesn't mind whom he upsets in telling it like he sees it. You can't help but be struck by his passion, by his humanity and by his sense of what is fair. You can't help but be struck by his grasp of detail, and his unflagging commitment to the cause that he's been interested in now for well over thirty years. You get a sense of shining honesty, and I think finally you have a sense of serenity.

So this conversation is going to be a great treat, and a treat also because of his interlocutor tonight, Philippe Sands: he's a barrister and distinguished QC in international law and human rights cases; he's an academic; he has a third career as a writer and journalist on legal matters and human rights; and he also has a further string, which is as a kind of activist. He believes passionately in these causes and combines his legal and forensic expertise, his academic knowledge and his writing talent with an ability to whip up concern and publicity and action around the causes that he champions. He has just written a book about Guantanamo and torture, which he approaches almost like a detective story. I really recommend it.

I want to give the biggest possible welcome to President Carter and Philippe Sands.

PHILIPPE SANDS: President Carter, firstly on behalf of everyone in the room, and everyone at Hay Festival, welcome to you and your family, to Britain and to this festival.

There's obviously a whole range of different topics that people in the room are deeply interested in, but I want to begin with a moment immediately after you ceased to be president of the United States in January 1981. You made it very clear in one of your writings that you were going to emulate President Truman, and engage for the rest of your professional life in public service. You've created The Carter Center, and you've been engaged in all sorts of activities. Which is the one of which you're most proud?

JIMMY CARTER: Well, I guess you mean since I was involuntarily retired from the White House by the election in 1980. Yes, I did have a choice to make about what I would do. And I think what The Carter Center has tried to do is adopt things that others didn't want to address. But if I look down the total of things that I've accomplished since I left the White House, I believe it would be the almost total eradication of one of the most horrible diseases that human beings have ever known, and that is Guinea worm disease. This is probably the 'fiery serpent' mentioned in the Bible – and it afflicted people in earlier than biblical days. We started out with this disease, which is relatively unknown and unaddressed, in 23,700 villages; we found 3.6 million cases. Now we have less than 5,000 cases left in the whole world and we know where every one of them is. We know who has the disease, and we believe that, before a few more months have gone by, this will be the second disease ever to have been eradicated from the face of the earth. And what makes it so important is that here were people who suffered, and yet very few people knew about them or cared that they even existed. So I think that's the most important thing that I've done.

PS: And you've taken on a whole raft of causes, some of which are very well known. Looking across the range of the political engagements you've been involved in in the last twenty-five years, how different is the world today from how it was twenty-five years ago?

JC: Well, what The Carter Center has had as a purpose is to fill vacuums in the world. This has led us into areas that, in the past, have not been addressed. Sometimes we negotiate peace agreements, sometimes we hold elections, sometimes we just ease tensions between people, sometimes we resolve suffering. And in the political realm, I think some of the most notable things we've done are the result of being willing to talk to people who are international pariahs or outcasts.

PS: To my mind, one of the very great achievements of your presidency was to put human rights on the international agenda in a way no other president had done. In relation to Iran in the late 1970s, there was a dichotomy there, wasn't there? Because you had a strong commitment to human rights, but you engaged in the *realpolitik* of dealing with the Shah, whose domestic human rights record was less than ideal.

JC: Yes. Well, when I made my inaugural speech as president, I pointed out that human rights would be the foundation of our foreign policy. Every ambassador on earth would be my personal human rights representative and in every American embassy on earth there would be a haven for people who were persecuted by their own government. And when the Shah demonstrated that he had lost the support of many of his people, and separated himself even from his closest advisers, who had formerly cautioned him against extreme actions, and let his secret police, SAVAK, attack those whom I considered to be innocent demonstrators, young people, I chastised him very severely in my back office, near the Oval Office of the White House. I told him I thought this was a serious mistake. I told him that he should let his people express their views against him. But he thought I was mistaken. I think that was an indication, quite early, that the Shah had lost touch with his own people and was using abusive violations of human rights to maintain himself in power.

PS: You gave an interview last October [2007] to Wolf Blitzer of CNN, and you surprised a number of people in the United States in what you said in respect of the United States' move towards torture. You said, I think, 'I don't think. I *know* [it's happening].' We've subsequently learned it was authorized at the very top. What's your reaction to that?

JC: One of embarrassment and horror and despair – and of hope, that the next president of the United States, whether Republican or Democratic, will permanently, and on a global basis, *vow* that our country will never again torture a prisoner. And that we will in the future comply with the terms of international agreements on multiple subjects in whose preparation the United States has been actively involved. This is something we have seen happen in our country in recent months or years – recent years – that is unprecedented in our history, and in my opinion it violates the basic principle that made our nation a great one in the past.

PS: You've been putting a lot of time in the past months and years into the Middle East. I know it's an enormously

important issue for you. We're going to have a new US president in January. What's your advice to that president in those
most important first hundred days on issues to do with the
Middle East?

JC: My first advice, not getting involved in details, would
be to begin a determined effort to bring peace to the Middle
East during those first hundred days and not wait until the
last hundred days that a president's in office. So my advice
to the next president is: don't wait till your second year in
office. Begin immediately to learn about the issues and to
follow, I would say, two things: follow the official policies of
the United States government. And if you read the official
policies of the United States government, it's to support the
United Nations Security Council resolutions, and also to follow the official position of the United States on the ultimate
goals on the Roadmap for Peace. There's no incompatibility
between those. And that means the withdrawal of Israel from
the occupied territories.

   I believe one of the greatest human rights crimes now taking place on earth is the imprisonment of 1.6 million Palestinians in Gaza, and the withholding of not only their freedom
but their right to adequate food, shelter, electricity, fresh
water in order to survive. And in this particular decision that
has been made, and is being implemented every day, I would
like for *Great Britain* to say that 'this is not right', and that
'we disagree, for one of the few times, with our friends in the
United States: and we believe the Palestinian people in Gaza
should be treated with all human rights.' Of that 1.6 million,
about 900,000 are children less than eighteen years old. A
million are refugees.

PS: We have an important presidential election coming up.

JC: I heard about it, yeah . . .

PS: You're familiar with it? It looks as though it's going to be a campaign between Senator Obama and Senator McCain. You're from a southern state; there have been interesting primaries in the last few weeks. Is America ready to elect an African-American as its president?

JC: Yes. And I don't think I would have said that so freely a few months ago. But I saw Georgia, my state, where I've lived all my life except when I was off in the navy for twelve years, vote overwhelmingly for Obama – and he got a majority of white votes. This would have been incomprehensible a few years back. He did the same thing in South Carolina, same thing in North Carolina. I think that proves that the answer to your question is yes. I think he's done quite well under very difficult circumstances as far as the race question is concerned. It's still, in my country, maybe even here, a subterranean, subconscious issue just to be naturally prejudiced against someone who has a different-coloured skin or something of that kind. So it's still there. But I think he has minimized the 'adverse effect' of his race, and I think America is ready.

PS: What does a President Obama or a President McCain have to do in those first few days to restore the confidence of the rest of the world?

JC: If the next president takes the oath of office, and the Supreme Court Justice sits down, and the next president walks to the podium and says: 'While I'm president of the United States, we will never again torture a prisoner. When I'm president of the United States, we will never again attack another country unless our own security is directly threatened. When I'm president of the United States, my nation will be at the forefront of protecting the environment against global warming, and every other challenge. When

I'm president of the United States, human rights will be the foundation of our foreign policy. When I'm president of the United States, every international agreement which the United States has participated in drawing up, we will honour. When I'm president of the United States, one of the earliest and most fervent commitments I will make is to bring security and peace to Israel and all of its neighbours, and I'll treat them on an equal basis' . . . That hasn't taken ten minutes to say, but if that series of resonating words goes throughout the world to more than a billion people who are going to be watching the television, then, almost instantly, the image of my nation will be changed.

Jung Chang

with Rosie Boycott

Hay-on-Wye 2004

ROSIE BOYCOTT: Good afternoon, ladies and gentlemen. I'm extremely honoured to have been asked to interview Jung Chang. When I first read *Wild Swans*, and was completely knocked out by it, there were so many little things I wanted to ask, and finally, over ten years later, I get my chance, which is wonderful.

In the introduction you say that your life changed in 1991, when you became a writer. Did you really not feel a writer until that?

JUNG CHANG: Well, I always wanted to be a writer. When I was a child, I used to lie on the ground and look at the clouds and compose fairy tales in my head. But, growing up in China, it was impossible to be a writer. Nearly all writers in China were condemned, denounced, in one way or another, and some were sent to the labour camps and some were driven to suicide. Even writing privately was dangerous.

When I came to Britain, for many years I didn't want to write this particular book because I wanted to forget all about China, and just enjoy Britain. I just felt I had come to this wonderful place; I didn't want to think back. And to write would have meant to turn inward and to think about the past, which I didn't want to do – until 1988, when my mother came to stay with me. For the first time, my mother told me the stories of her life, and the story of my grandmother. She stayed for six months. We talked every day, and she left me sixty hours of tape recordings, and that's how I started to write *Wild Swans*.

Before the book was published I was obviously very nervous about how it would be received. But then my mother wrote me and said: The book might not do well, people might not pay attention to it, but I was not to be anxious because, she said, writing the book had brought us closer together, and she felt I had come to love her more. It turned out the book was a success, and my mother, who had really just wanted to have her daughter understand her, now had understanding from millions of readers from all over the world. And I at last had become a writer.

RB: What I think was so amazing when you described all the things you didn't know about your grandmother, and indeed your mother, was that, it seemed to me, the three of you were clearly cut from the same cloth. There's a lovely phrase at one point about a woman with 'rebellious bones', a woman who won't quite do what she's supposed to do. Did you feel that you were learning about the hidden life of both your grandmother and your mother as much as about their public faces?

JC: Yes. For example, I always knew that my grandmother had bound feet. When I was a child, if I went out, say, shopping with my grandmother, after we came back the first thing she would do was to soak her feet in a bowl of hot water, and then she would cut dead skin from her feet with this little knife. And she would always say to me how much she lived in pain. Then my mother described to me how my grandmother's feet came to be bound, really crushed and bound. From the age of two, my grandmother lived in excruciating pain, and I remember when my mother and I were walking in Hyde Park and there were these piles of stones, rocks, and my mother said they used to put this kind of stone on top of the crushed feet, to really crush the bones and to stop the girls running away, and then do the binding.

RB: What I particularly learnt when I was reading *Wild Swans* was the level of brutality that, I suppose, went on all the time. It seemed to me that both your grandmother and your mother lived in this constant world of fear, and that they had grown up with that. There was no getting away from it.

JC: I grew up with fear. I left China in 1978 when I was twenty-six. When we first arrived in London I was still living in fear, because at the time China was just beginning to open up to the outside world. So when we first came, we were not allowed to go out on our own. We had to move in a group, and I remember I must have been be the first Chinese to ever walk into a British pub. The Chinese translation for pub is *jiŭ bā*, which in those days suggested somewhere indecent with nude women gyrating, so we were particularly told not to go into a pub. I was torn with curiosity, so one day I darted across the road from the college and I sneaked into a pub. I pushed the door open. Of course I saw nothing of the kind; I only saw some old men sitting there drinking beer. I was rather disappointed.

That first year in London was so exciting, because I did so many things that were not allowed, and I did them all the time in fear, not because I enjoyed fear but because I just couldn't stand living like in a prison in this wonderful world.

RB: You had worked incredibly hard to get to be the teacher chosen to go to London in 1978, because before that you had been turned out on to the land to be a peasant; and you'd worked as an electrician. Tell us a little bit about those experiences before you got to your vocation.

JC: When I was fourteen, the Cultural Revolution started and, like nearly all my urban contemporaries, I became a Red Guard. My generation was brought up in this intense personality cult of Mao – Mao was like our god. If we wanted to say:

'What I say is true', we would say: 'I swear to Chairman Mao.'

Since the publication of *Wild Swans*, for the last eleven years I have been writing a biography of Mao, and so I understand a lot more about him now. He used the Red Guard to create terror and he chose schoolteachers to start with as his victims. In every school in China, teachers were beaten up, tortured, driven to suicide, some tortured to death. I saw a lot of violence in my school as well, and it just went against my nature and I hated all this, so I soon left the Red Guard. And then we were exiled to the edge of the Himalayas and I worked for three years as a peasant, and as a barefoot doctor. Mao didn't want to put any investment in health and education, and he wanted to keep the whole country as a vast slave-labour camp. So he said that the more books you read the more stupid you become, and that was the guideline for health and education in those days. So as a barefoot doctor I didn't have any training. Later, I became a steel-worker, and then an electrician, and again there was no training.

RB: Could you choose what you did?

JC: There was no choice. But occasionally there were opportunities. One came in 1971 when I was able to get back to the city and enter a factory and, in 1973, again there was an opening, and I was able to get into university to learn English. It was a wonderful opportunity, and I had to fight very hard actually to grab it. I was twenty-three when we were sent to a port in South China to practise our English with some foreign sailors.

RB: You might have learnt some very dodgy words.

JC: This was, as far as I was concerned, my only chance. We would be seated in the café, the only café with a restaurant, and we would grab the sailors as soon as they came on shore, and of course we had no idea what must have been on their minds. My English textbook was full of propaganda: the very first lesson was 'Long live Chairman Mao'. The second lesson was 'Greetings'. Our textbook was written by teachers who had never spoken to foreigners themselves. They translated into English the Chinese greetings 'Where are you going?' and 'Have you eaten?' When I first came to Britain I used to go around and ask people where they were going and whether they had eaten.

It was like another planet. I remember at Heathrow airport I nearly walked into a men's toilet because I had no idea the figure wearing trousers on the door was supposed to be a man. In China, in my days, women were not allowed to wear skirts. And the man walking in front of me had long hair.

RB: Ah yes, 1978. But then you stayed in England and you went to York University and studied linguistics. I think you're the first Chinese person from mainland China to get a degree from an English university. Is that right?

JC: A doctorate? Yes. Until 1979 degrees were unavailable in China, regarded as a bourgeois thing, and I was in the first group of Chinese to come out of Communist China based on academic merit, because under Mao – he died in September 1976 – there were extremely few scholarships to go abroad, and all of them had to be based on political reliability, and of course I had no chance. And then in 1978, for the first time, scholarships for going abroad were awarded on an academic basis, and I was able to sit for a national exam. I did reasonably well, so I became one of the fourteen people in my group to come to Britain and then, the next year, I was offered a scholarship for York University.

RB: Amazing, but actually there was something that happened at York University that suddenly meant you had to write. There was a moment when you thought: I need to write my story, and those of my mother and grandmother.

JC: I used to tell people I was from South Korea because, in those days, mainland China was as fascinating as outer space. So people would immediately ask me what China was like and so on, things I just didn't want to think about. And also I didn't want people to be interested in me simply because I was Chinese. One evening, I was invited to a slide-show by a professor who had just visited China, and there he had seen that all the windows in the school he visited were broken. It was obviously freezing, and the pupils were wearing their padded coats in lessons. And so he described how cold and how hard their school life was, and afterwards there was a reception and there was a woman who was obviously trying to find something to say to me. She said, 'You must feel very hot here.' Now, I can laugh, but I was so upset by this innocent remark that I abruptly left the room.

RB: Was it partly because it felt like there were all these stories, and they were true, and the mistaken idea that people in the West can sometimes have which is that somehow everybody in China is inured to this now – they expect to be cold, and they expect not to feel things, and so it felt like a dehumanizing comment?

JC: Yes. I went by the lake and I had my first cry since I came to Britain. I really felt that people didn't understand how much the Chinese had been through and suffered. I thought of the life of my grandmother, my mother, my father who had died in the Cultural Revolution very tragically, and all my friends. I suddenly felt I wanted to write these stories.

Gillian Clarke

with Peter Florence

Hay-on-Wye 2016

PETER FLORENCE: Thank you very much for coming. I should say the best part of my job is that every few years or so, I get to sit down to talk to Gillian Clarke, with an audience. When we first started the festival in . . . 1767 . . . [audience laughter] . . . in 1988, the very first person we ever wrote to saying, 'Please will you come, we're starting a festival', was Gillian, who replied immediately with 'What a fantastic idea, yes of course'. After which nobody again would ever say no . . .

This is Shakespeare's 400th anniversary, and one of the things we wanted to do was to talk to writers about their relationship with Shakespeare – how he might have impacted upon their thinking and their style and their humanity. And this is particularly true of Gillian, because there is one great work of hers which has a keen and deep connection with Shakespeare, but also serves as a biographical poem, and an autobiographical poem. Introducing it and talking about it will allow us to talk about her work and her life and her evolution as a poet. So Gillian, firstly, thank you for coming.

GILLIAN CLARKE: Thank you for having me!

PF: The poem we're talking about is *The King of Britain's Daughter*, which had a rather wonderful genesis, but before we start talking about the poem, can I ask you to tell us first about sound and voice and radio, and then about your auntie?

GC: Well, my father was an outside broadcasting engineer

with the BBC. So he did a huge amount of work wandering about Wales, and he took me with him, and he used to talk to me in the car and tell me what the names of things were in Welsh, and I had a thoroughly lovely time. And I can remember at home, where they all lived together – my grandmother, my father, my mother, his three sisters, the husband of one of them – hearing from my upstairs bedroom several radios on, in different rooms downstairs, in different languages. And all of this big family would be laughing and shouting and arguing and joking in English and Welsh. Those sounds are crucially interesting and important to this little head that's taking them all in.

So the music of language was very important in my early childhood. One of my father's sisters – and over the years I realized I didn't thank her enough for what she did for me – was a railway clerk in Camarthen, and she discovered Shakespeare, and she read and read and read Shakespeare. She decided to take me to Stratford-upon-Avon. I was ten years old, and the first play that we saw was *King Lear* – which nobody would think was a good idea. But I was allowed to wear a party frock, and we went on a train, and in Stratford there was red velvet, swans on the river, little glasses you could look through . . . the whole thing was just so exciting.

And at the first interval she looked anxiously at me and she said, 'Well, are you all right?' And I said, 'Nothing will come of nothing: speak again'. And I just *loved* it, from the first moment. *Nothing will come of nothing: speak again* . . . I just loved it. Which shows that even if a child, or anybody, doesn't know exactly what something 'means', it doesn't matter; what comes first is the sensation, the music – in my head was 'nothing'; I muttered it, I skipped to it, I went to sleep dreaming of it, for years. But after the play was over, I said: 'He was stupid to make her say she loved him with all those people there', because I had a difficult father too, and then I paused, and I said, 'She was mean, though; she could've', because, while I recognized that my father could be a pain in the neck, I also recognized that I was a grumpy child who wouldn't do as he wanted. In other words, what that play is really about is a relationship between a father and a beloved child.

PF: It's also, crucially, the relationship between Lear, the king of the Britons, and *his* daughter.

GC: Llŷr, yes. As my father told me, Llŷr was the king of the Britons, and that is where Shakespeare got his story. Llŷr's children were Bendigeidfran, or Brân, the giant – he was one of the sons, and his daughter was Branwen. When I was growing up in my grandmother's farmhouse in Pembrokeshire, there was the news of a war on the radio on the windowsill, and there was someone called Hitler, and outside that window there were storms, and there was the sea, 200 yards away, breaking on the beach below. And I associated the stories that my father told me, the stories of Llŷr, the stories of something that must be overcome, with something that must be overcome in the big bad world we lived in – though that wasn't really real to me: Branwen and Brân were as real as Hitler and the other stories that I heard. Little by little, I thought I was Branwen. And I began to feel that my father was Llŷr, I suppose. Or was he Brân? So he was this heroic male figure, the brother in the legend, the father in the play, and they became associated with each other, so I was both Branwen and Cordelia, and I was in my little broken boat that I used to go and sit in down on the beach, it was full of pebbles, and I was sitting there by the sea not going anywhere . . . but I was setting off to Ireland . . .

Of course the Welsh-Irish story is this: Branwen had married the king of Ireland. She was living across the ocean, and the people in the court were very hostile to her, and made her life very unhappy. So she taught a starling to say her name, and she sent the starling across the sea, and the starling would land on Brân's shoulder and whisper her name in his ear, and at once he knew this was a cry for help, so he walked through the sea – he's a giant – towing all his ships behind him. The reality of it, and the myth of it, made no problems at all for me.

And as he left, he took something from his pocket and put it on the cliff, sometimes it's the apple from Brân's pocket, and sometimes it's the pebble from Brân's pocket, my father said. It was the rocking stone: if you touched it, you could hear the sea whispering. Long after, when I went back, the stone had gone. So it was a legend, it was a reality; and in the legend there was a war going on between Ireland and Wales – which of course was *Britain* then, and there was the war on the radio. So when I saw, at ten, *King Lear*, the language made everything more real than ever; the beautiful things that were said in that play, the rhythms, the sound of the language . . . I had no way of distinguishing between what was true . . . the word 'true' didn't exist.

PF: Flash forward, really quite a way, to 1990, and we're playing a game in Hay-on-Wye, and we say to you: 'We'd like you, over the next three days, please, to write a poem on a specific theme.'

GC: There's an essay I wrote called 'Cordelia's Nothing' describing all that: 'In 1990, at the first of the Hay-on-Wye literary festival weekend "Squantums", the plot offered to six poets late on Friday evening was 'Border: Fatherland, Motherland'. What I saw at once was that border country in the self where mother and father meet, an edge where there is both tension and conflict. At the same time it was the border where the two languages of Wales define themselves and each other, and the definition of self and the other was one of the most intriguing aspects of the subject.'

So my fellow writers and I were sent off to write, then terrifyingly we had to bring what we'd done before an audience, and then again on the next night – I don't know whether anybody else got a huge poem out of it, but I got a very long poem indeed, made of many short poems. Motherland, fatherland . . . I had thought of my beautiful mother from North Wales, who didn't want me to learn Welsh, and my father, always wanting me to speak Welsh. So for me the subject, 'Border', was very good.

PF: Could you describe just how the short poem you wrote that weekend then fermented into the much bigger work that it became? I think 'Rocking Stone'.

GC: On the headland is an absence
        where it fell some winter night
        between here and childhood,
        and the sea's still fizzing
        over a bruise that will not heal.

        A finger would rock it,
        Bendigeidfran's stone.
        My ear pressed to its flank could hear
        the footfall of a storm far out at sea
        long before the frown of it darkened the beach.

        It purred in wind, was warm against my back
        with all the summer in it.
        Apple out of legend,
        slingstone of Brân's rage against Ireland.
        Or so my father said.

PF: What I'd love, is for you to read a substantial bit of *The King of Britain's Daughter*. But just before you do could you just talk about the language that evolved to meet it, because it's quite specific, it's unlike the scale of most of your work, and I'm intrigued by how you approached it, and what rules you set for yourself, found for yourself while you were writing it.

GC: Rules: I don't know if I set rules . . . form . . . what I knew was I had a great many things to say; and the way to do it would be poem one, 'Rocking Stone'; poem two, no title; poem three, four . . . then nine is 'Giants' . . . Number two is me and father in the car and we were going to see my grandmother:

> We'd sing for a bit,
> the western sun in our eyes.
> Then rocked to sleep in the dark for a hundred miles

And then number three . . .

> Above the house a cat's-tail rises from the fire
> his mother lit a generation back.
> Beneath her plum-trees air takes up the slack
> in someone else's sheets.

The farm is still there, much changed. But what I'm using really is the *place*: as we walked on the beach, my father said: 'See that great big hole in the rock there, where you like swimming? That's the print that Brân made when he stamped the beach in rage, and set off towing all the ships to Ireland', and I've never believed anything more sincerely than that. But my father said, and I think everyone should do this, you have to say: 'This happened *here*.' So the child has a place, this beach . . . I think we should beware of absolute *fact*. Just listen to the stories, and allow the human imagination to do what it must do, because these stories are a kind of truth.

PF: Will you read a bit more?

GC: I'll read 'Giants' . . .

Giants

turn boulders into grains of sand,
a brimming horizon to a goblet,
capstone and orthostats of the cromlech,
a milking stool set slant
on the hills shoulder.

They loll on skylines,
their heads in the clouds,
warming their bluestone bones in the sun.
They tilt the earth, bring storms
when they breathe like rain on the sea.

They are the metaphors that shift the world,
make delta, Gulf Stream, sea-road
from a stream spilt on the beach,
and turn a houseboat full of sand
to quinquereme on a running tide.

Tonight, as Concorde folds her tern-wings back
to take the Atlantic,
I hear a giant foot stamp twice.
You can still see the mark he made,
a black space in the stars.

Now this is Branwen speaking:

Day after day
a starling comes to my hand,
both of us small birds at a window
he, with a dark rainbow
in every feather, takes seed
and crumbs from me,
touches my hands like rainfall

and I tell my name until
he holds its two syllables
of water in his throat
two pearls to bear across the sea

on a prevailing westerly.
I throw him into the wind
calling 'Branwen, Branwen'
to the far horizon.

And this is Brân:

Now stone and water rise,
the bay scatters with brokenness.
Wrecks in the deepest sea will crack
their carapaces under my foot.
My ships are gull feathers
towed over the drowned rocks of my rage.

Then Branwen again:

When my eloquent starling leaves my hand
I grieve alone, and for a month or more
my eyes never leave the grey and empty sea.

Then when the wind cries all night on the land,
huge waves breaking on the troubled shore,
I wake to hear my child cry in my dream.

At dawn swineherds run breathless to the King
with tales of an island, trees, two lakes, all
moving shoreward on the morning swell.

There, through the littoral, my brave Brân striding,
his tall fleet dancing at his heel
like giddy hounds at a huntsman's beck and call.

Then Brân:

> *I wear the shallows of the littoral*
> *which the long days have warmed. They steady me.*
> *I bridle the currents, wear the sea's cold iron*
> *for armoury, shoulder the hawsers of my fleet*
> *and set out through the sea to Ireland,*
> *taking the west wind to my heart like grief*

'Branwen's Grave' ... because she's rescued, but she dies:

> Lace of a winter ash-tree
> in a broken mirror
> where the river strums its stones,
> combing and combing
> its long green hair.
>
> There is weeping here
> in the cold stream,
> in the crumpled face of water,
> in the sob of wind,
> in a cry of water-birds.
>
> There's a whirr of air
> and a tambourine of birds
> rings in a cold sky,
> and the ash is leafed again,
> the starling tree.
>
> Her memory erased
> from the stones
> by the wind and rain,
> her name
> on the tongue of a bird.

The sea writes on the sand
in a scribble of weed and gullbones,
binder twine, coke cans, torn nets,
fish-hooks, broken glass, bladderwrack,
a freehand of mermaid hair and sea-ribbon,
polystyrene chip-trays, spatulas, flip-flops
and sometimes the drowned.
It discards, draft after draft,
each high tide a deadline.

Sonia Faleiro & Nimko Ali

with Laura Bates

Hay-on-Wye 2015

LAURA BATES: Hello, good evening, and thank you, all of you, for coming to this session – rather dauntingly titled 'Magna Carta 800: What do we want? Equality'. We've asked each of our two panelists what their Magna Carta for women would look like. So first, let me introduce them to you: Nimko Ali is an activist, a feminist, and the co-founder of Daughters of Eve, an NGO tackling female genital mutilation in the United Kingdom; Sonia Faleiro is a journalist and author of *Beautiful Thing* and *13 Men*.

Let's begin with you, Sonia, and let's start with the Indian justice system, which links in particularly to your recent work. Can you tell us a bit about that?

SONIA FALEIRO: I was very interested in a particular rape case that was reported last January. A young woman – she was nineteen years old at the time – went to the cops in the village where she lived in West Bengal, and said that she had been raped the previous night by thirteen men. She told the cops that they weren't just any men; they belonged to the village council of her village, and the decision to rape her, she said, was an official sanction handed down because the villagers were upset she was having a relationship with an 'outsider'. It was an enormous story, and of course in India we're hearing a lot of stories about sexual assault and rape. And a lot of us know it isn't because numbers have suddenly shot up; it's because women now feel secure and confident about actually reporting rapes.

I wanted to investigate this case because I thought it was interesting that no reporter had been able to interview this woman, and also that they hadn't sought access to the families of the thirteen men, who were immediately arrested and put in jail six months before the case went to trial.

I went to Bengal, and I got the chance to meet her. She was by then in a government shelter under high security. And I met the families of the thirteen men. What emerged was that *anyone* could have been lying, and *anyone* could have been telling the truth. There was no way of knowing. While forensic and DNA evidence was taken from the place of the alleged rape and while it was sent to the government forensic science laboratory, it somehow didn't make it to the court in time for the trial. So the trial began, and it ended, and the judgement was passed down, and nobody heard anything about this evidence – almost to the point where it was a 'he said, she said' case. But the judge was convinced that the young woman was telling the truth.

It's so interesting because certainly, in India right now, a lot of people feel women have not received justice for a very long time. And there is a question to be asked about whether some people are over-compensating for past mistakes or short-comings. Are we, in our attempt to make up for things that have gone wrong in the past, delivering an imperfect justice? This is not to say that the young woman *was* lying. But what we need is justice based on facts. And so *13 Men* is an exploration of the Indian justice system and how it treats women.

LB: Let me come to you, Nimko, and to the principle of bodily autonomy. From your perspective, working in the UK, why is this one of your key Magna Carta principles?

NIMKO ALI: We don't necessarily have equality in terms of how we get paid, or all of these other kinds of things. But you would assume that you have a fundamental right to your body and how you define it, how you use it, and how it's evidenced in a public space. And for me, coming from an FGM-affected community, I think if you want true representation and true value the first thing to start off with is control of your body. My *name* was written as 'evidence' in society; I was there on my birth certificate. But in terms of myself as a being, that was not something I had any control over.

I had FGM as a seven-year-old, and I didn't necessarily understand it was part of an issue around oppression, an issue of being a woman. I just knew it was a most ridiculous thing to happen, and I wanted an explanation. I remember the first instance of a separation between my physical being and my psychological being was coming back to school as a seven-year-old and telling my teacher this act had been carried out, and the reply was: 'That's what happens to girls like you.' I didn't necessarily know what that meant – 'a girl like me'. But at least she was very specific about my gender, and I thought to myself: OK, this is something I need to investigate.

But there were two spheres. One was very Western, where I was educated and accepted and invited to parties but at the same time dismissed and not understood. And then there was the *cultural* definition of what I should be, and who I should be. Growing up, I assumed people would bring those things together, and understand that FGM is something that manifests from a gender inequality position. That's the reason why I wanted to talk about my own experience, to change the narrative that FGM 'happens' within an 'ignorant' context, when really it's the same reason we're not paid equally: it's about gender inequality. And I think people found it quite weird when I compared those two. But it's two sides of the same coin.

LB: Sonia, coming back to you, and talking about young people, and about your going into schools: one of the things on your Magna Carta was about education?

SF: I'm doing a lot of reporting in North India, and one of the things that makes me very optimistic is that, wherever I go, in places that seem very remote, parents who are illiterate themselves, and whose parents were illiterate as well, want to educate *all* their children, sons *and* daughters, and they want to give them the best education. They have actually been able to see, because of migration between villages and towns, the impact of education. Their parents could not have known that education can fundamentally give you a better life, a better way of living. But they can *see*, and so they want better for their children.

The second thing is the fact that there's an enormous number of government schools in India. The down side is that the government pays a lot of lip service to education, but there's not enough follow-through. So schools exist but, in reality, half the time the teacher doesn't turn up. So the desks are there, and there are pieces of chalk, but there's no teacher. So this failure of follow-through is the great tragedy of Indian governance.

LB: Nimko, this lack of follow-through is something I hear a great deal, particularly working around sexual violence or sexual harassment. You hear: 'Well, no, that's not a problem any more; there's a law', and a perfect example of this, to bring us on to your next Magna Carta item, is the Equal Pay Act. What can we be doing to see change in these areas?

NA: Unless you have women who are truly affected by the laws there at the table when the legislation is being formed, it can be very inadequate. For example, the FGM legislation in 1985 was very much based on the fact that FGM is illegal; it's like: 'Great. (What does that mean?)'. One of the interesting things about the 1985 Act is it didn't have any territorial powers. You could be taken to Somalia, and have FGM: that wasn't a crime. It took till 2003 to change that.

LB: Sonia, access to health services is the third point of your Magna Carta principles. Is there, again, a disparity there in the way things look to be and the reality on the ground?

SF: In India you get excellent healthcare if you pay for it, but if you can't, and if you depend on government services, you know it can go quite, quite badly for you. The great burden falls on women because they do not have a good education, so oftentimes, even if they receive good service, they're not entirely sure what is going on with their bodies. They don't understand. There is no vocabulary that the doctors seem to be able to use that can convey the situation to women, and they receive prescriptions that they can't read; they receive copies of the results of various tests they have undergone that they don't understand. I think that increases their sense of vulnerability, and that sense of powerlessness has terrible repercussions on women's health and makes them reluctant to access services even when those services exist and are actually quite good.

LB: Nimko, the final point on your Magna Carta is equality of representation in decision-making. I know you mean that more broadly than just in politics. Can you tell us about that?

NA: I think always having women at the table is the foundation upon which everything should start. If women have been very involved in the forming of those conversations then I think that's where things become more equal – states and countries and societies need to be built where women are part of the equal *foundations* of legislation, governments, and so on. It's always men that are asked: we went into several wars saying we were going to 'liberate' the women of Afghanistan, and the women in Iraq and in Libya. But none of those women are at the forefront when it comes to peace.

LB: Here in the UK, Nimko is involved in the new Women's Equality Party. I'd like each of you to say a little bit about action. How can we effect the change? What can people in the room here today go away and do, to be part of the change that we need to see?

SF: I still feel like there's a separation, at least in India. If women aren't getting educated, or don't have access to education, that's a 'woman's problem': let *them* talk about it, or let a female politician talk about it or let a female social activist talk about it. If they're not getting access to healthcare, if the rape laws aren't effective enough, let people of that gender talk about it. It's not an 'Indian' problem. I find that separation very divisive, very dangerous in the long run, and I would like to see men take some ownership too, and see women as *fellow* citizens and see them as *fellow* human beings. Because I don't think some men do. I would love to see that change. I'd love to see *men* talking about it more. I think it's ridiculous that, instead of seeing these as issues around equality and justice and human rights, we still see them as women's issues. They're not.

NA: I think that's been one of the most amazing things in terms of the work I've been doing around FGM. You know, I could be standing here still shouting into the wind, but it was having other women who *weren't* affected by FGM, but ultimately understood the gender issues that came from it, standing with me. And there are great women out there today that are raising their voices, and it's about standing in solidarity. One of the greatest pieces of advice I ever got from Caitlin Moran was 'there's no such thing as oversharing', so I talk about my vagina a lot, and it's fine; it's that whole thing of it being a very pure and authentic thing, especially for young people, when it comes to consent, and education, and also the realities of the world we live in.

Christiana Figueres & Nick Stern

Hay-on-Wye 2016

NICK STERN: Thank you, thank you all very much for coming. We're in the presence of somebody remarkable, somebody who led the world in something that was astonishing, and we'll try to discuss, during this hour, what happened in Paris in December 2015, and why it happened, and what happens next.

CHRISTIANA FIGUERES: Could I just correct you? You are the remarkable person here.

NS: You can see we know each other quite well. This is an event in association with the British Academy. I'm the President of the British Academy, and we're very proud of our collaboration with Hay Festival. Christiana has been in her position as the Executive Secretary of the United Nations Framework Convention on Climate Change (UNFCCC) for six years, and she steps down in glory in July. Her successor will be Patricia Espinosa, the former foreign minister of Mexico who with Christiana led, brilliantly, COP16 in Cancún in 2010, which was your first COP [Conference of the Parties]. So Christiana has been doing this for six years, and it's been a hard road, because it began just after Copenhagen, which was complicated, cold, chaotic and quarrelsome. But it wasn't empty. It started us down a road which, just a year later, was Cancún, which was the most successful COP until Paris. So, let's arrive in Paris.

Could you tell us, before we get to the detail of COP21, something about the years before you took over? Now there's one thing that I will say because I'm a professor at the London School of Economics: we're very proud of our alumni, and of course a key ingredient was Christiana's master's degree from –

CF: Clearly! I mean there's no other answer. Next question? Well, you can look back and marvel at that amazing kaleidoscope of skills, experiences, exposures, that has given you a lot of the tools that you're going to need. I had worked on climate change from three different perspectives, first, supporting governments; second, recreating and leading an NGO; third, I had worked closely with some of the pioneering companies which, even before 2010, had decided that was the direction they wanted to go in. It was incredibly helpful to me to understand, over those few years that those were the components that had to come together.

NS: But Paris was really remarkable, and let me compare it to Bretton Woods in 1944, when the world got together under the leadership of John Maynard Keynes from Britain and Harry Dexter White from the US to put together the agreements for establishing the World Bank, the IMF and the WTO – to *collaborate* about development, macro-management and trade. There were forty-four countries – this was of course before decolonization – and one was dominant. Compare that with Paris: 195 countries, and it was good that there was no single dominant country. Nobody signed the Paris Agreement because they were browbeaten by a big dominant power. So, 195 in Paris, no dominant one; forty-four at Bretton Woods, and one dominant one. Think about the background to Bretton Woods: in thirty years, two world wars and the Great Depression. There was blood in the field, blood everywhere. You had to believe that this was a bad way to run the world, that we had to be much better at collaborating. So there's the United Nations, the International Declaration of

Human Rights, the beginnings of the European Union. Paris was very different, and Christiana was the one who led us and pulled us together and charmed and browbeat . . .

CF: Not browbeating – encouraging!

NS: . . . and blamed. Tell us how it happened, and tell us what you think were the main things that led Paris to happen?

CF: I think are were many factors. People have pointed to the incontrovertible fact that over those six to eight years, the cost of renewable energy had come down so precipitously that it was now technologically and financially possible to engage with climate change. And there are three factors that were, from a political perspective, absolutely key, and these are associated with three numbers: the number two, the number 195, and the number 'countless'.

The number two: as you say, there was no predominant country, but it is absolutely true that the Agreement would not have happened if the United States and China, as the two largest economies and emitters, had not wanted, first, to do something at home; second, to do something with each other, beyond what they could do individually at home; third, to role-model what could be done throughout the world. What was also key was that the stars aligned to have the political leadership in both countries understand in time that this was in their interests, and that they could do this together.

Then the number 195: I don't know how many of you have discussions in your family, your company, or whatever, when to get a unanimous decision between *three* people is actually quite difficult. So to have 195 countries coming to the unanimous decision that they now intend to change the course of the economy around the world is really pretty remarkable. How was this possible? Well, what was critical was that, over time, all these 195 countries had come to understand that we cannot pit the national interest against the global interest, and that it was in their *national* interest to address a recognized *global* need, through advancing on their priorities *at home*. That overlapping of the national interest with global need was very key, and that's different from Copenhagen. Because in Copenhagen we started with what is called the top-down approach, which is to say: here's what the globe needs and now let's pass it out, and everyone has to meet this responsibility. That's impossible. Whereas by the time we got to Paris, we understood this is about the sum of all the different parts. So I think that was a huge transformation.

And my third number, the 'countless' number: even those 195 countries understood that this is not just about central governments. The central governments are absolutely responsible for negotiating these excruciatingly detailed legal texts, every comma, every verb, and they're the only ones that can commit to it. But that is the centre, certainly not the boundary. The boundary is much broader, and needs to bring in sub-nationals, cities, provinces, states, the private sector, the civil society, the finance sector, the insurance sector, the NGOs, everyone. The opening-up of that space was one of the most difficult things. When I took over that system, there was no tolerance. Countries did not even want to have those groups in the room, let alone participating. In Paris, central governments were now able to understand that this was not a competition, not about taking their authority away.

NS: People saw that this wasn't a horse race between their own country's economic development and poverty reduction on the one hand and climate responsibility for the whole world on the other. In much of the language of the UNF-triple-c, the horse race had been locked in; that changed, didn't it?

CF: Absolutely. We had been locked into a myth that the only way to address climate was to decarbonize the economy but that this would mean that developing countries would never have a chance of developing. The use of fossil fuels has been the backbone of the industrial revolution and of any economic growth. The curve of greenhouse gas emissions, mostly from fossil fuels, and the curve of a country's GDP (but also global GDP) have been linked. In essence, the entire Paris Agreement is about decoupling greenhouse gas emissions from GDP. That is an extraordinary conceptual leap. You can understand a developing country saying: Well, show me a country that has already done that. So it remains a leap of faith.

NS: Let's talk a bit more about Paris. Can you explain the distinction between the bits that are legally binding and the bits that are voluntary? It is remarkable that when people come together to do something voluntarily, sometimes they'll be a lot more co-operative and a lot more mutually supportive, and indeed a lot more ambitious, than if they think they're going to be tied down and locked in.

CF: Let me start with a comparison. In the best of days, I'm a long-distance runner, though I'm ashamed to say I haven't run in a long time. With Paris, countries have committed to a marathon, and that is the legally binding part of it, and that is a long-term process. By the second half of the century we are going to get to the finish line, which is climate neutrality – the balance between how much the world is emitting and how much the world can absorb.

Now, when you run, you have checkpoints when people give you water and let you know how fast you're running. So here, the checkpoints are the legally binding bits: every five years you have to go and do an assessment to see how you're doing – can we do *better*? We also have the legally binding finish line. What is *not* legally binding is: how much am I going to run between one checkpoint and the next. That is healthy: it's very difficult to foresee how much each country will be able to contribute inbetween these checkpoints, and you don't want the 'numbers' to be so static that they can't be improved. With every five-year checkpoint, because technology will improve, policy will develop, finance will be shifting, countries will be able to increase their performance: every five years the expectation is *increased performance*. So it is about making the long-term path legally binding, because it has to set the direction; it has to set the expectation of increasing performance, constantly increasing performance; it has to set the expectation of collaboration, because none of these countries is going to do it on their own – in particular developing countries need to be supported in this huge leap that they're going to make. So all of that piece is legally binding. But the performance from each country for each five-year period is not legally binding.

NS: Very good. Now, we agreed, as a world, to hold the increase in average global surface temperature relative to the end of the nineteenth century, which is the usual benchmark, to well below two degrees. We always used to talk about 'two degrees'. One of the great advances in Paris was 'well below two degrees', and, indeed, 'we try hard in pursuit of one point five degrees'. Now that was a very strong agreement.

Secondly, we have to go to *climate neutrality* or *net zero emissions* or, in the Paris language, the *balancing of sources and sinks*. The reason for this is just the basic greenhouse effect – concentrations of greenhouse gases in the atmosphere preventing the infrared escaping, resulting in global warming and climate change. All the time that the concentrations in the atmosphere are increasing, the global warming effect is intensifying, and the temperature is going up. So even if you stabilized, at, God forbid, four degrees – we haven't been *there* for tens of millions of years; it would be absolutely devastating, but, just being the university professor here for a moment . . . to stabilize at four degrees, we'd have to be climate neutral, that's to say balancing sources and sinks, that's to say net zero emissions. Because all the while that emissions are net positive, the concentrations go up and the global warming effect increases, and temperature increases.

So *wherever* you stabilize, you've got to be net zero. Now, the earlier you hit net zero, the lower the temperature at which you can stabilize. For two degrees, it looks as if we have to hit net zero around 2070, 2080. For one point five degrees, we'd have to hit net zero quite close to mid-century. But it's very important, because net zero is *not* a political concept; the net zero emissions is what *the science* tells us, and you can see it's not some mysterious logic, it's the basic logic of the story of the increase in concentrations. What was different in Paris, I think, was the recognition, Christiana, that that basic science, that basic, very simple logic, had to be built into the commitment.

CF: Yes, for a very long time, there was science over there and policy over here, and never the two would talk to each other, and so integrating that was a huge success, and quite a process over many years. But, Nick, I think it's also very important to understand that while we need to be at that neutrality in the second half of the century, whether we get there or not is going to be defined *now*.

NS: Exactly.

CF: So it's not as if we can just sit back and say: let those who are going to be around in this beautiful world in thirty-five or fifty years from now figure out whether this is going to happen – or not. Let me raise the voice of alarm – and I have invited everyone since Paris to swallow an alarm clock, so you are not exempted. Here's my invitation for all of you to swallow the alarm clock before lunch, so that you remember it ticking. There is an alarm clock that says: over the next five years (or five to eight years even, pushing it), we must get to the maximum point of yearly emissions, which is called peaking, and from then we must start our descent, or we will not be in time for our 'well below two degrees' to be the temperature at which we are net zero.

I have had the insurance sector tell me they know that a world that goes over two degrees is systemically uninsurable. How would we ever live in a world that is systemically uninsurable? It's not about your house, or my little house. The entire economic system could not be insured. And then there's the loss of human life. And the loss of human habitat.

NS: And that leads us to post-Paris. At COP21, the sum total of countries' intentions for 2030, which was the date they were asked to put them in for, was around fifty-five billion tonnes of CO_2-equivalent per year – that's the 'flow'. We're now emitting about fifty. So looking fifteen years ahead to 2030, if you add up all the bits and pieces, country by country, that's an increase of ten per cent in the *flow* each year. Now for most paths that describe two degrees, let alone well below two degrees, by 2030 there should be, not a ten per cent increase, but a twenty per cent decrease. We should really be down to forty from the fifty we are at now: we should be down to forty billion tonnes of CO_2-equivalent global emissions a year in 2030. That's an indication of how fast we have to move; people came with their promises, they were sincere, they were different from anything like business as usual, but they were ten per cent *up* fifteen years from now, where they need to be twenty per cent *down*.

So that's another way of underlining the alarm clock, and the peaking, and the next twenty years are absolutely critical – twenty years when urbanization is moving very quickly, twenty years when we're going to be building our energy systems: if we get the next twenty years wrong – we lock in high-carbon infrastructure, we lock into cities where you can't move and you can't breathe, and any chance of two degrees has gone. So: net zero by the end of this century, or by the second half of this century, doesn't, shouldn't, take away from the urgency now. The urgency is the next twenty years. If we go on, and we don't accelerate the next twenty years, we'll be lost on two degrees. So we can be excited and positive – I guess we're positive people – you certainly are, Christiana – but we mustn't underestimate the magnitude and the urgency of this challenge.

So let's see – one word on how you felt. Was it eight-thirty on 12 December, when Laurent Fabius, the French foreign minister – he was chair of the COP – whacked down the gavel? How did you feel?

CF: You know it really is indescribable. I actually received a scroll, just before Paris, with 2.8 million signatures from people who had prayed, walked, fasted, sung, worked – everything – towards this, and that was just a representation from around the world, let alone all the people who were there in Paris and had been very personally involved. So for me, it was such a celebration of team spirit, such a true confirmation that when humanity sets a goal for itself we can stand up for our highest purpose – if we do it together. What was most moving was the fact that everyone in Paris – and so many people outside of the halls – felt it was their personal success. That's the beautiful thing about it.

That's what is transformational about the Paris Agreement, that there is not *one* person who can be credited; this is a shared standing up for who we are as a *human race*. This might have seemed impossible, but as I like to say, impossible is not a fact, it's an attitude. With all of us together, we are able to change this attitude, and take this moonshot, and say: We don't know exactly how we're going to do this, but *this* is the moonshot. We know that for our children, for their children, for generations to come, this needs to be done, so we're just going to put it out there.

NS: Now let's talk about the leaders, the practicalities, in terms of the players, and the private sector, and so on. Let's start with the leaders. Of course leaders have to respond, at least we hope they do, to pressures. It's the pressures as well as their own vision, or lack of it, that bring the decisions and the movement. How do you see that leadership taking place? We've got moral leadership, *Laudato Si*, and the Pope . . .

CF: God bless the Pope!

NS: My father would never have thought that I would ever be an enthusiast for a Pope . . . but I am! And the political leaders . . . of course the United States, China, extremely important, but also India and Indonesia and Europe and Africa and Latin America – your continent – and so on; let's start with the political leadership, and of course we have an election in the United States at the end of this year . . . [reaction from audience].

CF: Could we have silence in the room about that one [laughing]? I don't know why people started to get a little bit uneasy when you mentioned that one . . .

NS: It's a serious subject, no jokes: as James Taylor said, this is no time for levity. I don't want to obsess about that election . . . You worked so closely with all these leaders up to Barack, help us to think through the leadership from Paris.

CF: At several levels, certainly at the national government level, it is going to be fundamentally important that these 155 heads of state that came to Paris – under one roof, on one day, on one topic, for the first time in history – really understand that the decisions that they make now must be seen in the context of what we're collectively trying to do. But it's not just the national leaders. This is also about sub-national leaders, cities, provinces, regions, at every single level.

For example, if we're looking at more energy generation, which is critically necessary in the developing countries, they cannot make those decisions in the absence of the under-standing that we have to decarbonize. If we're looking at the construction and the development of more cities, which China, but not only China, is looking at every single day, that cannot be done outside the context of what we're trying to do globally.

So what is important is not to look at climate change as a silo over there, and then we're going to do our real world over here. The fact is that the accelerated decarbonization that we need has to be the guiding light for almost every decision of human endeavour. It needs to guide what are we going to do on agriculture, transportation, building, energy, health. We have been doing all of this in a high-carbon context. That is no longer possible. And for me this is the toughest part of what we have to do now.

NS: Another way of expressing that: in 2015 the world agreed the Sustainable Development Goals, which are the succes-sors of the Millennium Development Goals. The Millenni-um Development Goals really did have an effect on the way people understood development as much more than growth and income. It was about education, health, gender and so on, and the MDGs had a big part in that. And the Sustainable Development Goals will guide us from now on as well, and they were agreed in September 2015, a few months before Paris. So a way of saying 'it's everywhere' is to say the Sustain-able Development Goals and the Paris agenda are the same.

CF: Yes

NS: Could you tell us something about the private sector

and cities? You mentioned the NGOs and they were important clearly, but the private sector and the cities were not only a big part of Paris; they were also absolutely at the heart of what we have to do next.

CF: Absolutely at the heart. Both the private sector and the cities had a very antagonistic approach to this whole negotiation in Copenhagen. It was one of the many reasons for what I call one of the most successful failures of the UN. This antagonism had built up between national governments on the one hand and cities, regions, provinces and the private sector on the other. So opening up this space was absolutely fundamental.

I come back to this fascinating reality: as long as they can understand that the global interests aren't pitted against their own, companies will see that global interests are also their interests – because who wants to do business on a dead planet? There's not much business to be done.

NS: Firms now take much more seriously not only their moral responsibility, but also the fact that their customers, their shareholders, their investors, are looking at how they behave, partly because they care, but partly from the point of view of *risk*; that investing in hydro-carbons, fossil fuels generally, is a very risky business. And we'll do our best to make it still more risky. This is nerdy stuff, but there's a Financial Stability Board which operates through the bank of international settlements, chaired by the governor of the Bank of England, Mark Carney. And they have woken up very strongly to the riskiness that's embodied in a system that depends so much on fossil fuels, which not only disrupt and destroy so much, but are also on their way out. Mark Carney asked Mike Bloomberg (the former mayor of New York, and the Bloomberg of Bloomberg LP) to put together a financial protocol whereby finance companies will have to report at the end of this year about the riskiness of their activities from the climate point of view. Now that could well be a game-changer in the private sector.

CF: Yes. We have turned the risk equation completely on its head. A few years ago the predominant understanding was that it was much more risky to invest in clean technologies and renewable energies than in the incumbents like coal, oil, gas. Because of physics or because of policy, it is much more risky today to continue to invest in high-carbon, and especially in high-carbon-high-cost (because there is also high-carbon-low-cost), and increasingly the more interesting investments are in the clean technologies and the renewable energy sectors. We now have renewable energy that is not just competitive, but is actually cheaper than fossil fuel – three cents per kilowatt hour, compared with six or seven cents from fossil fuels. And it also is this new technology, this decentralized capacity to generate electricity, that is essential to the eradication of poverty.

NS: But we do have to remind ourselves that were moving far too slowly, and there's still opposition. Can you say something about the opposition?

CF: Well, I think one of the species that should be on the CITES list of our species in extinction is the climate change denier.

NS: We don't want to prevent *that* extinction do we?

CF: [laughing] No that is true. It is very difficult now to be a climate change denier and remain credible, given the incontrovertible science. However, there is a very ingrained lethargy, which we all have as human beings or as institutions. We have developed a comfort zone over the past 150 years as individuals, and the fossil fuel companies particularly behave as if they've got it cracked. To face the challenge of completely changing their business model if they want business continuity, they need to invest today, not tomorrow, in renewable energy. They need to transform their understanding of themselves from being fossil fuel companies to being energy companies. They have a huge technical and engineering asset base to devote to this, but they need to retrain, and deploy their capital differently. Many other sectors that are not as energy-intensive, and certainly are not *producing* these fuels, are already on their way to being transformed, and some are already 'a hundred per cent renewable'.

We've been talking about this transformation in technological terms and political terms, but there is something much deeper here. I think we began to see the seeds of it in Paris, and for me that has to do with giving up the need to blame, and giving up the need to compete. We are fundamentally much more interdependent, and so the thought that it was possible for you to lose and me to gain, or for me to lose and you to gain, is being questioned now. Our interdependence is pushing us into a space in which we either are all going to sink the ship or can all be better.

That change in understanding was perhaps not in the legal text of the Paris Agreement. But it really is the spiritual underpinning of a new kind of being with each other, and the underpinning of how governments are going to work with each other, how corporations are going to work with each other. I know that it sounds a little bit 'apple-pie' (and how is this actually going to function in reality?), because we're all fundamentally egotistic. But I think there is huge space for us all to be better human beings, and better governments, better corporations, and I don't think we have any other option. There is a huge shift in values, a tectonic shift, as you can see in the way that countries came together in Paris, and will continue to do so.

Stephen Fry & Christopher Hitchens

with Joan Bakewell
Hay-on-Wye 2005

JOAN BAKEWELL: Welcome everyone to the Blasphemy Debate. Well, it's called a debate, but there's no motion, nor proposer and opposer, because this has segued into a discussion, in which two extremely brilliant minds – well-informed, with backgrounds reaching across the globe – are going to present what I hope will be a subtle analysis of the problems arising from, as it says in the brochure, 'freedom of speech' – that includes laws of libel, invasion of privacy, things like that, 'religious tolerance' – and I'm sure we all have in mind the proposed law against incitement to religious hatred, and then, the brochure adds, 'multiculturalism' and 'orthodoxy'. So this is a broad canvas, and no people more broad than my two guests today: Stephen Fry, actor, film-maker, broadcaster, chairman of *QI*, one of my favourite programmes – and a promoter of tea . . .

STEPHEN FRY: . . . Just come out with it and say: 'Whore!'

JB: And Christopher Hitchens? Well, I hesitate to describe him, so can we leave that to someone else? And just say that in his own book, this remarkable collection of reviews and essays called *Love, Poverty and War,* he himself tells us that he comes from a long line of naval and military types, and that he wakes each morning hoping that he's not fallen prey to premature curmudgeon-hood. The word I question is 'premature'. But he does use a phrase that will indicate what he will speak of tonight when he talks about 'the most toxic of foes:

religion'. So, before we start debating blasphemy, I thought I would ask each of them to set out their own picture, to give us a background to their own beliefs, faiths, and how this background has developed or been rejected, to show us where they're coming from. So, Stephen?

SF: Well, I would like to be able to offer a tidy description of my views on spirituality and religion and sectarianism as regards my own history, but it's been a very messy one. When I was about thirteen, I became enraptured by the Anglican Church. I was born, technically . . . if one can be 'technically' a Jew that's what I am, because that's what my mother is, a Jewess with Jewish parents and grandparents. I wasn't brought up in the Jewish faith; I was brought up with no faith at all. But, as I say, I became enraptured by the Anglican Communion and also by the English mystics – Mother Julian . . . the author of *The Cloud of Unknowing* . . . Aquinas . . . and so on. I don't know why. I can't explain it – I was a child of fads. Simultaneously, I managed to immerse myself in Wagner and P G Wodehouse and Sherlock Holmes. There is no special pattern that I can discern.

I have always believed that everything that is said from authority has either the authority of one's own heart, one's own brain, one's own reading, one's own trust, but not the authority of someone who claims they're speaking for God and knows the truth because it's written in a book. So that, essentially, is where I come from. I just want to add, on the blasphemy side, I've never believed there was any problem with blasphemy, and it is obvious nonsense to have a law suggesting that blasphemy is a crime. It's often an offence against good taste; it's often unkind. But so are many things humans do; we don't have to make them outlawed.

JB: Thank you. Christopher?

CHRISTOPHER HITCHENS: Well, I've no intention of being that brief. You asked me an autobiographical question; I have a captive audience – they're not going to leave while Fry is here. Settle down. I hope you all have a drink and a smoke, as I'm going to have.

I consider myself in some ways to have been fortunate, in that my father came from a very strict Baptist – a Calvinist – family. The misery of those Sundays was maybe one of the things that made me run away and join the Royal Navy. I've also had to work it out like Stephen, backwards as it were, in retrospect, not knowing any of this in childhood. My mother's family also comes from what we now know as the 'whiplash' of the Polish border, of the German frontier – when they left it was Germany; it's now Poland. But she, for innumerable reasons, didn't want to be Jewish. She wanted to assimilate, and wanted her sons to be English gentlemen, and you can be the judge of that . . . comrades. So neither of my parents wanted to inflict religion on me at all, and I think the fact that I was baptized on a submarine in the Royal Navy in Warsaw, the most Catholic country in Europe, was because they hoped to move into the middle class, which again you can be the judge of. So nothing was inflicted on me, I have nothing to rebel against, no grudge against it, and no grudge even about being forced to go to Bible classes at school.

But I do remember exactly when I realized it was all balls from beginning to end. And that was – Mrs Watts, who taught us the scripture class, and also did our nature walks, and biology, and introductions to flowers, birds, etcetera, when I must have been not much more than nine. One day I remember distinctly, she said, with perfect sincerity, it seemed to me: 'Look, children, how the trees and grass are so green. Think how good that shows our Lord to be, because what if the trees had been . . . mauve, or electric blue? How unrestful that would be to the eye.' I knew nothing then about natural selection or about the human genome or the theory of evolution but I remember thinking very clearly, in my little corduroy shorts: That's bullshit. The argument of design . . . it's impossible to believe in the creationist view or the revealed view of any faith, unless you concede to the argument of design. Without it religion is . . . well, no religion is without it, actually or implicitly. And if you can tell at the age of nine that it's much more likely your eyes have adapted to the vegetation than that the vegetation has been created for the pleasure of your eyes, you don't need any more.

I wish we had a true believer here because it sounds a bit complacent for me to say this, but I have exposed myself to the argument a good deal. I'm perfectly certain that I'm right. But even if I was completely wrong, and there was revealed truth and we were designed by a benevolent dictator – excuse me, creator – who took a benevolent look at all our actions and supervised us from cradle to grave and beyond – in other words, if we were to live in a celestial North Korea, why people should *want* this, I don't know. I'm an anti-theist, not an atheist.

Suppose it was true, there would still be no place for a blasphemy law. The important thing, the essential thing, would be the right of people to say it's not true at all. So we could, in fact, adjourn.

JB: No, you're not getting away that easily. What I want to know is, if we're going to have to deal with people who are religious in this world, devout people – and perhaps there might be some in the audience who will speak to their faith, do you know what it is to have a religious impulse? Can you understand that? Have you ever experienced it or is it simply weird, somewhere else – 'I don't need to bother'?

CH: I've met people whom I consider to be morally superior to myself.

JB: That's not the question. I'm talking about the spirituality within yourself.

CH: I've been forced to confront it by meeting people morally superior to myself, braver than myself, who live in terrible countries, or very dangerous situations, and do witness in a wonderful way for the rights of others, and are self-sacrificing. I don't mean the Mother Teresa racketeers and frauds; I mean people who really do it, and, when they say that religion is their motivation, I'm obliged to agree with that or to respect it, and I do. I don't myself have any hope about death or any fear about it. I consider myself to be as subject to the laws of biology as everybody else and I may be lucky in another way – I have been born without whatever gene it might turn out to be.

JB: I want to hang on to these very good people you've spoken of, doing selfless deeds because their faith has inspired them to do so. What do you believe religion is?

CH: In only this respect am I an orthodox Freudian: I think Freud, in *The Future of An Illusion*, says it's *ineradicable* in us or, at least, it's not eradicable until we cease to be afraid of death or of dying. Cease to be afraid of the dark. It's the highest form that wish-thinking takes, wish-thinking being the cheapest form of our emotions and our ambitions. It's the most elevated form that cheap, narcissistic and solipsistic ambition will take, and I think when writing *The Future of An Illusion* he condemned us to go on living with it but taught us what we already knew, which is that it's a curse. That's why Freud is right because, until we cease to fear death, or rather until we evolve a bit more, because nothing proves evolution more than the survival of religious belief, we are still fearful, partially formed animals, with a terror of death and the dark.

JB: But there's a theory by Robin Dunbar, whom I heard expand this theory at Hay last year in a book called *The Human Story*. His theory – I'm no authority on it but I'm fascinated by it – is that religion is, as it were, hard-wired into the human consciousness, and is part of a programmed pattern which we cannot avoid.

SF: Yes, there is a theory that it's congruent to or deeply parallel to the development of consciousness in the human mind, because as far as we can tell tree frogs don't have a religious impulse, or seem to yet. Of course, we don't know.

CH: They behave as if they do.

SF: Yes.

CH: They behave like moral idiots from dawn till dusk.

SF: Yes, because they are prelapsarian. Whatever the myth of Genesis means, it is essentially that of consciousness, of understanding. And they are either very lucky or very unlucky, in that they spend one hundred per cent of their time being tree frogs and being supreme. They don't have to *become* tree frogs; they don't have to wake up the next morning saying: 'Was I a good tree frog?'

CH: Nor do they sacrifice baby tree frogs to idols that they've made.

JB: Nor do they want laws of blasphemy. We have to come back to this!

CH: Religion *is* in our consciousness. This theory may turn out to be inadequate, but for now I'd be willing to accept it. I believe religion is an ineradicable impulse, but for that reason

I believe it's a combatable one. It can be . . . not defeated . . . it can be negated, it can be ridiculed, which is the first impulse not of the blasphemer, by the way, but simply of the critic or the rationalist. Marx did not say that religion was the opiate of the people. What he said was, and it's in the introduction to his critique of Hegel's *Philosophy of Right*, he said that 'religion is the sigh of the oppressed creature, the heart of a heartless world, the spirit of the spiritless situation' . . . the criticism of it has 'plucked the flowers from the chain, not in order that men shall wear the chain without any consolation but so that they may break the chain and cull the living flower.' And the history of our civilization has been that it starts when theocracy ends. Only when people separate the church from the state can art or science or philosophy have a chance. There are no exceptions.

JB: You have a problem, gentlemen, here, because you have highly brilliant views about the place of religion – which is to be *nowhere* in society. You clearly hope it will die out . . .

CH: No, no. I don't believe that at all. One must have the policy, the position that I think is adumbrated by Thomas Jefferson and Thomas Paine and is enshrined in the First Amendment to the American Constitution, which says that 'Congress shall make no law respecting an establishment of religion, or prohibiting the free exercise thereof': the state is utterly neutral. All religious belief is therefore equally protected and not protected, and this is the same amendment that guarantees absolute freedom of expression and allows the state not to abridge any form in which the people may petition or assemble or speak for the redress of grievances. It understands that freedom of expression in religion is the origin of free expression. You may not qualify. You must assume that people will always believe in God. But you must not let them run the state. Unluckily, the American Revolution, which was an English revolution, was never completed. The Americans got away from the Hanoverian monarchy and the Church of England – under which we still live. And to which we still pay tithes . . . Wake up, by the way! We have traditions instead of rights. Which means that the law can say you may not offend someone's religion but they won't say which one it is, or they'll keep changing which one it is. That's preposterous, that's doomed.

JB: Well, we have a proposed law which will outlaw – criminalize – incitement to religious hatred. These are the words going into law and are being revised now on the agenda for the next parliamentary session, and there are voices raised against it. This law is likely to go through. Christopher, what will happen?

CH: Well, anyone who has any understanding of the English language can see incitement of religious hatred must, if it means what it says, mean incitement to hatred *by religious people*; it can only mean that. That's the plain meaning of the first thought. Well, a part of me wants that to be banned, but no part of me would make it illegal. People often incite hatred *in the name of religion*. Isn't that what they mean? If not, it's deadly hostile to free expression.

JB: Stephen, the nature of comedy, the nature of wit in language, all languages – but we're familiar with English jokes and humour – involves the use of this word 'offence'. Giving offence. Comedy is to give offence. You will therefore offend people who will have on their side a law enacted by this government that will allow there to be prosecutions brought for comedy. Salman Rushdie would certainly be prosecuted.

CH: Irony. He'd be prosecuted for irony. In England.

JB: How is this to be stemmed? We can object, we can be passionately against it –

CH: No. Repudiate. No tolerance for that.

JB: Simply refuse to obey the law?

CH: You cannot grant the first premise of it, either.

SF: I think we have to separate out all kinds of things. I'm sure we all have the same horrified feeling about what newspapers like to call 'Mad Mullahs', or the fanatical end of any religion, whether they're fundamentalists in America and other parts of Christendom, or the absolute intolerance and hatred that's felt by some members of the Muslim population towards people like me – the desire to see people like me killed. And it's horrifying to think there is that much hatred out there for me and for things I believe in, and it makes me very cross, naturally. And I will not bear the idea that I can't discuss it openly and freely.

But when it comes to *inciting* hatred, I'm rather pleased we have a law against inciting racial hatred . . . there are all sorts of clichés, like the Holocaust began not with the first hut built at Auschwitz but with the first stone thrown on *Kristallnacht* . . . of course, that's rather banal, because you can't stop people throwing a stone. But we're alert to the fact that the incitement of hatred is not good. And I think sometimes, on our side of the debate, which is to say the secular side, we can rather over-read the mass of what religion is, and alienate it all the further, and drive a wedge between it and a secular world – a world of reasoning, educated people like ourselves, who can happily quote all kinds of philosophy and are familiar simply with the *mechanics of logic*. Which of course are alien to the vast quantity, it seems, of religious people who have no respect for logic. Which for us is tiresome in the extreme, because it means there's no basis for argument.

But if we accept that there are people who fall on their knees in churches and who don't wish to be mocked with whips and scourges for doing so, that's fine. I would always hope to be tasteful enough never wantonly to offend anyone. However, simply to say: there is a religious world, and there is a secular world, and the two are enemies, is a hopeless thing, it seems to me. It seems to me the greatness of our *reason* – if it is great – is that it can accommodate and teach and enlighten. The Enlightenment should not be considered to be over; it's a project that will never end.

JB: We applaud, and we rightly do, the expression of the in-heritance of the Enlightenment, which is characterized by tolerance. We wish to extend to others the rights we claim for ourselves to the expression of ideas. When they express ideas that damage that tolerance, how do we persist in *our* tolerance of that critique?

CH: I think one *must* hear from people who dislike others. It's essential that Ian Paisley is a member of parliament, and a member of the European parliament, and that he says Catholicism is the work of the devil. It's essential to hear what Catholics really think about Protestants, and Jews, and others. I know what they think about you, Stephen: they say they hate your sin but they love you as a sinner. They say your essence is hateful, in other words. What a stupid, casuistic thing to say. What a crappy euphemism. Don't put up with things like that. But I want to hear it from them. I want to hear people say that the Holocaust never happened if that's what they think. I want to hear Jews say Arabs have to clear out of Palestine to make room for them if that's what they think. I'll defend this for anybody. But if I'm going to defend it for everybody else, I'm going to insist on it for myself too. I'm going to insist they respect me back. How bad is that? That's all we're asking.

The government says: 'No, we'll check that right away. We apply it selectively.' You never know in advance what it will be you're going to say that someone might not like or some cock may misinterpret. That is illegal. In America, it would be unconstitutional. We have to defend ourselves. I will go on to say to those who are prepared to use violence, or the threat of it, to enforce this law, that what they are essentially saying to Blair is: 'Do you want this law, or do you want violence in the streets that would split the Labour vote?' That's what they're saying. It's plain incitement. I'm not going to have that. I won't be talked to in that tone of voice. Would you?

JB: But we're addressing the extremism of people who wish to impose on us – we, the tolerant, and tolerant of them, too – their way of thinking. And this is a growing phenomenon of world politics.

SF: I think it's fair to say, almost every failure of humanity is a failure of imagination to some extent, a failure to penetrate the minds of others. G K Chesterton – he was, of course a religious man, as we know, not an entirely nice one – but he said some very good things, and one of the things he said was that the trouble with atheism, as far as he was concerned, is that when you stop believing in God, you don't believe in *nothing*; you believe in *anything*. And perhaps we do live in a culture where reason and so on are not glorified, deified, as perhaps they should be. However, I don't think the spiritual and the beautiful and the noble and the altruistic and the morally strong and the virtuous are in any way inventions of religion, or particular or peculiar to religion – there is absolutely no monopoly on beauty and truth in religion.

I suppose that's one of the reasons that I'm so fond of the Greeks. And one of the reasons that the great radical and poet Shelley wrote his *Prometheus Unbound* was because he understood that the Genesis myth, which had bedevilled our culture, the Western European culture, for a very long time, indeed for 2,000 years, is essentially a myth in which we should be ashamed of ourselves. God says: 'Who told you you were naked?' What possible reason have we to believe we are 'naked', or that if we are naked there is something to be ashamed of? That what we are or what we do is something which we should ever apologize for? That we should apologize for our dreams, our impulses, our appetites, our desires? These are not things to apologize for. Our *actions* sometimes we do apologize for and excoriate ourselves for, and rightly. But that's the Genesis myth for you.

In the Greek myth of Prometheus, who stole fire from heaven and gave it to his favourite, mortal man, the Greeks were saying we have divine fire; whatever is divine is in us as *humans*. We are as good as the gods. The gods are capricious and mean and foolish and stupid and jealous and rapacious and all the things Greek mythology shows that they are. And that's a much better explanation, it seems to me. And for that, the gods punished Prometheus and chained him to a rock in the Caucasus and vultures chewed away his liver, which regrew every night because he was immortal. And Shelley quite rightly understood – and interestingly his wife, of course, wrote *Frankenstein* as the modern Prometheus – understood, as the champion of a real humanity and a real humanism, as we've come to call it, that *we* are captains of our soul and captains of our destiny, and that *we* contain any divine fire that there is, divine fire that is fine and great.

It's perfectly obvious, if there were ever a God he has lost all possible taste. Forget the aggression and the unpleasantness of the radical right or the Islamic hordes to the East. The sheer lack of intelligence and insight and ability to express themselves, and to enthuse others, of the priesthood and the clergy here in this country, and indeed in Europe, are enough:

think, God once had Bach and Michelangelo on his side; he had Mozart. And now, who does he have? People with ginger whiskers and tinted spectacles who reduce the glories of theology to a kind of 'sharing'. That's what religion has become, a feeble and anaemic nonsense. Because *we* understood that the fire was within *us*; it is not within an idol on an altar, whether a gold cross or a Buddha or anything else. That *we* have it; the fault is in *our* stars but also the glory is in *us*. We take credit for what is great about man, and we take the blame for what is dreadful about man. We neither grovel nor apologize at the feet of a god, nor are so infantile as to project the idea that, as human beings, we once had a father and therefore we should have a divine one too. We have to *grow up*, which is partly what Christopher was saying.

JB: That is the most wonderful tribute to the human spirit.

Stephen Fry's Alphabet

with Peter Florence

Hay-on-Wye 2010

PETER FLORENCE: This is Stephen Fry. We're going to invent an alphabet tonight. I'm going to make some of it up, and Stephen's going to make some of it up, and we're going to need you to help us with some of the letters.

We're going to start with *AMBITION*. Stephen, what is it you would most now like to do?

STEPHEN FRY: Now, it's very hard to answer. If I was to say my ambition is to be happy that would be very dull. There is no one I'm ambitious to go to bed with, no one I'm ambitious to meet. I suppose what I'm ambitious for is not to turn into a bitter, angry old person. I'm now fifty-two, and would hope as I got older I got more accepting of things so that if, in thirty years' time, there's a modern Lady Gaga – incidentally, when is the video coming out? It's just driving me mad! – rather than saying, 'Oh, tunes used to be better in the past', I want to think: Tunes are so much better *now* than they ever were. All things are better than they ever were. They may not be, but they're almost certainly not worse.

I think it's dangerous to the human spirit to believe that your island of youth was privileged as better, richer, more fulfilling, more artistic, more creative, more innocent. I think the best ambition anyone can have is to get younger as they get older. To be more accepting, and to be less closed.

PF: 'B' is for *BORED*. What makes you bored? You work at a higher speed than anyone I know, so what holds you up?

SF: I suppose it's very interesting, being in the public eye. The modern culture of celebrity is a terrible thing, but nonetheless, when I was a teenager watching *Parkinson*, I wanted to jump into the television and be part of this glamorous world of extraordinary people. I fantasized about being stopped in shops and asked for an autograph. But if you want to know what bores me now it is being at a signing-queue for a book. It used to be fun to be able to go and ask: 'What's your name? Where are you from?', sounding like the Prince of Wales – to 'fall into a conversation' was really good fun. Now, that's impossible, because the moment someone arrives at the queue, they're looking at the person next to me and going, 'Is it all right if I have a photograph?' And *they* want to be *in* the picture, so they give their camera to that person next to me, and that person is like someone who has never seen a reptile being given a chameleon and it's 'what . . . so . . . what . . . oh I think I've turned it off . . . oh!' If I could have back the hours in which I've gone, 'Well, get on with it for fuck's sake!' – through smiling teeth – I would be very happy.

PF: *CAMBRIDGE*. What kind of transfer was that for you?

SF: It was a very extraordinary thing for me. When I was seventeen, I got arrested by the police and went to prison, and I emerged from a custodial sentence with two years' probation, and my parents were understandably at the end of their tether. When I arrived back home on probation, I said: 'I want to do some A levels.'

By then I had screwed up every other opportunity. So they said: 'It's fine if you really want to, but it's up to you. We're not going to do it.' I knew that Norwich City College did a one-year A level course, so I went . . . literally the day I got back from Pucklechurch, which was the name of the prison I'd been in. It sounds like a beautiful bed and breakfast somewhere in the Lake District. In fact, it was such a hard place . . .

So there was this queue, and it was the second day of registration for this college, and I was at the end of the queue, and there was a little man, his name was Peter Butler, I'll never forget him, with silver hair and bright blue eyes, and he said: 'What do you want to do?' And I said: 'A levels. English, French and History of Art.' He said: 'Oh, I think there may be one place left in French, but the other two have gone. You'll have to pick something else.' I said: 'No, those are the ones I want to do.' I looked at him, and I said: 'If you let me do these, I will get A grades, and I will get a scholarship to Cambridge. You must let me do this.' And he looked at me, and there was a pause that seemed like eternity, and he said: 'I don't know why I'm doing this. OK. You're signed in.' That was the moment, I now realize, looking back, on which my entire life pivoted.

PF: *DARTS*.

SF: Now you've got me going. Phil Taylor is probably the greatest sportsman alive on the planet. You may question the use of the word 'sportsman' next to a darts player . . . But he is fifteen times world champion. He's broken every possible world record – I don't think any other sport in the world has a *fifteen-times* world champion. There is an unwritten embarrassment about darts being a pub game, and a working-class game, and it is a very male game. It's obviously not very attractive to see these overweight, sweaty men with tattoos, except for the fact they are so good at their sport, and that the scoring of darts is so exciting that you get fantastic games. As I said on live television, I'm like a pig in Chardonnay.

PF: *EROS*.

SF: Oh, *Eros*. Sore backwards, by no accident. It's also an anagram of rose. When you're a child and you watch films on television, you tend to wonder why it is that the action, the comedy, the adventure stops every now and again for this bewildering, baffling nonsense that is *Eros*, that is love. And then, when you pass through childhood into adulthood, there's a part of you that sometimes questions why there is any other subject in the world. It is all there is to think and talk about: love. And the extraordinary thing, there are many shapes to it. I remember seeing a man of 106 being interviewed on television on his 106th birthday, and the interviewer said: 'Is there anything that makes you unhappy about being old ... all your friends ...?' And he said: 'It's not friends. I still miss my mother.' And I thought: Wow, of course you would. My mother, I'm happy to say, is still alive, but I'm sure I'd miss her and I'd miss my father if he went. If you love someone, you love them for ever.

PF: *FOLK MUSIC.*

SF: I'm very fond of folk music. Folk music is roots music. Some of the most talented musicians, Kate Rusby, people like that, in Britain are folk musicians. And the music is deep and complex and exciting and unusual ...

PF: *GENOME.*

SF: I'm lucky enough to have done that BBC programme *Who Do You Think You Are?* where you can go back to your roots. We have two parents and four grandparents, eight great grandparents, 16, 32, 64, 128, 256, 512, 1,024 ... it soon becomes a gigantic number in a very short time, so it becomes obvious that, if you have any English blood in you at all, you must be directly descended from William II, if not, from Henry III ... because you have more ancestors going back to then than the population of the country. So you must be. There's no possibility that you aren't, even allowing for quite a lot of incest. You have thousands of ancestors, and each one of them is as responsible for your existence as any other. What do we base our identity on? I don't know my own genome, apart from it's probably very similar to yours. *We're* certainly related, and we're all related in this room, and if that sounds like a hippy-ish way of saying we're all brothers and sisters, well, why not?

PF: *HITLER*. You wrote a novel called *Making History*, which is one of the very few works of fiction, works of art, at all that satirizes Hitler. Why is that so difficult? Why is the taboo so strong?

SF: He's our bogeyman. We decide on whatever 'evil' means, and, whatever it is, we pile it on to Hitler, and for me that lets the human race off. The point of my book was: suppose Hitler had not been born. Can we be sure that the world would be better? The same? Worse? It's a science fiction 'what if?' book. But let us just suppose . . . let us recognize some of the facts of anti-Semitism, Pan-Germanism, that there were in, say, the 1890s: there were over a hundred regular anti-Semitic publications just in Vienna. There were more than that in Munich: Hitler was not alone.

So let's suppose that, instead of Hitler coming to power through the struggles of the German workers' party in Munich in the 1920s, it had been somebody else – who probably hated Jews too. And let's suppose that person had said: 'Well, let's keep them here. We don't like them, but, my God, they've got some clever scientific things.' He would have had an atom bomb by 1940. America wouldn't. And who would have ruled the world? That is the premise of the book, at least. It makes it sound like we're saying 'thank God we've had Hitler', but how is anyone to know, not that history is benign, but that even worse history might not have taken place?

PF: *ISHERWOOD*.

SF: Auden was a great hero of mine, and Isherwood to some extent as well. He wrote a book called *Christopher and His Kind*, which was very influential on me. It was an autobiography in which he treated himself as a third person, Christopher. And, as it happens, probably his most famous work, *Goodbye to Berlin*, was very instrumental in my being expelled from school. It started my downward spiral into prison. He wrote a short story involving this woman, Sally Bowles, who was a rather self-fantasizing figure, and that was turned into a play called *I Am a Camera*, which was then turned into a musical, *Cabaret*.

I was at school in 1970-something, at the age of about fifteen, and I got permission from my housemaster to go to London for a meeting of the Sherlock Holmes Society, which I was a member of, and I was to stay the night and come back the next day. I went to London, went to the Sherlock Holmes Society meeting, and the next day went to the first screening in a cinema of *Cabaret*. And I was so overcome by the experience, I thought it was so fabulous, that I stayed to watch the next screening, and some rush of blood got into my head and the next day I stayed for *A Clockwork Orange*, and *Fritz the Cat*, and various other films. It was about three days after that that I woke up out of my mad daze and realized I ought to get to school. They said: 'Fry, you've delighted us for long enough.' And I was expelled.

PF: *JONATHAN IVE.*

SF: Hands up if you know who Jonathan Ive is . . . He's probably the most influential – well, the *second* most influential Englishman alive, the first being Sir Tim Berners-Lee, who invented the World Wide Web. Jonathan Ive was a young British designer, and in 1992 he joined Apple, at the time run by a man called John Sculley. It's one of the great stories of the twentieth century, certainly for a fanatic of digital things such as me. In 1984 the Apple Macintosh came out. Then, over a difference of opinion between Steve Jobs and the board of directors, Jobs was fired in 1985 and had twelve years away from Apple. But while he's away Apple is spinning around in a terrible state. In 1992 Jony Ives joins and is very frustrated. He's a very good designer but there's not much he can do, because Apple is going from crisis to crisis: it brings up products that are very remarkable, but nobody buys them. So by 1997, they'd not made a profit on a line of computers for a long time, the inventory was piling up, the stock price was on the floor – there was no hope for it. They brought back Steve Jobs.

Steve Jobs looked round this company that he'd founded that was now in great trouble – nobody would give it the time of day – and he saw this young British designer, Jony Ive, who'd had a terrible time of all his ideas being rejected or not really going anywhere, and he saw some of his work, and he picked up the phone, and said, 'Come up to my office.' Jobs said, 'I've had a look at some of the things you're doing, and I think they're very exciting. Whatever you need it's yours. Go away, and come back with something new and exciting and different that will make people happy.' And Jony Ive designed this extraordinary one-piece machine called the iMac in 'Bondi Blue' transparent plastic – really remarkable. And it was the first computer that Apple made a profit on and had done for twelve years. Then he designed an MP3 player of such simplicity and beauty and pleasure to use that it utterly transformed the music market, called the iPod. And then he designed a phone, here it is. And then – it's backstage – a 'pad'.

He is so talented and so charming and so modest and so extraordinary; it is remarkable to me that he hasn't been knighted [Jonathan Ive was knighted in 2012]. Not because he would like a knighthood, but because it would recognize that designers are at the very heart of our culture, that they have altered the way we look at things and do things. He's as aware as you are, and I am, that not all technology is perfect. There are complexities and ambiguities about what the digital age is doing to us as a society, as a community, as individuals, but you could not be prouder of any Briton, I think, than of Jony Ive. He is worshipped in Britain and in America as the greatest industrial designer of our age. But only a few hands went up when I said his name, and that's sad to me, because I think he's a great man.

PF: *KNIGHTHOOD*. Since you brought it up, why have you not been knighted? Would you approve of the system?

SF: Oh Lord, it's terribly embarrassing even to think about such things. It would be embarrassing to reveal that I'd been offered it and turned it down – if that were true – because that would sound sniffy and ungrateful. And it would sound bad if I said: 'Yes, *I* can't understand why I haven't been, either.' There is, however, a famous story of a philosopher, a quite well-known philosopher, who was asked by one of his students: 'There are statues of Nietzsche and Spinoza. There's no statue of you. Why's that?' He said: 'You know, all my life I have believed it is better for someone to ask why there is no statue than why there is.' And it's a lot better for someone to say, 'Why on earth haven't they knighted you?' than for them to say, 'Why did they knight you?' I'm very happy being Mr Stephen Fry, thank you, but it's very charming that you might ask such a thing.

PF: *LAMBETH WALK*.

SF: Oh my, there's a thing, yes. In 1984-ish, a man who was my agent, Richard Armitage, invited me to his house in the country. He was a very old-fashioned, rather growly English-man, and he talked. He said, 'My father was called Reginald Armitage,' and I said, 'Well . . .' And he went on, 'And my grandparents made their money making Pomfret cakes in South Yorkshire, but my father Reginald was very musically gifted; he went to Cambridge and then he went to the Royal College of Music, and he was an organist at St Anne's church, Soho, and he heard a lot of modern music being played in his day. Jazz music. And he turned out to have rather a facility for composing tunes.' And I said, 'Gosh that's interesting.' He said, 'Yes, but he thought it was rather embarrassing to the family name to use his own name, so he invented a pseudonym under which he could compose, which was Noel Gay.' I said, 'Right.' He said, 'I know it's an odd name now, but right for the time, it was very 1930s. Under that name he was a very successful composer, and he wrote many songs – "The Sun Has Got His Hat On", "Hey Little Hen", "Let's Have a Fiddly At The Milk Bar", "The Lambeth Walk", "Leaning On a Lamp-Post", and so on.' I said, 'That's a great litany.' And he said, 'Yes. And many of these were written into a musical called Me and My Girl.' I said, 'Wow . . . it's getting late. I'm going to bed.' And he said, 'Here it is!' And he gave me this typescript.

I read it, and the next morning he said, 'What do you think?' and I said, 'Well, it's very interesting.' It was the most successful English musical in the 1930s that there had ever been. And he said, 'I want you to rewrite it for the modern age – in the 1980s.' I had never had anything to do with musicals. I didn't know anything about them, but, to cut a very long story short, I did it, and it was performed at the Leicester Haymarket, and transferred to the West End where it ran for twelve, thirteen years I think. And then to Broadway where it ran for nine years. I was three years out of university when I started work on it, and it was extraordinary, because it was also performed in Mexico and Japan and Hungary and Australia and France, and every day there would be a flapping noise as another envelope hit the doormat full of cheques, and I was suddenly absurdly rich. I can't put it any other way. My friends began to hate me and, in equal measure, to borrow money from me, and it was the most bizarre thing to happen to someone. There's not much one can say about it, except I've never dared do a musical since.

PF: *MIAMI.*

SF: Miami is not *mon ami*. When I did a documentary where I visited all the states of America, I drove in a London black cab from Maine all the way down the coast, and round, and up, until I ended up in Washington State. When people say, 'You've been to every state in the union – which one did you like best?' and I try and answer that, I never know quite what to say. I say, 'I like 'South Kentana' – a mixture of Kentucky, South Carolina . . . Maybe Northern California would suit me; it's very hard to pick a favourite.' But then they say, 'Which one did you *dis*like most?' And I always say Florida. It has its charms. North Florida is 'the South'; North Florida is like Alabama or Georgia which border it. But South Florida, where Miami is and Orlando is, to me is a hell. It's rude and brash and nasty and glitzy and unpleasant, and I couldn't wait to be shot of the place.

PF: Now, *NORWICH CITY.*

SF: We've gone up! We're champions of League One. I come from Norfolk so you might, if you're in the west, support the Linnets from King's Lynn, but it's more likely – because you want to watch professional football of a reasonably high standard – you'd support the Canaries, who are Norwich City. I think there's some real pleasure in supporting a team like Norwich, rather than having the burden of Arsenal or Chelsea or ManU or Liverpool, because you so *expect* them to win that when they do it's somehow not quite good enough. Whereas a local team . . . when Norwich win, it's like, 'Wow, did you see? They *won*!' And if they lose, you make a joke about it and you sort of don't mind – the risk–reward ratio is so fabulous.

PF: And on that sweet note: OSCAR.

SF: Well, you can probably tell, I can talk about him for ever. As Richard Ellmann says at the end of his biography, he stands before us now so wise, so kind, and so right. He symbolizes the fact that it was the life of the mind, it was art, and it was imagination, that would set people free. He was a kind of prince of Bohemia – to students in particular, who are given for three years the keys to the kingdom of Bohemia, and I hope they will always keep them, and never be seduced into a world of false morality, and false closed convention, and never close their minds, but keep them open. Oscar stands as a symbol for that more than any other man, I think.

PF: PSYCHOTHERAPY.

SF: That's a good 'P', that. Golly. I've had a bit of experience with psychotherapy. I think it's a happy thing now – and I speak as an honorary fellow of the Royal College of Psychiatrists. It's a happy thing that all psychiatrists agree that the better outcomes for most people who have a mental health disorder of one kind or another are the result of a mixture of physical diagnosis and treatment, if necessary, and talking therapy. But psychotherapy is easy to mock if you're British, partly because the only people you ever hear about who get psychotherapy are those you hear talk on television and people like me, so you're bound to think psychotherapy is just something rich celebrities do, like they might play polo.

But, in the meantime, it's been given to hundreds of thousands of people who don't actually appear on talk-shows and talk about it, so I think what's unfair, sometimes, is people thinking it's just a designer accessory for those in the public eye who can talk about how unhappy and miserable they are.

Actually, if you've ever been to somewhere like Homerton in the East End of London, you realize mental health is a problem for the homeless, the dispossessed, the immigrant, the uneducated – the underclass, if you like. That is where the real mental health front line is.

PF: *QI*.

SF: I thought you were going to say 'queer'. Right, *QI*. Gosh. Well, it was the brain-child of a man called John Lloyd, who is a remarkable fellow. He was also in the Cambridge Footlights back in the same time as his friend Douglas Adams, and he started off doing radio comedy – he started *The News Quiz*, and then he made the jump to television with a show called *Not the Nine O'Clock News*, which made stars of Rowan Atkinson and Mel Smith and Griff Rhys Jones.

I got to know him because we had mutual friends, and he asked me to be in *Blackadder* II. Then at some point in 2002, he took me out to lunch and gave me the idea for a show about things being so interesting, and you could have a quiz show about the universe and history. I particularly liked the idea as I was beginning to get tired of television's incessant interest in popular culture, in pop music and politics. I loved the idea of a quiz show that wasn't about the week's news, wasn't about Jordan whoever she is, and it wasn't about *Big Brother*, nor was it self-consciously about art and things. So I said, 'I'd love to be involved as long as I don't have to be the host,' because I had the idea that being the host was a miserable job, and he said, 'Yes that's fine, you won't be the host.' So that was agreed, and then he called me up and said, 'The BBC are interested and we're going to do a pilot. Trouble is, I can't find anybody to be the host . . . so for the pilot will you be the host?' And I said, 'OK, if it's just for the pilot, I'll be the host.' About three weeks later: 'There's really good news. The BBC love it. They want to do it as a series, but on one condition . . .' So I've been the host.

PF: *ROWLING.*

SF: As in J K? This was again one of the odd gigs you get. Many years ago, my agent called me up and said, as she often does, she said, 'There's an audio book . . .' And I liked audio books – I often used to think that if I got an Equity Card, even if I never really got any good parts, to read stories into a microphone would be terrific fun. She sent it over, and it was a novel – 90,000 words – and I was slightly startled. But I thought there were fun parts to play. I turned up at the studio at lunch-time and the author, this nice woman Jo Rowling, also turned up. We shook hands, we chatted. (I wasn't really this patronizing, but it's better for the story if I was.) I said, 'Jolly good story,' and she said, 'Oh, I'm glad you like it. I'm writing a second one.' I said, 'Good for you!' And so it won the Smarties Prize: very, very good.

When I was doing the fourth one, Jo Rowling herself had done a signing tour of America, and she'd just taken off there, and by this time these were the most famous children's stories of their time. She talked about the signing-queues, we've talked about the photographs, also that people have presents for you and they're very sweet. Anyhow, she was in a shop in New York, and there were the 700 little boys with scars on their foreheads and little goggle spectacles . . .

But, every now and again, someone, a stranger, would come up to her and say, 'Oh, Miss Rowling, I have this for you.' And they would hand her an envelope, and the person from Scholastic, her publishers in America, would grab the envelope and say, 'Thank you', and snatch it away. This kept happening, and after the last book was signed and she was rubbing the callous on her finger, she said, 'By the way, you were very rude to those people who had things to give me. You just snatched them away like that; I thought it was a bit offensive.' And they said, 'No Jo. These people have written their own scenarios, in which Hermione does *this*, or Ron does *that*, in which *this* happens to Dumbledore. They've written little plot lines and whatever, so when your next book comes out, and there is some similarity, they will attempt to sue you. But they will not be able to sue you, because your fingerprints will not be on the envelope. You will have never seen what they wrote. We can depose before witnesses that you never saw any of this – it will be signed and sealed in a safe – and that you have not read it, and it will save you a lot of hassle.' And that's when she thought: This is not normal for children's authors, is it? This is a new territory. And sure, of course dozens of law suits came: I gave you the story about Hermione and you used it! And they would get a letter back from Jo's lawyer, in legalese of course: Fuck off out of my face, you mad bitch!

PF: Can I ask the audience for an 'S'?

AUDIENCE MEMBER: *Sex.*

SF: Well . . . it was the first thing that was called out. Not my natural area of expertise. I created a strange rod for my own back when, in the 1980s, I was called up by a marvellous man called Jonathan Meades; at the time he was a features editor at *Tatler* magazine. I was not a well-known person – I'm talking about 1985 – but I was well known *in a small circle*, because I was doing a bit of journalism, some radio, a little bit of television comedy and the writing mostly. He said: 'I'm commissioning some people to write an article about something they *don't do*. Gavin Stamp is doing something about the fact he doesn't drive; Brian Sewell is doing something about the fact he doesn't go on holiday; somebody else is doing something about never having a pet. Is there anything you don't do?' I said: 'Oh, gosh. I like to think I do almost everything . . . Sex, I suppose. Would that count?' And there was a pause. 'Four hundred words by Thursday.'

I've talked a bit about love, which is the important thing.

I'd had a partner at Cambridge and we stayed together in the first year after leaving. But he was much more interested in the sexual gay world in London in the early 1980s. I loathed gay bars and clubs, just because I can't stand being looked at in that 'inspect-you' way . . . that raking eye . . . and I feel so inadequate, and I just want to have a conversation, and I certainly don't want to dance, or grind away in some dark room. I just want to say, 'Which is your favourite Evelyn Waugh novel?' There aren't any bars for people like me, unfortunately, so I gave up on the whole idea of sex.

PF: *TWITTER.*

SF: Twitter, now we have a particular thing to say for this, because you sweetly asked if I would judge your competition.

PF: We did. The competition was to find a beautiful tweet, the most beautiful tweet of the last month. And what are the criteria by which you judge beauty?

SF: Unbelievably difficult – you've got a very small canvas on which to create your work of beauty. But if you ask someone to be beautiful in 140 characters, you can't expect something Keatsian, some beautiful, sensuous, exquisitely sensual line. I think that would be inappropriate to Twitter.

PF: Who would like to offer a 'U'?

AUDIENCE MEMBER: *UPPINGHAM.*

SF: Uppingham. That's rather scary and very quick. Are you all hugging to yourselves V, W, Xs, Ys and Zs . . . ? Uppingham is a reference to a school that gave me part of my so-called education back in the day. It was founded way back in the Elizabethan era, resolutely middle-class, middle-brow.

I have nothing but the most fond memories of very nice people running it, but I think no matter what school I'd been to, Winchester College or a local comprehensive, I would have had exactly the same problems. It was the strange aura of insane adolescence that I carried around with me, and the troubled nature of my mind and spirit was not *made* by that school – but they did their best with me.

PF: *VILE BODIES*.

SF: *Vile Bodies* is the title of Evelyn Waugh's second novel. He wrote it in 1928 about the society in which he himself had become embroiled, that of the Mitfords and Brian Howard and Harold Acton, and those people known as the Bright Young Things. In the early part of the millennium, I wrote the film version – *Bright Young Things*. It didn't set the box office on fire, but I'm still pleased with the film and the extraordinary cast I managed to assemble. It's very difficult to cast young, because if they're young and *well* known the chances are they're booked up, because the system is so greedy for young talent, and if they're young and *un*known it's hard to be sure if the money-people will be satisfied with them. I cast Michael Sheen, whom I'd worked with in the film *Wilde*.

Then – I'd had literally a day and two-thirds looking at young actors, some still at drama school – and then I had two in a row. They were both Scottish, and one came in, and he had done just half a line, and I thought: That's him. He left, and I turned to the casting director and said, 'He's so brilliant. What's his name?' David Tennant. Right. David Tennant. Brilliant. And then this other one comes in, even more Scottish, if that makes any sense, and even more brilliant, if that's possible. And I thought: Am I hallucinating because I've been here for two days and I'm so desperate? Or . . . this guy is brilliant. I said, 'What was his name again?' James McAvoy. What an extraordinary cast. I was really lucky to have that.

PF: *WAGNER.*

SF: I recently made a documentary about Gutenberg and the invention of printing, and the kind people at BBC4 who screened it said, 'If there's another individual project like that that you're interested in, we might talk and see if we want to do it.' So I said, 'Well, would your heart sink if I said I was interested in Richard Wagner?' and they said, 'Oh, no, no. That could be interesting.' I said, 'I know.' Anyone who likes Wagner is used to seeing a film glaze over people's eyes, even before the 'g' of Wagner is out of your mouth, because he's not to everyone's taste.

I wrote a regular column for *The Listener* magazine, and I happened to write a review of a book by Bryan Magee that is one of the greatest books written on Wagner. A week and half later, I got a letter headed 'All Soul's College, Oxford'. It went, 'Dear Mr Fry, I read with interest your views on Wagner, your views as a Jew on Wagner, your views as a non-religious person on Wagner, your views as a Wagnerite on Wagner . . . perhaps a lunch would interest you. I have a club in London called the Garrick and we could meet there. Yours etc., Isaiah Berlin.'

PF: Can I skip 'X' for a second, and replace it with picking up something you said about the letter from Isaiah Berlin? Why is it that an Irishman can make Irish jokes; a Jew can write about the Holocaust. Why is the author of an art work's identity important to the work?

SF: You're so right. It's very peculiar you mentioned, when we were talking about Hitler, my book *Making History*. It received a complete savaging at the hands of *The New York Times*. I happened to be in New York when it was out, but I didn't know this. A friend of a friend, Bret Easton Ellis, the novelist, was at a party and he came up to me and said, 'Give me a hug.' And I said, 'What?' And he said, 'You managed to get a worse review than my *American Psycho*.' I said, 'Oh, no. Really?' He said, 'It's a stinker. You made fun of the Holocaust; you laughed at the dead Jews.' I said, 'Does she honestly think that? Does she think I'm making light of the Holocaust? As a Jew, do you think I could hold up my hands to my friends and family?' He said, 'Are you Jewish?' And I said, 'Yes. Sort of. My mother is, so I kind of am. I'm not religiously so, but yes – Hitler would think I was. He'd put me in the oven with the others whether I liked it or not, so I might as well say yes. I am.' He went, 'Ahh . . .' Like that.

So I think he told her, and she then wrote a review of my next book – which was my autobiography – in which she described *Making History* as 'sadly misjudged'. But it did set me thinking. The actual knowledge of who made it completely transforms something, even though it is, molecularly, exactly the same thing. So knowing that a book that says this about the Holocaust is written by a Jew, or knowing it's written by a German, *matters*, and this is true of all things in art. So when you know George Eliot was a woman and a Victorian, does it alter your view of *Middlemarch* if you'd previously thought that George Eliot was a man? I don't know. It probably does.

PF: This may be a bit of a twist for 'Y' – I think you might have said 'teenage Stephen'. But I would like you, if possible, to reprise just a little of the spirit of the letter that you wrote to 'YOUNG STEPHEN'.

SF: I was asked to write a letter to my young self by, I think, a gay magazine. It was reprinted by *The Guardian*. It was because of the fact that I had written a letter to my future self when I was fourteen, and it was a very angry and a very convinced letter, saying: I know you will blush when you read this. I know you will think I'm being hysterical. I know you think the world is about this that and the other, but I know where I'm writing from *now* is right, that who I am *now* is right, that how I feel *now* is the truth, and every day I grow away from this moment and this age is a betrayal of who I am.

I had this very peculiar sense of the primacy of the emotional world of the adolescent. When nature and poetry and love first explode in you, it may make you or unmake you, but it certainly transforms you. And there was nothing to endorse or vindicate who I was or how I was, except literature. There was nothing but the library to tell me I wasn't alone. Rock music didn't tell me I wasn't alone; it might have done to people like me later, or I might have changed genders or names or that sort of thing in a lyric and say, 'That does apply to me.'

But for the direct experience of lives similar to mine and the intensities and pitch of life as I felt it, there was literature. At the age of fourteen, this was all new to me, in the way that every month is five years when you're that age. So I wrote this letter to myself. A year or two ago, I wrote a letter back, and in it I pitied the abject misery of myself then, his ferocity, his certainty, his – we would now say – authenticity. The primacy he gave to emotion and the rawness and nakedness of his feelings.

I've never believed that feeling comes before thought, and that feeling alone makes us who we are. But if you love you love. You then have to *recognize what it is* you're feeling. But feeling comes first. I think as an adolescent I knew that, and so I was hugging myself and saying, 'It's all going to be OK. It's going to be fine. You'll be amazed at how lucky your life will turn out to be. You'll be amazed that actually the world does not belong to the strong, rugby-playing, thoughtless and unkind rejecting people. The world belongs to you if you want it to. It belongs to writers and artists, to kindly people, to cheerful people, to people who want to help. And there isn't so much to despair about. There is room in the world for you, so long as you allow yourself to believe it and don't sink into an attitude of self-pity and pessimism.' That's sort of what I wrote.

PF: Tell you what. If we do 'Z' it means we've finished. So why don't we hold that for another time and pick it up again. Stephen Fry's been here for two hours, and has given, and given in the most extraordinary, generous and wonderful way . . . we've had two hours, and it's been the highlight of my festival. I'm deeply grateful to you for doing it. Thank you very much.

Germaine Greer

with Peter Florence

Hay-on-Wye 2015

PETER FLORENCE: Thank you all for coming. It's great to see you, and it's a huge pleasure and delight to present to you the great Germaine Greer.

Can we start by thinking about what is maybe one of Shakespeare's most challenging portrayals of women – in *The Taming of the Shrew*. It's relatively early, and we find it difficult. Producers find it difficult to deliver.

GERMAINE GREER: Do they really? Well, I think the problem is that they don't pay attention [audience laughter]. For example, they tend to allow Petruchio to knock Kate around, and the most important thing about it is that he *doesn't*. What he does with Kate is try to give her psychotherapy, try to get her to abandon her self-defeating posture of rage and opposition, and come to understand what *she* wants from life. But the only way he can do that is by completely confusing her.

So, first of all, he comes to the wedding on a horse that's a mess, so he is a contradiction in terms: he is a dashing bridegroom on a decrepit, spavined horse; he's got all the wrong clothes on; he arrives late. Meanwhile, Katherina, who has been angry about being married from the very beginning, and was prepared to kick the place to bits if she had been put through a proper wedding, is out-foxed by this guy: he's trashed her wedding, so there's no opportunity for *her* to trash it. So then he tucks her under his arm and takes her to the country. And then, in the country, he again confounds all her expectations. She half-expects to be raped, she half-expects him to insist upon his rights as a husband, but they haven't actually been married, and he doesn't do that. What he does is spend time with her, trying to get her to start thinking differently: so, Katherina, you think you know what's going to happen . . . And she resists and resists and resists.

He calls for new clothes for her and then he says he doesn't like them, and he throws them away. She's startled, and she thinks: Wasn't I meant to have a nice new cap? But he knows perfectly well that if she had a nice new cap, she'd say it was rubbish, and stamp on it. And so it goes on like this, until she begins to understand the game.

And then he says we'll go back to town, and they go off together, and they see this old man standing by the road, and Petruchio pretends that this old man is a gorgeous young girl, and he tells Kate to go and speak to her. Kate wants to say: Are you mad, it's obviously an old man. Yes, Kate. It *is* obviously an old man. So why is he asking you to behave as if it's a young girl? She gets it. She goes up to the old man and says:

Young budding virgin, fair and fresh and sweet,
complying with Petruchio's

. . . thus the bowl should run,
And not unluckily against the bias.

So there they are in the middle of the street, and he says to her: Kiss me, Kate. She hesitates in front of all these people, and then she kisses him. That's it. Done. It's a bit like the big challenge of drawing the sword out of the rock, and you get the prize of the magic horse that you have to train. Well, Kate's the horse. But what makes it special is the sexual tension between the two of them. It's such a sexy play, and you want him to prevail, you want her to bend her neck to him, but you want her to do it willingly and to have joy in it, which she's not going to do at the beginning because she's wrapped in such rage.

PF: Have you ever seen a production that gets that across?

GG: No [audience laughter]. Everybody jumps to the obvious conclusion: you're at the end of the play; the three husbands are there and their wives are not there; they've had to summon their wives, and their wives don't come, but Kate does come and she says: This is the deal, and his part of it is that he would be ready to protect me, to die for me and my children.

PF: Is it reasonable to observe that that particular relationship is unusual in Shakespeare?

GG: I don't think it is, really. Kate is the most obvious case, but all the women in the comedies have sinew; they're all tough, they're all plain-speaking, they're all highly sexed.

PF: Let me just develop from 'plain speaking' to the first moment in any of the great plays that he, Shakespeare, finds his full voice, which is in *Romeo and Juliet* . . . His first big hero/heroine – the star part – is not a king or a prince, but a fourteen-year-old girl.

GG: A child.

PF: He gives her the most spectacular language of the time . . . in the theatre . . . in literature.

GG: Yes. And that's an amazing thing for him to do. The way Shakespeare does this is so masterly – you don't see her at the beginning of the play, and then you meet Juliet, alone, with her nurse, and her mother comes in, and her daughter is much the same age as she was when she was married, and her mother doesn't know her, and is ill at ease with her, and Juliet listens to them talking about her *while she's in the room*, and they have that big joke – the last thing you want people to talk about when you're *fourteen* is your sexuality. . . I mean, excuse me,

do you *mind*? Juliet is thinking: Where is this *going*? Then her
mother says:

> *How stands your disposition to be married?*

And Juliet says:

> *It is an honour that I dream not of.*

Then her mother utters a sonnet, a bad sonnet. Remember,
the characters are *what they say* . . .

Then, when everything goes wrong, Juliet enters into that
blank verse, that extraordinary verse, she talks about her images of horror, what life will be like in the grave, she talks
about the importance of the death of Tybalt . . . entering into
all the horrors of the situation. And she holds the stage.

PF: Juliet is the star.

GG: Shakespeare's heroines of comedy too. His women
always go more than half-way – Shakespeare's idea of the
generosity of women, the *faith* of women, is extraordinary.

PF: Come to Cleopatra for a moment. For an actress, some
might say this is the big Shakespearean part that they would
like to play. It's got some of the greatest language. Line for
line, it's the longest female part in the whole of Shakespeare.
It comes quite late in the canon, and part of what that makes
one think is, actually, there are very few really good parts for
women in these plays, maybe four or five in the tragedies
– maybe only *two* in the tragedies; that isn't a great hit-rate
for someone who is the most compassionate, the most
understanding, possibly the most, it seems to me, *feminized*
playwright or writer – certainly male writer – of all time.

GG: The funny thing about your saying that is it sort of re-
lieves me a bit. Because I'm sick and tired of being told that
Shakespeare created these 'amazing women'. What Shakespeare actually did was make amazing plays, and the women

are the *words they speak* in the plays, and their vibrancy also comes from what other people are saying and the situations in which they say things. Cleopatra is a very interesting case, I think. What is fascinating to me is that we are told at the beginning that Antony has become the bellows and the fan to cool a gypsy's lust. When you see Cleopatra, you are told she can hop forty paces through the public street, that she has a thousand games and foils, she is almost fantasy, *erotic* fantasy, and the erotic fantasy of someone whose virility is waning. It's like elderly sex (sorry); it's full of quirks and changes and novelties to keep it interesting. It's pornographic in its way, and she is using it to manipulate Antony before she decides she's fallen in love with him.

But then you have the problem of is she really in love with him? Or is she going to turn it into heroic passion? Has this become the meaning here? There's no relationship, there's no possibility of marriage, there's no possibility of children, it's not embedded in the social order, it's these two alien people manipulating each other, and how does it become heroic? It becomes heroic when they decide to take it as far as death – and that itself is perverse.

PF: There are two other women I really want to bring in. One of them is Elizabeth I. We're dealing with a country that is ruled by, for the first time . . . the most sublime joke ever played on Henry VIII, or any man who wanted a son, is that the 'greatest British monarch' has taken the throne, and has done it really rather well, and is a *woman*. Isn't it rather unusual, or unexpected, that he wouldn't have wanted to represent hugely powerful women – as a matter of tribute to *her*?

GG: I don't know . . .

PF: She's a great patron, why would you not?

GG: Well, she's not actually a great patron. The great patrons are the people we know about, Lord Hunsdon, the patron of Lord Chamberlain's Men, and so on, but Queen Elizabeth doesn't have her own troupe of players – James, her successor, had a troupe of players, but she doesn't have one. *A Midsummer Night's Dream* was probably played for her, it's about marriage, it coincides with the time when the country is really anxious about the *queen's* marriage. *She's* probably already decided at that point that she's married to England. There's a very interesting symbolism in the way she presents herself. When she is first crowned, she wears the clothing of a matron: her bodice is buttoned up to *here*; her cap and her hair are hidden; she is married to England.

PF: Do we know all that from contemporary written versions, or do we know that from subsequently painted portraits, which were obviously formalized and were presenting a particular image?

GG: Well, you could say that the crown is just an image, and that would be true too, but the thing about being a monarch, before we had photography and film and so on, is *you* were the icon. And we talk about other great women, whether Elizabeth would want them celebrated. What she did with her own ladies-in-waiting was to send them away if they looked more impressive than she did. None was taller than she was; they had to wear more sober colours than she did. *She* was the blaze of glory, and she was very smart about that. No one was going to say, when she appeared in a street procession, that one of those ladies-in-waiting was the queen.

What happens later on is she begins to dress as a virgin. She begins to make a big issue, in iconographic terms, of being a virgin. So she wears her breasts exposed. They probably weren't, they were probably covered with gauze, but she wore the low-cut stomacher, she wore 'gutta-percha' gilded hair in ringlets on to her shoulders. Only unmarried women show their hair and wear it loose. She is, in a way, always playing a part, she is a great performer, but she's never a more extraordinary performer than when she's actually in parliament arguing, presenting her case, speaking Latin, pretending she can't do it properly and then knocking them flat with her Ciceronian, pretending that she's a weak woman but she has the heart and stomach of a king. She's a consummate role-player, and Shakespeare knew that, everybody knew that, I think, who was anywhere near her.

PF: And yet he doesn't anywhere represent it . . . I was also going to ask about Anne Hathaway. You've written an entire book – much of which has to be speculative – about Shakespeare's wife Anne Hathaway. We know that she was much older than he was.

GG: Six years. He wasn't of age. His parents must have agreed the match, and we know they had to go and ask permission from the Worcester episcopal court to get the licence for them to be married. The thing that concerns me about that is it's generally thought it was because Anne Hathaway was pregnant, because she gave birth the next – whatever it is – May, I think.

When you actually look at parish records, which almost nobody ever does, you will see that one-third of the women married that year at Holy Trinity church in Stratford gave birth within nine months, some of them within three months, and as for carrying a belly being a shame in the church, you couldn't tell because they wore wooden stomachers that came straight down the front of you. It simply wouldn't have been why they needed to be married – in the forbidden season of Advent: there's got to be another reason, which we haven't yet found, and the whole thing with Anne Hathaway is that there's got to be a trail there. There's got to be a trail. It is an extraordinary thing for a woman of substance, as Anne was, to marry a boy of no expectation.

PF: But presumably, again speculative, a brilliant, attractive boy with a hell of a gift of the gab. I mean, he'd be a good date.

GG: If I say to myself what did Shakespeare have to offer Anne, there's one thing I know he had. Poetry. Why ask for anything else? But then you have to ask: Who is this woman who likes poetry? And she's a *puritan*. But puritans read the Bible – every day, and she would have read the Geneva Bible, which is the one that's inspired all our Bibles since. And the best poetry in it is the poetry of Coverdale and the people like Coverdale who made their own translations of the Psalms. Now, the Psalms represent a whole stripe of our literary history that we never consider, and they're probably the most important body of poetry in our culture and in our language. If she read them every day, she knew what poetry was, and if he came to her – and the thing about the Psalms, by the way, is they're extremely dramatic, they're all in terms of conversation – if he came to her with offerings like that, and if she loved them, and she loved him, then that's a good reason for them to be together. And she had the substance to let him *work*.

David Grossman

with David Aaronovitch

Hay-on-Wye 2012

DAVID AARONOVITCH: David Grossman, welcome to a British summer . . . you know, it's the price we pay for all that green.

It's an enormous honour to be here with somebody who is such a renowned writer, and such a terrific writer. Many of you will have read several of his books, and many of you will have read his latest book – which was published in Israel in 2008 and over here in an English version in 2010, *To the End of the Land.*

David, the book starts in a hospital in 1967. The very first thing that you're aware of is that there is a voice on the radio, saying that Israel may be 'obliterated'. And that sets the tone for something, I think, that happens right the way through the book, which is what we call 'precariousness'. This notion that life, political life, but personal life particularly, at a certain point is very, very finely poised: anything could happen, the certainties have gone. Were you aware of that theme when you were writing?

DAVID GROSSMAN: You know, I was aware of that probably as a fish is aware of the water. This is one of the basic feelings of being an Israeli. But I think even before that, I remember from a very young age, the age of four I think, when I realized that people are going to die, that everybody dies in the end, and I think that had a very strong effect on my life. Living all your life among wars, amidst terrible violence, all the time almost, that is directed at you, that you perform against others . . . Israel is a country that has a very long and some-times heroic past, and a very agitative present, but our sense of having a future is very problematic. The *fragility* of Israel as a state, as a nation, when it comes to having a future, is really amazing . . . and maybe people from the outside cannot really understand it, because what you see on television is the iron fist of Israel, the militant country, the very strong country, the superpower of the region. But almost every Israeli feels first and foremost this fragility, this lack of promise, of guar-antee, that Israel will exist. I think maybe we shall get to it in the end, but, for me, the hope for having peace for Israel is the hope for peace as existential solidity. To know that we are there, that we shall be there.

DA: You began the book three years or more before one of the major and most tragic events of your own life. It feels like a coincidence – I don't know how else to describe it. Maybe the best way is if you begin by telling us how you came to write this book, which is about a woman escaping the news, or any possibility of the news, that her son, who's gone into the army, may have been killed.

DG: I'll describe the plot of it just to make it more clear. It is a book about Ora, who is fifty-something years old, an Israeli woman, a very typical Israeli woman, if there is something like that. In the beginning of the story, she takes her son to the gathering point of the army, from which he will be sent to a military operation in the West Bank. She brings him to this place, to the gathering point, and she comes back home, and she starts to await the 'notifiers' of the army.

Now in Israel there is a very developed machinery of notification, because of the tragic experience that we have. When they get the final confirmation of the death of your beloved one they come and knock on your door and come back every hour until they find you in. And she sits at home, and she waits, and she knows they will come. She has this very poignant intuition . . . and then suddenly, it occurs to her that it takes two for bad news, one to deliver and one to receive, and what if she's not there to receive? Maybe the whole machinery will be reversed for a day, until they find her, or a minute, or a second, even a second is enough in such a situation, and she runs away from home, she will not be there to wait for them. And she runs to the end of the land. To the very northern border between Israel and Lebanon, Israel and Syria, and on her way she takes, she almost kidnaps, a man called Avram, who was the love of her youth, and maybe he is the love of her life, and Avram is a broken person. He was like a volcano of ideas and imagination and creativity and sensuality when he was fifteen, and twenty, and twenty-one . . . and when he was twenty-one he fell captive to the Egyptians in the 1973 war. He returned from captivity broken in his body and his soul. He doesn't want to have any contact with life. Yet Ora keeps some contact with him, and he is the one that she chooses to take with her on this journey towards the north.

She tells him the story of the life of the son that she took to the army. She tells all the minutiae, all the small moments of how she used to breastfeed him, with this intimacy of breast-feeding, when she looks and she feels how she's imprinted in the pupils of his eyes and she knows that never again in her life, or never before, has she been, or will she be, so beautiful as she is in this moment. Those moments that we all know . . . those first moments, when he stood up on his feet as a baby . . . She tells Avram all these stories.

I thought, when I finished the book, not when I was writing, why did I choose this idea of telling the life story in order to protect the son? And I thought that when we take care of our children and we try to be good parents, or good enough parents, we do it because it's important, and we want them to grow up as good human beings, and we want to provide them with all the conditions to feel good and be well ... But there is also another very delicate layer, in which we make a deal with God, or with the devil or with destiny ... and we say: 'Look, we are doing our share, by taking him to the ballet, to kung-fu ... you, God, devil, destiny, you do your part. Spare this child.' But when danger hovers above the head of our child, there is an immediate feeling that all the good that we have infused into this child, all our part of the deal, that it fades out suddenly. That it's not there, it evaporates. And what Ora does in the book is to re-infuse significance and strength by *telling the story*, by mentioning those little moments of accumulating this person into a human being.

DA: That's a wonderful answer, but not to the question I asked you. But that's fine, because it's difficult, obviously it's difficult, to answer. You ... after having begun a book about a woman who was on the run from the 'notifiers', you were notified. After you'd begun the book.

DG: Yes. Three years and three months after I started writing it, our son Uri was killed in the war in Lebanon in 2006. It's almost six years now.

DA: How had your book, your writing, in a sense anticipated this possibility, and how did you then manage the book which had begun with this theme in the period afterwards?

DG: It's hard for me to answer. I know that I started writing this book also because of anxiety for him, and I remember when I started writing it and we spoke about it in the family, and I said, 'I want to accompany him as much as I can', because I knew he was going to be a combative soldier, I knew he will have to serve in the Occupied Territories. I knew that he's going to face harsh situations, both physical and moral, and all kinds of dilemmas; I knew that for him being a leftist in his opinions, it will be even harder than usual because he really will be trapped, even in kind of inner dilemmas. And I felt that writing the book will allow me not to shield myself from what he will go through . . .

You ask how it was to go back to the story? I went back to the story a day after the *shivah*, the seven days of lamenting that we have in Judaism. And I went back because writing is the way that I always knew in order to understand my life. I of course have never had to use it in such an acute situation, but, OK, that was the situation and I did what I could in order to understand. I felt if I was doomed already to be thrown into this accursed land, at least I will map it as much as I can, and for me mapping is writing about it, and I remember very strongly in the days after . . . you know, sitting and looking for a word or a metaphor or something like that, and then I suddenly ask myself: Am I an idiot? All around me the world has collapsed and I am looking for a word. And then, you know, when I found the right word there was this feeling that I did something right in a world that had turned to be totally wrong. In a world that was then a big mistake for me, and finding the thread of the story again, and being able to imagine, even, to imagine or to fantasize, and to infuse my characters with love and humour and passion . . . After a while I understood it is a way to act against the gravity of sadness, of grief, and to choose life in the end of it.

DA: But also to find the only meaning you can, to make the only sense of it you can?

DG: I'm not sure I thought at all, it was a very intuitive choice. Writing makes things more relevant. Usually so many things in our life, they are imposed on us by 'irrelevant' people, by irrelevant coincidences or arbitrariness, but if you write a story – even if in the beginning I do not understand: Why do I have to write this story, why do I have to write this character? I have nothing to do with this character. And then after a while I understand how I could have been this character. Maybe I was spared from their destiny, but I want to try and understand the relevance between me and this other human being, and what it tells me, what it reveals to me about myself.

DA: Well, that's interesting in this instance additionally, because this is a book about a woman. Do you remember the moment when you said: 'OK, I'm going to be a woman'?

DG: Yes, the answer that I can give you is that I just surrendered to the option of Ora within me. And of course it was very natural to write from the point of view of a woman in a story like that, where so much of the book deals with family life and the primal connection between a mother and child. I always feel – forgive me, maybe it's incorrect – but I always feel that this connection between mothers and children is more primal than the connection of the father and the child, and I say it as a father who is . . . was . . . is very involved in the life of my three children. But I regard myself as a motherly father, yes, and when I say that I already indicate what I think.

But there was another thing. I also thought that a man will not escape the notifiers. Men . . . basically, I have this intuition that they will sit and wait obediently for the system to get them, you know, for the machinery of the army to get them. Maybe also because it is men who have created most of those machineries, yes: the armies, government, state, war. All those systems that reward men even more when they kill. When I look at some women that I know, I feel they have this slight scepticism towards these boys' games of army, war, etcetera. I always think of this episode in the Book of Genesis when God came to Abraham and He told him: 'Give me your son. Your only one. The one that you love. Give me Isaac, to sacrifice him. To kill him.' Now God is very intelligent. He came to Abraham, not to his wife Sarah. He knew. I just think of her reaction to such a terrible suggestion ...

DA: In the end, the fact is she can't escape, can she?

DG: I don't know. The ending is open in the book. We don't know if she managed to save her son or not.

DA: I mean in the sense that we can't escape.

DG: Of course we cannot escape the totality of death, we cannot. But we can have our stand in front of death. Writing gave me the illusion that I am not frozen in front of what has happened. Of course things are irreversible, but at least I do not stand in front of that helpless. This is one of the things that is so difficult when you are confronted with such an occurrence, that you feel fossilized ... death fossilizes not only the dead ones but also the people around the dead one. Writing allowed me this illusion of flexibility, and when I had this feeling I suddenly stopped feeling a victim of what happened, even by just giving my private names to the situation. Which again ... it is the heart of writing I think ... we all write about things that thousands of people in thousands of years have written before us but the ability to give our own words, and not to use words of other people, and not to use the cliché of the media, or the cliché that was given to us by the government or the army or the situation or our fears – this is the heart of writing, and of course after what I have experienced this ability seems to me really a way to be, with a capital B, in such a situation.

Yuval Noah Harari

with Anita Anand

Hay-on-Wye 2015

ANITA ANAND: I am Anita Anand, and this is a very special Talking Books session brought to you at Hay Festival. In this series, we talk to very serious, successful authors. And they tackle meaty subjects – they always do. Few, though, have the ambition, and – may I say? – sheer *chutzpah*, to decide they're going to tell the story of the entirety of humankind. But that is exactly what Yuval has done with his new book, *Sapiens*. It is an international bestseller. It is one of those books that right from the get-go takes your breath away, because it asks the really big questions: How did we come to be here? How did we come to be like *this*? Are we really happy? Was there a time that we were happier still? Please welcome the great Yuval Noah Harari.

Although it exploded on the scene, this book had been brewing for some time, because you are a serious academic and this is something that you teach, and have been teaching, honing and refining, for about eight years.

YUVAL NOAH HARARI: I was teaching a course at the Hebrew University of Jerusalem – 'An Introduction to World History' – for seven or eight years before I had the idea of taking the lecture notes and turning them into a book. The university asked me to teach a course, and I had to say yes because I didn't have a permanent position and, at that point, you do whatever they ask you to do. They asked for an introduction to world history, and that is what they got. But on a deeper level, I think that you can't really understand anything today about the world if you don't take the big picture.

AA: So you decided to go to the very root of us . . . the very root of what makes us who we are. It wasn't that long ago that we were not alone; we had cousin species. Tell us a little bit about that, and why you think it was *Homo sapiens* who managed to break through and evolve into this audience here.

YNH: For more than two million years, the earth was populated by several different species at the same time. If you go back, say, 70,000 years, you have our ancestors *Homo sapiens* in East Africa, but there are Neanderthals in Europe, and *Homo erectus* in East Asia, and other species in other parts of the world; and it's only the *current* situation when you find just one single species of human all over the world. As our ancestors spread from East Africa, we pushed the others out of existence. We caused the extinction of all other humans.

AA: There must be something special, then, about *sapiens* right from the start. What set us apart?

YNH: Our real advantage is not our brains. Neanderthals had bigger brains than *Homo sapiens*, and even *Homo sapiens* 70,000 years ago had bigger brains than we have today. Our brains have been shrinking for the last 10,000 years at the same time as we have become more and more dependent on networks of co-operation – we need to know less individually, and the real advantage is exactly those networks of co-operation.

We are the only animal that can co-operate flexibly in very large numbers. Ants and bees can co-operate in large numbers, but only in a very rigid way. Chimpanzees and wolves can co-operate flexibly, but only in small numbers because, in order to co-operate, chimpanzees need to know one another personally. Only humans – or *Homo sapiens* – can co-operate flexibly with millions upon millions of strangers, and what enables them to do that is their *imagination*. If you examine any large-scale human co-operation exercise, you always find at its basis some fictional story. We're the only animals that can not only invent fiction, but believe in things that don't exist anywhere except in our own imagination.

AA: Now, if you haven't read the book, you'll think: Oh, he's talking about one of these cohesive forces that pulls people together, like religion. But it's more than that. It's about money, it's about society. You call these part of the myth. Tell me why.

YNH: Well, with religion it's easy. It's easy to understand people coming together to build a cathedral or fight a crusade because they all believe in the same fiction, which is something no other animal can do: you can't convince a chimpanzee to give you a banana by promising him that after he dies he'll go to chimpanzee heaven and receive lots and lots of bananas. No chimpanzee will believe such a story. Humans *do* believe such stories, which is why we control the world and not the chimpanzees.

But it's not just religion. You find the same thing happening in the legal sphere, the economic sphere. Similarly, with money. Money is probably the most successful story ever told. Again, it's not an objective reality. You take the pound or the dollar bill: it has no objective value. You can't eat it, you can't drink it, you can't wear it. But then you have these master storytellers – the big bankers, the finance ministers, the presidents, and they come and they tell a very convincing story: Look, this piece of paper is actually worth ten bananas. And if I believe it and you believe it and everybody believes it, it works. It *is* worth ten bananas. I can take it, give it to a stranger in a supermarket, and he will give me real bananas in

exchange, which I can actually eat. Try that with a chimpanzee. It won't work.

AA: Just as you to start to sit back and congratulate yourself on the cleverness of all that, suddenly Yuval will describe
sapiens as ecological serial killers. That's a real indictment.

YNH: It's justified. We tend to associate ecological degrada-
tion with the modern age, and it's all the fault of capitalism
and industry and modern science, but *Homo sapiens* caused
the extinction not only of all the other human species; our
ancestors caused the extinction of about fifty per cent, half,
of all large mammals of the world before the first agricultural
revolution (which was about 10,000 BC). Again and again, you
find *sapiens* spreading to a new environment, and their arrival
immediately leads to a wave of extinctions. So when we say
sapiens are serial killers, it's simply a truth about our species –
not in the last 200 years, but in the last 50,000 years.

The problem is, no matter what we achieve it never satisfies us. At the deepest level of the human mind, we react to
achievement, and even to pleasure, not with satisfaction, but
with a craving for more. We want more, and even more, and
this causes tremendous destruction all around us. More than
ninety per cent of the large animals of the planet are either humans or domesticated farm animals that we have enslaved and
that we control. If you ask yourself how many domesticated
dogs there are in Germany, the answer is five million. If you
think about birds, you have fifty million penguins remaining
in the world, which sounds a lot, until you compare that with
chickens. You have between twenty and fifty billion chickens
in the world.

AA: You describe this domestication of animals as enslave-
ment. That's how you see it?

YNH: Yes. These domesticated animals are at one level the most successful species ever: if you measure success in evolutionary terms of survival and reproduction, the chicken is the most successful bird in the history of planet earth. But if you go down from the collective level to the *individual* level, at the same time it's probably the most miserable bird that ever existed: if they did an Olympic competition along the lines of 'who is the most miserable animal that ever existed on earth?', I think the gold medal would be contested by the chickens, the pigs and the cows.

AA: One of the most contentious things that some scientists have identified in your book is the idea of a 'cognitive revolution'.

YNH: Until about 70,000 years ago, humans of all species, including *Homo sapiens*, were insignificant animals. We tend to think about ourselves as the most important thing in the world but, for more than two million years, humans were merely insignificant apes minding their own business in their corner of the world – with not much of an impact on the ecological system. And then, quite quickly in evolutionary terms, *Homo sapiens* breaks out of East Africa, spreading all over the world, reaching areas where no humans have reached before. Something must have happened. We don't see any change in the physical look of humans. If you look at *Homo sapiens* 50,000 years ago, they look exactly like us, so the best theory we have is that the change was something about the internal structure of the brain that happened 70,000 years ago, plus or minus some years. This idea of genetic mutations leading to a cognitive revolution is, as I say, the best theory we have at present.

AA: I am fascinated with the way you deal with those epochs of human development. We were foragers and then, suddenly, *agriculture.* You say of the first agricultural revolution that it is history's biggest fraud.

YNH: Individuals had a worse life in many respects after the agricultural revolution, compared with what happened previously. If you abandon the perspective of the king, of the priest, of the philosopher, and look from the point of view of the average person, the average peasant in Ancient Egypt, the average peasant in Ancient China, life was much harder than 30,000 years previously.

First of all the job is harder – what you actually have to do to is make a living. As a hunter-gatherer you woke up, you went to the forest to look for mushrooms and run after rabbits. This is what our bodies and brains evolved to do for hundreds of thousands of years. As a peasant, you wake up, and go to the canals, and bring water from the river, and plant the wheat, and harvest the wheat, and grind the corn, and so forth. This is much more difficult for the body; we see it in evidence from skeletons. And it is so much more boring to the mind. If you think about the nature of this monotonous, backbreaking job, it's not as interesting as going to the forest to look for mushrooms. Even today, what most people are doing for a living is more boring than going to the forest to look for mushrooms.

And, in exchange for all this hard and boring work, people got a worse diet. Hunter-gatherers lived by eating dozens of different plants and animals and berries and mushrooms and whatever. The average medieval peasant, say in China, ate rice for breakfast and rice for lunch and, if she was lucky, she had enough rice left for dinner. So the nutrition was much poorer in vitamins, minerals and so forth. Also, peasants suffered more from diseases. And on top of all that, you have agriculture which meant empires, and you have all these cultures with a tiny élite controlling and exploiting everybody else.

AA: Thinking back to the way you were describing us as spreading across the planet and destroying so much that we touched . . . A virus ends up killing its host . . . Is that inevitably in our story, then? Is that the only thing we do? Is that the only thing we *can* do?

YNH: No, because I think it's more likely that, in the next 200 years or so, *Homo sapiens* will upgrade themselves into some kind of completely new being – divine being, if you want. Either through biological manipulation, genetic engineering and so forth, or by the creation of cyborgs, beings which are part organic and part non-organic. Or the third option we are seeing developing is the creation of completely non-organic life. Like artificial intelligence. From this perspective, what we are heading towards is not only the greatest revolution in history. It's also the greatest revolution in biology since the appearance of life.

AA: I wonder, when you've got these big things knocking around in your head, how do you sort and sift and end up a man quite at peace with yourself? Because these are massive, massive thoughts.

YNH: I meditate for two hours a day, and it gives a lot of clarity; you can really focus. Because the main thing when you try to get hold of these big issues is to remain focused on what is important. It's like, maybe, the job of an editor on the news: so many things happened today; what will be the five items that we mention on the news tonight? So it's the same when we try to understand the whole of history. Everything is pulling your attention this way and that. We have to stay very, very sharp. This is the really important thing; let everything else just go away.

Seamus Heaney

with Gwyneth Lewis

Hay-on-Wye 2006

PETER FLORENCE: I have with great delight ceded my place tonight to the national poet of Wales, Gwyneth Lewis, who, aside from being a great poet herself, has for many years been a great friend and admirer of Seamus Heaney's. Having him here is the fulfilment of a long-cherished wish; it is the most exciting thing, I think, that we've ever had at the festival. Please join me in giving them both a very warm welcome.

GWYNETH LEWIS: Well, good afternoon everybody. You know, it always irritates me when people who are presenting somebody say that their guest needs no introduction. This is *almost* true of Seamus Heaney, but not quite.

Seamus has become a *necessary* poet, and not just to readers in his native Ireland. He was born into that poetic aristocracy, a farming family in County Derry, and his first book, *Death of a Naturalist*, was published in 1966. Since then, twelve collections of poetry have appeared, alongside translations and collections of criticism. One could say that it started with a description of a spade and ended with a Nobel Prize, which Seamus Heaney won in 1995, but, of course, it isn't over yet.

I first met Seamus more than twenty years ago at Harvard, where he was Boylston Professor of Rhetoric and Oratory; he had more hair then, and I think I had more hair myself – longer hair certainly – and, as far as I was concerned, he was the only good thing about Harvard in that year. I was lucky enough to take his workshops, and I *lived* off those from week to week, I can tell you. This afternoon we have an hour, and

Seamus will be reading from his new collection, *District and Circle*. Seamus, you mentioned that there was some uncertainty about the title of the book.

SEAMUS HEANEY: Well, it's one of the sweetest uncertainties in any writer's life, as you'll know, if you have a volume, and you think it's more or less ready to go, and you're thinking of a title. I think if you get a title about half-way or two-thirds of the way through, it helps you to go for the ending, and my problem was, I had several titles. And I thought of calling it, at one stage, *Planting the Alder*: there's a poem about planting an alder tree; I love the tree itself; I like the slightly weepy cadence of the title. And then Paul Muldoon said to me: 'Oh, yes. I can just see the reviews – alder man Heaney . . . the alder statesman', and so on . . . And then I had another title which suited, because iron for some reason comes into several of these poems so I was thinking of –

GL: Iron man Heaney?

SH: No, no! . . . So I was thinking of calling it *Midnight Anvil*, but I thought that was too heroic, and that no book could really live up to it. Anyway, I ended up calling it *District and Circle*, because I wrote a poem about going into the London underground, and this was in May last year, May 2005 . . . It's two sonnets. And it began with a true-life situation, as they say: sometimes you're going down into the underground, you're confronted with a fellow playing a tin whistle, and quite often he's an Irish chap, and quite often he might half-recognize me. And it placed me in a dilemma: will I demean him by throwing money at his feet? Or will I elevate him to the status of 'the circle'? . . . I'm serious, he's playing there, he's good at it . . . So that's where it started.

And then it went deeper down, and of course once you negotiate with money at the entrance to the underground

you could be with Charon any day. It did not *start* with any
of that myth stuff at all; it started precisely with the situation
with the busker, and then it went deeper down. And it did
then get a sense of – being transported in the underworld on
a death journey, if you like. Aeneas in the underworld and all
that was there. Then, in July last year the bombs occurred on
the underground, and I thought, my God, if I keep this title,
which I liked, the poem will be scrutinized for all kinds of relevance. And so I built in three more sonnets, so it's a little set
of sonnets called 'District and Circle'.

GL: Well, I think that is actually a very good description of
your preoccupations; it's just a more indirect and less heroic
one perhaps, but the *district* in terms of a specific location, and
circle in the sense of indirection, which I want to talk about
a little further. It's subtle but it's definitely a very good self-
description of you as a poet, I think.

SH: See how we had such a good workshop . . .

GL: Whenever we go into a Seamus Heaney landscape, I'm
never quite sure where we are – if you're in Ireland, or if you're
in a mythological place, or both. You've had, throughout your
writing career, a remarkable persistence of gaze on a certain
type of subject matter, a lot of it to do with your childhood on
the farm. The way you write about that, you can still hear the
sounds of it, the feel, the judder of a blow through the arms.
And yet these landscapes are never quite what they appear
to be. They may be local, but they're also in a different place.
Would you like to expand a little? Is this book a departure
from that type of material? It seems to be, but I suspect it's
not.

SH: I don't know. The same places are revisited, I agree, but
I think . . . when I began to write I was in my twenties . . .

I'm now in my sixties, and the forty years of looking changes things a bit. I don't think it's a nostalgic view. I think it is one with an awareness of the oddity of my experience. I feel what I lived through in the 1940s and 1950s in County Derry – of course it was *lived* experience, but it has a quality of once-upon-a-timeness merely because if I say 'well', or 'milk', or, I don't know, 'cow' even, or 'field' or 'pump' . . . you know, they have physical credibility to me. They have thing-ness. But I think for a lot of people they are diction of a sort. I don't know if that answers your question. In fact, I'm uneasy about making too clear to myself the answer you're asking for.

GL: One of the most remarkable things about your work to me is the way that it comes out of a physical memory of *things*. As you say, objects are not just words. I remember reading a very small thing, an endorsement that you sent for *The Reader* magazine in Liverpool, and I thought when I saw this: This is typical Seamus Heaney; rather than saying, 'I like this maga-zine', or something anodyne like that, you said, 'I always get pleased when I hear . . . ', and it was 'the thud of the magazine on the doormat'. And I thought: Nobody else but Seamus would have said that . . . no, it wasn't 'thud'; it was a better word than thud . . . but anyway, I think your inner ear has a memory for blows and weight-shifting . . . can you tell me, is that something that you recognize about your own method of working as a poet?

SH: Yes – though 'method' would be a strong word for it. It's the necessary start for a lot of what I do.

GL: 'Thwump'! That was the word for thud. The 'thwump'.

SH: There it is . . . yes. Quite often the poems begin with memories. Which aren't just words; they're physical. It's like the nervous system comes alive.

GL: I once heard you say that the term 'an established poet' is a contradiction in terms. You're very, very, very established now. Does that make it more difficult to write, in some ways?

SH: I don't know the answer to that. I think since *Death of a Naturalist* was published . . . it was well received, which was a good thing, and then it has its anxieties, as you must know. So self-forgetfulness becomes the *sine qua non* of successful secret action, and that is really the test, as far as possible: to *forget* yourself. Now, that is helped by having friends, I think. You don't need a large number, but two or three talented, fond mockers – very, very useful. And also, desperation now and again to write something. 'Established' covers everything that has happened, but, as you know, it doesn't mean a thing, because we're anxious about the next poem . . . and I think anxiety is part of the drive also.

GL: I think I should congratulate you on behalf of the whole of our culture that you're outselling Jamie Oliver at the moment. You must have a huge amount of, or a huge capacity for, self-forgetfulness, in that case?

SH: I have, I have.

GL: You have travelled a lot – do you find that poetry's quite a portable art, or do you need to be close to the magnetically charged accents of your Ireland to write well?

SH: I think those are in my ear all right, the accents. I don't think I need to be in Ireland to write well, but the fact is I've written very little anywhere else, chiefly because most of the time I spent out of Ireland was spent on that 1982 to 1996 one-term-a-year Harvard appointment. And, as I say, when I was there I was teaching, I was grading, and so on. I don't feel I need to be in Ireland to write, but I feel I need this noise in my ear. But it's established; it's already in my ear. I can't get rid of it now.

GL: So it's not a question of having to renew it?

SH: You renew it, I think, by writing poems that you like yourself, don't you? I mean that's the best renewal any poet can have – the sense that he or she has 'done it again'. And your sense of confidence and self-trust is renewed. I was quoting last night this George Herbert line from his poem 'The Flower', which, as I was saying, he was, I think, in his forties or maybe not even, when he wrote it:

> How fresh, O Lord, how sweet and clean
>   Are thy returns!

And he's renewed, and he says:

>   And now in age I bud again,
>   After so many deaths I live and write;
>   I once more smell the dew and rain,
>   And relish versing . . .

That seems to me to have the complete, sweet electricity of the gratitude and the fulfilment in it.

GL: At Harvard, I remember one time you asked us to write a poem about our favourite word. And there were some very weird and wonderful words that came out of that workshop. It's gone out of my head now, the word that I did, but you've got a very strong fondness for Anglo-Saxon: snubby, snagging, turnip – 'snedder' words. Are these words . . . I mean do you look them up? You know so many of them!

SH: I can honestly say I never look them up.

GL: Where did you hear them?

SH: They were all part of the first language . . . but 'snedding' is a wonderful word; it means the slicing off of turnips or sugar beet. I once knew a fellow in County Derry who wanted his pencils sharpened; he said: 'Sned that for me.' Of course he was being ironical, because it's usually used for a bit of a more hefty engagement of materials. No, actually, I suppose politically speaking, the vocabulary factor was a little way of pushing back against the centre.

GL: It's a political choice, that type of vocabulary?

SH: Yes . . . but I wouldn't want to go too far down that political protest. It's just part of the culture of the *verity* of certain things, to hold on to.

Eric Hobsbawm & Niall Ferguson

with Philippe Sands

Hay-on-Wye 2009

PHILIPPE SANDS: Good afternoon everybody, and thank you for coming out on this warm and wonderful Hay day. We're delighted that you're all here to listen to a conversation between Niall Ferguson and Eric Hobsbawm on the 1919 Treaty of Versailles. I'm not a historian; I'm a lawyer, and I came across the Treaty in 1980, for the first time, in the first class I ever had on international law. We all – all three hundred of us – thought: What on earth has this got to do with the present day? And that is the topic of conversation for this afternoon. Without further ado, I'm delighted to introduce Niall Ferguson.

NIALL FERGUSON: I thought I should begin by warning those of you who've come for some kind of ideological Punch and Judy show that, in fact, Eric Hobsbawm and I *agree* on a great many of the points that we're going to discuss about the Versailles Treaty. One other rather academic point – we're going to take 'Versailles' to mean the whole complex of peace treaties agreed at Paris in the wake of the First World War including, for example, the Treaty of Sèvres that was supposed to regulate the future of the Ottoman Empire. Over to you, Eric.

ERIC HOBSBAWM: Why do we discuss the peace treaties after the First World War? It's a war that won't go away, for two reasons. There is, for Britain and France, the reason of *memory*: it was the 'great war'; in memory, it *was* the greatest war, and the most murderous war, in which these two countries were involved. That is not the case for Germany or for Russia, who had a worse Second World War. Second, we are still living with the results of Versailles – that's the subject now. Look at the Balkans today: virtually all the problems in the Balkans are Versailles problems. Look at the problems of the Russian frontiers in the west and in the south. They're problems that go back to after the First World War. Above all, look at the Middle East.

Now what we're talking about, just in case details have dropped out of your mind since school, it was, or it became, a war between the so-called four Central Powers – the German, the Austro-Hungarian and the Turkish (or Ottoman) empires, plus Bulgaria, on one side, and most of the independent states of the world on the other. The British, French and Russians were the main belligerents – although the Germans knocked out the Russians – with Serbia, Greece and Italy being drawn in, joined by the USA. But, in addition, don't forget that China, Japan, Siam – which is now called Thailand – were also in there, and so were a half-dozen Latin American countries, though probably only for the record.

As you may remember, the war lasted a bit more than four years, chicken-feed by the length of modern wars. It was fought as a total war, the first of its kind, the model, if you like, of the barbarous wars of the later twentieth century, and harbinger of a century of barbarism. But it was also still an old-fashioned war, declared officially and ended by official peace treaties. It was also, I think, still a war which in theory, even in practice, focused on killing soldiers – soldiers killing soldiers – and not on killing civilians, although as a matter of fact the idea of *starving* civilians, not an entirely new idea, was something which really did develop quite sharply during the First World War too.

A brief word about the Peace. There were three urgent problems. First of all, there was the breakdown of the German,

Russian, Austro-Hungarian and Turkish empires, which produced a situation of revolution in Europe, and indeed an actual revolution in Russia, in which the Bolsheviks came to power. You cannot understand the peace-making without thinking that this was in the minds of all the people that made peace. It was certainly very much in the mind of President Wilson.

Second, there was the more long-term problem of Germany. In fact, as in the Second World War, Germany, single-handed, beat the rest of them – almost. And consequently, the peacemakers in 1919 were terribly worried, particularly the French, whether Germany would do it again. Essentially, the attempt to control Germany failed. Niall and I may disagree on how far this helped to bring about *Hitler*, but certainly it was a strong element in the rise of Hitler. Plus, of course, the Depression.

Third, remember the peacemakers didn't break up the empires. They were already breaking up. They had to pick up the broken pieces, although it must be said they did their best to *go on* breaking up both the Russian and Turkish empires as far as they could. Versailles contributed, I think, one fatal element in trying to pick up these broken pieces – that is, President Woodrow Wilson's 'right of self-determination', that's to say, the right of independent, sovereign-state sovereignty for peoples or nations defined as being essentially ethnic – which means that all these states were supposed to have one, as it were, 'state people', and the rest were *minorities*. Now, in actual fact, this couldn't work. It couldn't create ethnically homogeneous states, but mini multi-ethnic units rather like the maxi multi-ethnic units that there'd been before, such as the Austro-Hungarian Empire, which today exists as *eleven* different states in Europe. Same with the Russian Empire, same with the Turkish Empire.

Ethnic homogeneity and ethnic states, as we discovered after the Second World War, can only be based on mass ethnic expulsion or genocide. And so this was pioneered in the First

World War, and particularly in the Balkans in the early 1920s. It wasn't systematically applied until after the Second World War.

In the Middle East, however, the basic principle of peacemaking had nothing to do with self-determination. Indeed, self-determination was a pure *hypocrisy*, because it was perfectly clear that, where it didn't suit the victors, it wasn't applied. In the Middle East it was a straightforward imperial carve-up, except in the two cases that were favoured by Britain, both of which had rather dangerous results, and one of which was the notorious Balfour Declaration that created a national home for the Jews in Palestine, and we know the long-term results of that.

PS: One of the themes you touched on was the weakening of Germany and the reparations issue. Niall, why don't you focus our attention on what the consequences of Versailles were in that domain?

NF: Well, of course the reason that the Versailles Treaty has a bad reputation, in this country particularly, is John Maynard Keynes, who wrote an extraordinarily influential polemic, *The Economic Consequences of the Peace*, more or less before the ink had dried on the Versailles Treaty. It was one of the great bestsellers of 1919. I'm sure if Hay Festival had existed in 1919 Keynes would have filled many tents this size. He had actually been at the Versailles Peace Conference as a Treasury representative, but had walked off in a sulk after his ideas had been rejected on the specific question of reparations – how much the Germans should be made to pay on the basis of their declared responsibility, their 'guilt'.

Keynes's argument was that far too much was being asked of an exhausted Germany, and that the effects of doing this would be to plunge Central Europe into chaos, and, in the wake of this chaos, something very bad would happen: 'Vengeance, I dare predict, will not limp' is one of the most memorable lines from *The Economic Consequences*. And it is quite tempting to look at the subsequent decades as a vindication of Keynes's critique of the Treaty.

Now, how does this look in the cold light of historical retrospection? I've worked on this subject for years – in fact it was part of my PhD thesis, so I'm perfectly capable of boring you all for hours about it. I'm going to resist that temptation, and make simply one point. In historical perspective, this was a debt crisis, but not an *exceptional* debt crisis. In effect, the Germans had a large debt imposed upon them at the end of the First World War, notionally to pay for at least part of the costs that they had inflicted particularly upon Belgium and northern France. Now, inflation, which Keynes wanted to blame on reparations, was already well advanced in Germany by 1919, and it accelerated in 1921, and reached a climax in 1923, when the German currency became entirely worthless. But the critical point to notice is that it can't be blamed entirely on reparations. Indeed, the Germans quite deliberately allowed inflation to spiral out of control in the misconceived belief that this would persuade the Allies to reduce the reparations further. Historical research has uncovered, among other things, the very successful efforts the German delegates made at Versailles to persuade John Maynard Keynes of this. It actually turns out that Keynes was quite nicely captured by the Germans. Their argument at Versailles became *his* arguments. But on closer inspection, what caused the German hyperinflation was not purely reparations.

What caused the German hyperinflation was the way that the Germans ran their own domestic affairs. Remember, as well as an influenza epidemic at the end of the First World War – which was a very important part of the war, as it was one of the reasons the German army's morale collapsed in late 1918 – there was also a Bolshevism epidemic. It wasn't only in the Russian Empire that Bolshevism gained ground. There

was a period of time in 1918–1919 when it seemed it was going to sweep the whole of Europe. In my own home town of
Glasgow, tanks had to be deployed when the red flag was flying over the City Chambers. Berlin had something approxi-
mating to it; Hamburg briefly had a soviet republic too.

Although that Bolshevik wave receded, not least because
the Poles defeated it militarily when the Red Army swept
into Poland, it left a legacy in Germany of left-of-centre
government. The Weimar Republic was essentially based on
a compromise with social democracy, designed to contain the
revolutionary threat, and it was actually the extraordinarily
expensive welfare state the Germans set up, more than
reparations, that drove the hyperinflation. The Germans
were printing money in 1919 and in 1920, before reparations
had even been fixed, and they carried on printing money in
1923 when they'd stopped paying reparations. So Keynes was
actually wrong. We have to remember that, ultimately, the
Versailles Treaty was a case not so much of can't pay, but of
won't pay.

PS: Let's turn to another aspect of the 'unfairness' of the
Versailles Treaty. There was no law of human rights in its
modern sense. Yet this treaty put in place, for the first time,
principles dealing with the rights of minorities. What was the
impact of that move on the world that came subsequently?

EH: I would say, not very much. There had been attempts,
by getting all the powers together to limit the effects of war,
before 1914, but even those didn't really have any real punch
behind them. It was Wilson who introduced, I think, the idea
of a 'league of nations' which, except for him and some of the
smaller countries who benefited from it, most of the other
leaders didn't think much of. The League of Nations managed
to sort out some small disputes in places without any great
'importance' – between Finland and Sweden, or around the

coasts of Greece and Albania. But basically, the League of Nations, although there was a great deal of enthusiasm for it particularly in this country, was a flop, which is why, in fact, when the United Nations was set up in 1945 it was set up on a completely different basis.

NF: The League of Nations did better than I think you're implying in the 1920s. We remember it because of its great failures in the 1930s over Abyssinia, over Manchuria, but in fact its record in the twenties of, for example, implementing plebiscites in contested territory was really not bad. It was only in the thirties that the wheels really came off. I think the biggest defect of Wilson's project wasn't his failure to carry the ideas in Washington; I think the biggest defect was one concept that he, more than anybody else, brought into the mainstream of international relations, and that was the concept of self-determination – the notion, which Eric already mentioned, that states should be congruent with nations, with ethnic communities.

Wilson's notion that you could redraw the map of Europe on the basis of self-determination was a tremendously naïve notion based on an almost complete misunderstanding of political geography. Once you look at the ethnic map – particularly of Central and Eastern Europe in 1919 – you see what a tremendous patchwork it was. You might draw up these grand-sounding treaties and documents creating a legal protection for, say, the Jews or the Germans in Poland, but it was impossible to implement. In almost every single country created after the war there was discrimination against minorities, even in the most liberal and enlightened, which was Czechoslovakia.

PS: Would it have been better – I put the question to both of you – if Germany had won the First World War?

EH: Well, this is an issue on which, curiously enough, I think Niall and I are among the minority who think it would not have been *worse*. Germany wasn't a liberal democratic state, but it *was* a civilized state, and what the Germans call a *Rechtsstaat*, a state in which the rule of law operated. And, OK . . . the Germans would have imposed, no doubt, their own carve-up. They might or might not have succeeded; after all, *we* didn't really succeed in convincing the Poles to accept the frontiers which we wanted, and the Poles went on fighting the Russians and extending their frontiers and making themselves more vulnerable to future division without anybody knowing – the same with the Turks. I don't . . . think . . . it's a particularly interesting question . . .

NF: . . . Ah [laughing], there we do disagree . . . I think it's a very interesting question. I wrote a whole book about it . . . I suppose I published *The Pity of War* eleven years ago now, on the eightieth anniversary of the Armistice, and at the heart of that book is the counterfactual question: What if Britain had stood aside, had not intervened in 1914? – which was an option open to the British cabinet on 2 August 1914. That's a counterfactual that's quite easy to play out because we know pretty much what the Germans intended to do: they drew up their war aims. And one *can* imagine what they would have done if Britain had stood aside, which they rather expected the British would do – they didn't really see how Britain would gain from intervening with its very small expeditionary force in 1914.

I took a rather facetious line that got me into trouble at the time: I imagined 'the Kaiser's European Union' as the upshot of this counterfactual. The shorter war would have been over much more quickly of course, probably by 1916, if Britain had stayed aside, and this would have been a European Union primarily carved out at the expense of the Russians, who were after all the main target for German aggression in 1914: it was a war, mainly waged in their minds, against Russia. So my counterfactual's a very cheerful one in many ways – for the reason that you say, Eric: because Germany in 1914 was a very different country from Germany in 1939. And perhaps that is what makes this counterfactual so hard to sell.

Bettany Hughes & Hannah Critchlow
Hay-on-Wye 2015

BETTANY HUGHES: Good afternoon everybody. How utterly delightful to see you here. I don't know if you noticed when you came in that there was a Greek word on the screen, which was the word *idea*. This seems to me one of the most doggedly tenacious and exciting arrangements of four letters that we have in our human experience.

What is interesting is that when the word first appears in the fifth century BC, it actually doesn't mean a 'notion'; it doesn't mean a 'thought', or a 'concept'. Rather brilliantly, it means a gorgeous, oiled, pumped-up young man. Hold that thought for a moment: I'll explain. When the word *idea* is first set down in a historical record, it's by the brilliant poet Pindar, and he writes an Olympian ode in, we think, about 474 BC, so almost exactly twenty-five centuries ago. *Olympian Ode 10*: 'And I praised the lovely son of Archestratos, whom I saw at that time beside the Olympic altar winning victory with the valour of his hands. Beautiful in form ... [and the Greek here is *idea te kalon* (ἰδέᾳ τε καλόν), that is, 'beautiful in form'] ... He blended with that youthful bloom, which once kept Ganymede from shameless death, all the gifts of [the gorgeous sex-loving] Kyprion Aphrodite.'

So we are left in no doubt at all that this young son of Archestratos was pretty gorgeous, and that he inspired Pindar to use this word *idea*. What it first means when it enters the written record is a 'real thing', a 'form'. Then, with the birth of philosophy as we know it, slightly later in the fifth century BC, Plato takes this word *idea*, and he uses it in his 'theory of forms'. And he completely changes it. For him, suddenly *idea* isn't a gorgeous young man; instead it's a perfect version of something. So it might be the perfect version of my pair of spectacles, or of a pencil case, or of something bigger – the perfect version of beauty, of love, of valour, of truth. *Idea* moves from being a 'solid' thing to an abstract notion of the ultimate form of something, and then, very interestingly, it becomes something that is powerful enough to change reality itself. So very quickly, within one generation, the possibilities of *idea*, and of ideas, are monumentally exploded.

But also, 400,000 years ago, something happens which is arguably the defining characteristic of who we are as a species, as *Homo sapiens*. What happens is that we genetically mutate *specifically* so that we can communicate abstract ideas: that is, we develop *language*, so that we can express these abstract ideas, and, if you think about that for a moment, that's a massive quantum shift. What we're doing is sharing an idea before we can imagine the consequence of that idea. You can imagine how that exponentially expands the possibilities of us as humans, because even if we don't know that something has practical use, we think that it's worth communicating an idea and that somebody else within the group will enact it, and generate something beautiful and wonderful from it. Ideas are essential to us physiologically . . . I think we all know the excitement of when we think we've had a new idea.

I know what it feels like to have an idea. But Hannah tells me she can *show* you what happens when I have an idea.

HANNAH CRITCHLOW: Over the last few decades there's been a revolution in technology, allowing us to peer into the brain as never before. And, with that, we're starting to understand more about the functioning of our brain, our behaviour, and also how ideas are generated. There are some interesting points that Bettany raised there in terms of beauty, how beauty can possibly help to inspire ideas, and we're going to be examining Bettany's brain as she's thinking of ideas. I'm going to rig her up to an EEG – electroencephalogram – machine, which will measure the electrical activity in her brain as she thinks about a problem she is having with a chapter in her current book. We will visualize her electrical spark of ideas in real time.

We know that there are around a hundred billion nerve cells in our brains. That's about fourteen times the number of people on this planet, so . . . a pretty vast number. Each one of those nerve cells is connected to about 10,000 other nerve cells, so there are about a hundred trillion connections in the brain, making it one of the most complicated and intricately designed circuit boards that you could ever imagine. And this circuit board changes all the time. As you learn new things from your environment, as you meet new people and discuss new ideas, your circuit board will change.

BH: Which is very interesting if you think of what it is to communicate an idea: so an idea isn't a thing, or in a place; it's the result of a network and exchange within the brain.

HC: If you imagine your brain has this complicated circuit board, and you have this framework of experience as you go about your day-to-day life – for example, you might meet new people, come across new environments . . . well, that circuit board can actually change, and you can bring together new connections within the brain. Nerve cells communicate within a circuit board – basically they pump sodium and potassium ions in and out, and that causes a flow of current.

So, what have we got here? Earlier, Bettany was talking about beauty, and about the early concept behind the word *idea*, and how it was tied in with beauty and admiring male physiques. Well, look at these alpha waves here – I don't know whether you've noticed this, but sometimes you have more creative, innovative ideas when you're having a relaxing time. So maybe you're wandering in a park, or you're going for a jog, or you're having a cycle, and that's when these ideas come to you, when you're in this peaceful, relaxed, appreciating-beauty state. Alpha waves are a particular frequency of electrical waves in the brain that are associated with ideas and relaxed thinking. Beta waves, in blue here, are associated with more focused thought. The more relaxed Bettany is, the smaller the blue will . . . wow! . . . the smaller the blue will be.

Bettany can't actually see what's on the screen here at the moment. The green is the raw electrical activity of those nerve cells in Bettany's brain that we're picking up, so all of the different frequencies; that nice pink colour there is gamma, which is associated with being able to filter out lots of information – all the signals that are coming in through Bettany's ears, her eyes, her sense of touch, her sense of her own self – you have to filter that information out if you want to concentrate on a particular task. So we've just been looking, in a very crude way, at the generation of thought and ideas in Bettany's brain – which I think has been a first for Hay, maybe!

BH: Definitely. (Can you unstrap me now?!) I think it's very interesting, the fact that you can 'read' it, and the notion that we invite unexpected experiences into our lives, kind of neurologically and physically. Now, as you will know, there's a huge amount of interest in the brain and how it works, and people are trying to monetize that and commercialize it, aren't they?

HC: Yeah, so there have been studies, in the last couple of years really, that have been using electrodes that deliver electricity through the scalp and through the skull to actually innervate particular circuits within the brain, electrically stimulating the right-hand side of the front of the brain, which has been thought to be involved in creative thinking, and relaxed thinking as well. There's been quite a lot of debate among scientists about whether it's true that this part of the brain is involved in creativity; however, when researchers induced this side of the brain with a small electrical current for about ten minutes, they actually found that the volunteers *were* exhibiting slightly increased amounts of creative thinking. Manufacturing and marketing companies have leapt on these findings, and companies are now selling over the Internet – and this hasn't been endorsed by the scientists in any way whatsoever – these little kinds of 'bike helmets'. Basically, there's electricity 'strapped' to these bike helmets, and people wire themselves into one and zap themselves, thinking that they're going to become more creative. It's quite concerning that there's so much commercialization going on in what's a relatively new area of neuroscience – that is, looking at creativity and ideas.

BH: I know that the patent and commercial licensing business is worth $600 billion per year, and that's just for intellectual property. I'm sure none of you in the audience will go out and buy your brain-bike-helmet because you think it might make you brainier, but, as a historian, that's something I see time and time again: we are often pulled into new experiences, and into dangerous experiences. It's almost as if we're compelled to invite the unknown across our threshold.

There's a rather brilliant word or idea that sums this up in Ancient Greek literature called *xenia* (ξενία). It's a strange word because it means lots of different things – it's a very difficult word to translate, but it's also a word absolutely full of promise and potential. *Xenia* basically means a kind of guest–host friendship, the notion that as an individual you are compelled to invite strangers, and the strange, over your threshold. The Greeks rationalized this in all kinds of ways: as you'll all be aware, in Ancient Greece gods and goddesses and demigods and spirits were everywhere – they often took on human form. So you didn't know, if a stranger turned up at your door, whether it was actually Zeus or Hera or Heracles in disguise. It would be very bad news to turn Zeus away from your door, for instance. And this was how they explained *xenia* to one another.

But it has much deeper roots, and it really seems to me to be the basis, in a way, of civilization as we know it. Because, if we trace this strange word *xenia* back through time and look at it in the Bronze Age, when we first get the proto form of Greek on those Linear B tablets (we're talking about 1400 BC), this gives us an idea of how people interacted with one another across the eastern Mediterranean and the Ancient World: one of the words on these Linear B tablets is KE - SE - NE - WI - JA 𐀐𐀫𐀩𐀸𐀊 which then becomes *xenia* in classical Greek, and KE - SE - NE - WI - JA seems to refer to special cloths that people would exchange with one another to establish a formal, diplomatic trade agreement and relationship.

But what's even more exciting about this word, and the notion that we have to open ourselves up to welcome strangers and new ideas across our threshold, is that it has a much earlier, proto Indo-European, so really prehistoric, integration in the word *ghosti*, which comes down to us via the Germanic route as the words *guest* and *host*. Originally, a guest and a host were one and the same thing, because of a particular unspoken etiquette: imagine we are a tribal group on the Siberian steppe, for instance, and we see a cloud of dust on the horizon; rather than automatically assuming that the people approaching us are enemies who are going to bring something malign into our settlement, there is an understanding that we will take a risk and welcome those people in because of the notion that they will bring new goods, new ideas, and, physically, new blood and new genes into our settlement. There seems to have been just such a notion, which actually held together the whole of the Ancient World, and I think it is, in a way, what allows us to be civilized and unprejudiced: very, very early on, when we're forging our civilization, we decide it's a good idea to invite the unknown, the strange, the unrecognizable across our thresholds. And, I wonder, is that mirrored in any way in what's going on in our brains?

HC: Definitely. There are different areas within neuroscience that have this idea of *xenia*. And this hospitality and welcoming of strangers across the threshold is incredibly good for your wellbeing. It really does boost brain health and promote resilience, which is increasingly important for people as they get older: as your brain cells start to die or become more rigid within your 'framework', if you explore new environments and meet new people, if you share ideas with people outside your existing social group, outside your normal tribe, you can actually get new connections to form between those hundred billion nerve cells, get new circuits to form, which will enrich your brain and help you to have different ways of thinking, which in turn can promote happiness and resilience.

BH: I would say one of the most tenacious therapies that I see in historical records is comedy and laughter, something that actively makes lives better and solves problems: as human beings, when we start to live together, we have to try to find a way to get along with one another.

HC: It seems as though laughter is a really important form of social bonding, and actually what happens when you peer into people's brains while they're laughing, while they're being told a joke, is the release of endorphins, which are feel-good hormones in your body and your brain. But laughter also engages a social aspect of your brain; you're trying to figure out what other people are thinking of you, how the joke fits with your existing knowledge and outlook on the world. And your brain engages to get to the bottom of this intrigue.

BH: I think my two favourite things about laughter and comedy are, one, that physiologically animals are laughing the whole time, and, two, that when we laugh we're the only species who, in a kind of Darwinian struggle between breathing and laughing, *choose* to laugh, so you know that thing when you say, 'I was helpless with laughter'? We actually *are* helpless with laughter. So you go to watch Stephen Fry, and then a tiger walks into the back of the tent; you wouldn't get up and run, because you would choose to laugh rather than to stand up and breathe. There's something very hopeful, I think, about that.

Kazuo Ishiguro

with Francine Stock

Hay-on-Wye 2000

FRANCINE STOCK: Ladies and gentlemen, hello. I don't think Kazuo Ishiguro needs much introduction, but I will just give you the barest bones of one before we start to talk. He was born in Nagasaki in Japan in 1954, but came to this country at the age of five and was brought up in the south of England. His first novel, *A Pale View of Hills*, was awarded the Winifred Holtby Memorial Prize by the Royal Society of Literature. The next novel, *An Artist of the Floating World*, was Whitbread Book of the Year in 1986. In 1989, getting better and better, he went on to win the Booker Prize for *The Remains of the Day*, which of course Merchant Ivory subsequently made into a film with Emma Thompson and Anthony Hopkins. *The Unconsoled* followed in 1995, and his new novel, *When We Were Orphans*, is just published this year.

In this new novel the hero, Christopher Banks, is a detective, or so he tells us, anyway. I wonder whether with all your books, because they are, in a sense, about a degree of self-deception, you are inviting the reader to be a detective, to pick up the little clues that show the gap between the way the narrator, or the principal character, sees events and the way that the reader might do?

KAZUO ISHIGURO: Yes, I guess so. I think in all my books, to some extent I ask the reader to be a detective in that way. And I suppose we're all quite used to this, aren't we? We've become quite sophisticated about the way we listen to politicians, say, or about the way we listen to each other; we don't always take what people are saying at face value, and I think, particularly in this day and age, when we see a lot of people on television or hear them on the radio, we're very tuned in to trying to find out what people are really saying behind the words, or whether they are covering things up. We have become quite expert at being detectives in this sense, so I feel in a way I'm not asking anything unusual in making this assumption that people can do this. They can encounter a person and immediately start asking: Well, where are they coming from? Are they telling the truth? Why is this person saying this? Are they being defensive? Why are they saying that? Of course, in this latest novel, the man thinks he's *literally* a detective, and I suppose that's more incidental than anything else.

FS: But is the element of self-deception that characterizes a number of the figures in your novels – is it always to do with that discrepancy between the way life really is and the way that they rather hoped it might be?

KI: I don't know if it's quite that gap, actually. The self-deception of my narrators in my earlier books, I think, is the self-deception that is perhaps necessary when, quite late in your life, when it's too late perhaps to substantially change the course of your life, you start to realize that there are some grave shortcomings about yourself, and I guess in that situation, yes, you have to have a certain amount of self-deception. So people like Stevens the butler in *The Remains of the Day* – he seems like a very self-deceived man, but I suspect that he's no more so than many of us would be if we faced the possibility that perhaps we'd failed in some big, profound way. I don't think we'd go: Oh, yes, it was all a bit of a disaster, but I'll accept that. We'd all spend a long time struggling with ourselves, trying to persuade ourselves it's not quite so bad. In the end I think there's a kind of dignity, something admirable, when people do finally come to terms with what they did do or with the shortcomings in their life. But you often have a lot of self-deception to wade through before you get there.

FS: You say there's something admirable about coming to terms with it. You must think that's the state people should be aiming towards?

KI: Well, there's a part of people that wants to see things honestly. It depends what it is, what's happened in your life. But I think there is a big impulse to be honest, perhaps not to the outside world, but to yourself. So if you suspect, for instance, that you've been an awful parent or an awful spouse or an awful son or daughter, I think it's quite difficult to put that away and pretend it's not happening. This is what makes people very interesting to me; they have this impulse to be honest and to try to figure out what really did happen, and, certainly in my earlier novels, there is this battle going on between the impulse to see their lives clearly and to assess themselves clearly and this other voice that says: No, no. It was all right. Don't worry; you've been a great guy.

FS: Your first two novels dealt with Japan in the aftermath of the war. Was that discussed at home? Because your parents had come from Nagasaki, and, as I said earlier, you settled in the south of England in the early sixties. But was the war still a topic at home?

KI: Yes, it was, but not as a kind of 'subject'. It was just there, in a very natural way. So, for instance, if my mother was telling me about a relative or a friend of hers at school, it would often naturally slide into war experiences. But she wouldn't necessarily say, specifically, 'Look, I want to tell you about the war.' War in any case tended to be Nagasaki and the atomic bomb, so it had perhaps this extra dimension to it. I must say I didn't realize there was anything that special about the atomic bomb until I was quite old. I grew up thinking every city had an atomic bomb. I only discovered about all that, really, in Guildford when I was at school, and I was eight years old, and I looked it up in an encyclopaedia to find out a bit more about this atomic bomb, and read that Nagasaki was only one of two places in history to have been atom-bombed. I remember discovering this with an odd sense of pride. But it was very much that way round. War was there as part of what had happened, rather than a big subject on its own.

FS: But what about the other boys at school? When you went to school in Guildford, they must have been so aware of the discrepancy between your family's history and theirs.

KI: I don't think *they* were. I think I was. Perhaps we should reveal at this point that you're from Guildford too: perhaps you can bear witness to some of this. A lot of my friends . . . well . . . I suppose Britain in those days wasn't very sophisticated about things like multi-culturalism and so on – there were no other foreign people I met at all, for about the first five years of my life in England. And so the only way people could really relate to me was as an honorary English kid. If they liked me they said, 'Oh, he's English', and I remember there were these awkward moments where in the playground people wanted to play war. Perhaps that's died out from playgrounds in this country now, but in those days this was a very popular thing to do – you played war. Basically, you divided up between the English and the Germans, and occasionally 'the Japs', and I do remember feeling slightly ambivalent when 'the Japs' came into it. I would always try and persuade my friends, let's have it against the Germans. But they didn't seem to sense anything particularly odd about this.

I did sense very much that, for my friends, war – the Second World War – as they'd heard about it was a triumph; it was something they were proud of. Their parents talked about it as a triumphant, successful thing, and I only knew about it

as a tragic, sad thing. I had it from the loser's point of view.
I was too young to sort out things like who was the guilty
party in the war or whatever; it was just about winners and
losers then. But I did sense there was something profoundly
different about the attitude of my parents, particularly my
mother, towards war. I wouldn't say it was a *pro*-war feeling in
Britain then, but it was certainly quite different to the attitude
that exists towards the Second World War today. It was seen
as something triumphant, good to be playing it out or talking
about it. And it *was* one of the large areas, I suppose, where I
felt a distance from English society as a whole. I played along
with it, but that feeling that you're slightly acting here, that
inside you there is another person who is distant from this – I
think that's one of the big areas where that was true for me:
around war.

FS: In *When We Were Orphans*, the hero Christopher Banks
has a friend who is Japanese, and there is some discussion
of – well, quite lengthy description of – the childhood they
spent together. The fascinating thing about Akira . . . there's
quite often the prospect he will be returning to Japan, and he
is encouraged by his parents to be more Japanese. Was that
something that you ever felt?

KI: I don't know if it's fair to my parents to suggest they ever
wanted me to be more Japanese. But I think I was so rapidly
turning English that they might have at least tried to deceler-
ate the process slightly. But my parents' attitude was always
one of visitors. They always thought the family was about to
return to Japan at any moment, and they would tend to discuss the odd, curious customs of the natives of this country, at
a kind of great distance, with quite a lot of respect as well, but
it seemed to be very much observation: we'll tell the people
back home about how the English behave, so let's remember
this. It was more that than: here we are living in this country
and this is the way things are done in this country; perhaps

we should adopt this way of doing things. It wasn't that kind of thing at all.

And I suppose in that sense, in an unconscious sense, I always held the assumption that a lot of the English traits, the English etiquettes, a lot of English rules, somehow didn't quite apply to me. And that definitely came from my parents. But they didn't consciously try and make me more Japanese. But certainly, if I reported, 'At my friend's house they say grace before eating. Don't you think we should say grace?' they'd be quite respectful about that; they'd say, 'That's what people do here in England' – and they did, they were always saying grace . . . and I'd think: So it's not something that applies to us; it applies to the English.

FS: But do you think that helped with that degree of observation that any novelist is bound to have?

KI: Possibly, yes. I'm not sure how observant I was as a child, but it gives you a certain emotional distance. And it's not just little things like saying grace, it's bigger things like relationships. I did notice that the relationship of a lot of my friends to their parents was actually very different from my relationship to my parents. So it wasn't just sort of itemizing the rituals that the English went in for; it ran deeper than that. I sensed that their position in their world was different to my position in what I thought was my world, and so I suppose something like that does give you a certain distance from things. But of course, outside the home I was obliged to function in this world; I went to an English school, and, to some extent, I remember I kind of pretended that at home it was the same for me as it was for everybody else. If my teacher or one of my friends said something that didn't really apply in my house, I wouldn't immediately say, 'Ah, we don't do that'; I would go, 'Yeah, yeah', pretending that was the case. And so you do find yourself, without really meaning to, becoming a bit of an imposter at times, an impersonator.

Judith Kerr & Michael Morpurgo
Hay-on-Wye 2013

MICHAEL MORPURGO: Good morning, Hay. This is one of the most special mornings I think I've ever lived . . . I'm going to have the honour of interviewing one of the great writers of children's literature, not just in this country but throughout the world. She's a remarkable lady, no question, who's had the most remarkable life. She has produced the most extraordinary range of books. There is no one, no one, who has written so well for children who are older, and for grown-up children, and for very small children. Anyone who has written *The Tiger Who Came to Tea* and *When Hitler Stole Pink Rabbit* in the same lifetime, that is truly extraordinary.

First of all, can you please welcome on stage the wonderful Judith Kerr.

JUDITH KERR: Thank you.

MM: Now, what you may not know before we start is that Judith is ninety in a very few days' time. So listen, Hay, I thought it would really be good if you people would get to your feet now, and we are going to sing, extraordinarily loudly, a wonderful 'Happy Birthday' to Judith Kerr [audience sings 'Happy Birthday'].

Well, Judith, you're not ninety yet?

JK: No, it's a bit early.

MM: I'm going to start, if I may, by quoting back to you something that you wrote in your wonderful new book, *Creatures*, which is a gentle, touching autobiographical essay – story – about your life and your writing and your drawing. It's the most extraordinary mix, I suppose, of everything that has been Judith Kerr. And in this book you describe your father remembering your words as a child: 'Isn't it lovely being a refugee?'

Could you give us some sense of your beginnings and how you arrived in this country?

JK: Well, my father was a writer who was very, very well known and anti-Hitler from an early stage, and he made fun of him, which is always the worst thing you can do. So we had to leave secretly. He had to leave overnight, in fact, although he was in bed with flu, because somebody warned him that they were going to take away his passport. So he got out of bed with his high temperature and caught the next train out of Germany, and my mother didn't know what to do because they hadn't had time to talk. So she went to Prague where he'd gone and had a few hours with him, and they decided we must all be out of Germany by the elections – which brought Hitler to power. We weren't allowed to tell anyone that he'd gone, and we weren't allowed to tell anyone that we were going be-cause he was afraid that the Nazis, even though they weren't yet in power, were going to hang on to us to get him back.

MM: What would have happened to you and your family if you had not got out when you did get out?

JK: Well, we wouldn't have survived very long. My father, I think, would have been killed – tortured first and then killed very soon. I suppose my brother and I might have survived a little while in a concentration camp.

MM: I noticed you dedicated this book to 'the one and a half million children who didn't have my luck'. It's an extraordinary story. Much later you wrote *When Hitler Stole Pink Rabbit*, which is often misunderstood as *pure* autobiography.

JK: I thought about it for a long time. I thought of writing it in the first person. But if you do that it has to be absolutely spot-on accurate in every detail otherwise you're cheating. I didn't think I could do that, and I thought also that some bits were a bit boring. So I wrote it in the third person. But it's totally true – as true as I could make it in all the essentials. But I cobbled a few bits together – I dramatized some bits.

MM: Changed your name?

JK: Well, not altogether. I'm called Anna Judith. Actually, I'm called Anna Judith Gertrude Helen.

MM: So you didn't change your name! What a good idea you didn't use Gertrude.

JK: Well, I thought that was a good idea.

MM: And you arrived in 1935?

JK: Thirty-six. Early 1936.

MM: You've been living in this country all that time since. You've journeyed hither and thither. But you are a German Jew. Was there a moment when you felt, I think you put it in your book, a Brit?

JK: Yes. I think it was perhaps not one moment. But it was during the war, because people were so incredibly good to us.

MM: In spite of the fact that you would have spoken with a German accent.

JK: I didn't, and my brother didn't, but my parents did, and nobody ever said anything bad to them. We were in London during the Blitz and people were being killed right and left, and yet everybody was just terribly kind.

MM: You started drawing very young. Who encouraged you on that road?

JK: Well, my mother was very proud of the fact I was doing all this, and she'd collect the better ones. I don't think anybody at that stage particularly encouraged me. I don't think I encouraged them to encourage me. When I got to college there was a marvellous man called John Farley who was an illustrator himself, and a good painter, and he helped me a lot, and he helped me to get a scholarship, which was the most important thing because we had no money. And then when I went to art school you had to have a 'trade' because my scholarship was a trade scholarship, and he suggested that I should do illustration. I just wanted to draw from life, and he said: 'That's all right. Just sign on in the illustration class every morning, and then do whatever you like.' Except that about a couple of months before the end of my course some bureaucrat suddenly decided we must all get diplomas, and for this we must have a show of our work and write a thesis, and of course I was supposed to do it in illustration. I hadn't done any, so I failed . . . book illustration . . . When my nieces and nephews worry about exams, I say: 'I failed book illustration.'

MM: At some moment you wanted to write this book, and were having difficulty, it seems to me, getting into this book, and your husband seemed to encourage you just at the right moment to give you the helping hand you needed.

JK: I started writing it and it took me for ever because I'm very slow, and I'd written three chapters in three or four months, and, I don't know . . . the cooking sort of *despaired* really. I always forgot to buy food.

MM: This is probably why he helped you. He maybe thought, well, perhaps I can get a meal on the table.

JK: No! It was the opposite. It was terribly unselfish of him, because I gave him these first three chapters to read, which were all scrawled in pencil and stuff, and he was quite busy at the time and he read them and said: 'No, this is good. You must finish it.' Which meant another nine months of terrible meals. What a man.

MM: We've got to talk about this, I'm afraid. Cats. You have written one or two cat books, and I don't like cats very much.

JK: Oh, no! And I'm associating with you . . . they didn't tell me . . .

MM: . . . No, no, they're appalling creatures. But I was told I had to interview you, so I thought fine, talk about Mog. At some point, you sat down and you wrote your first Mog book. Can I ask you, first of all, why you wrote the book?

JK: Well, because I always hankered after a cat and I didn't know any at all, and I couldn't have one, obviously, as a child, and Tom had always had cats. He was good with cats.

MM: So he introduced you to cats, really.

JK: I'd always wanted one anyway, so we got one once we had a house with a garden, and we got this cat, which we called Mog, and like all cats it was very weird.

MM: The first book was called?

JK: *Mog the Forgetful Cat.*

MM: And I know what some of you are thinking, I'm think-ing it too: It's really easy to write a story like that. You try it! It was just pitch-perfect. I'm going to read something now. Actually it will make you sad.

> *Mog was tired. She was dead tired. Her head was dead tired. Her paws were dead tired. Even her tail was dead tired. Mog thought, 'I want to sleep for ever'. And so she did. But a little bit of her stayed awake to see what would happen next.*

Most of you who know Mog stories, and that's most of you, will know that that's the moment that Judith decided that was Mog's last dance, so to speak, and it still upsets people. I was there once, I witnessed it. I don't know if you remember it, but we were in a line-up and the Duke of Edinburgh came along. Do you remember that?

JK: Yes.

MM: And he said to you: 'Why did you kill off that cat?' And I thought: This guy reads *books*! You know? . . . But the nation . . . It's not a joke really, because what Judith did wonderfully well . . . and it's so hard to deal with grief, to deal with death in a way which is not sentimental but which somehow gives young people a sense that this is what happens.

I want to, if I can, come on to a book I know you're very fond of, which was written after the death of your husband Tom – *My Henry*. Would you like to tell us something about *My Henry*, because I know it's a book you treasure.

JK: Well it's quite a short book, which is good. It's about an old lady . . . well, it rhymes. It starts with:

They think I'm sitting in this chair
Just waiting for my tea.
In fact I'm flying through the air
With Henry holding me.

My Henry died and went to heaven,
But now he's got his wings
They let him out from from four to seven
And we do all sorts of things.

And then they do ridiculous things, like riding on a dinosaur and climbing Everest and swimming with mermaids . . . But then she says:

But sometimes we prefer to give
The world a miss, because
We picture how we used to live
And think how nice it was.

And they're just quite ordinary things, like gardening and watching telly and carrying the children about, and then in the end she's back in her chair, and they bring her her tea. I don't know that I was thinking of Tom so much as . . . a lot of my friends are widows, there are an awful lot of them about, and just thinking of a very ordinary, very happy marriage, and you see an old lady sitting there and you think, well, yes, OK, that's an old lady . . . I know about them and there's all that stuff inside them of what they remember and what they feel. I don't know, it seemed just a good idea.

MM: What's wonderful is you shared that in a way everyone here can understand, I would say young and old . . . and what's wonderful about your stories, what's wonderful about you, is that you resonate for young people, very young people, not just Mog-lovers, and the older ones amongst us too.

Mario Vargas Llosa & Julian Barnes
on Gustave Flaubert
Cartagena 2012

MARIANNE PONSFORD: What has changed for you in your appreciation of Flaubert in the past twenty years?

JULIAN BARNES: I suppose there are two parts to the answer: what has changed with Flaubert, and what has changed with me. Rather surprisingly, Flaubert, despite being dead for 133 years, is still changing. That's to say, the corpus is still expanding. In the last twenty years, the magnificent Pléiade edition of the *Correspondance* has been completed, and so we can now read almost every single letter of his that has survived. And the correspondence is the place to find Flaubert the human being, and is to be read side by side with the novels. It's a great work of art in itself. Other things that have been published: the Pléiade produced the *Oeuvres de jeunesse* for the first time, in a complete format – everything he published before *Madame Bovary*. It's a fat volume that has more words in it than all the books he published in his lifetime. And it also proves that if Flaubert had died in 1850 or 1851, before he'd started writing *Madame Bovary*, no one would say: We have lost a genius.

Also what has changed with Flaubert is new translations – some of them are an improvement and some of them are not. I don't follow the academic discourse, but in the world of amateur Flaubert scholarship amazing books keep coming out. One arrived on my desk the other day: it is a dictionary of all the words that appear in *Madame Bovary*. In order. Every time the word crops up, it is listed. So you get to 'l' and you have la and le and lui, and there are eleven pages, each of six columns – 2,027 entries in all – going 'la la la la la' – like we're in a demented opera house. You look at it and you think: What is this for? There's a very French introduction to it, which says: This is perhaps a work suited to the Oulipo school, whereby if we put all the words of *Madame Bovary* into a book, in alphabetical order, you the reader can then manufacture your own novel using only the words that are in the original. Crazy, or what?

So that's how Flaubert has changed. For myself, I continue to read him, and I find that I do read the books differently, still. I go back the most often to *Madame Bovary*, and I still find, in its adamantine perfection, that there are new things to discover, things I had not noticed before.

Bouvard et Pécuchet now stands clearer and greater in my mind, because I think I'm beginning finally to understand what it's about. It's not a book to read when you're a young man.

MARIO VARGAS LLOSA: No.

JB: So partly he's changed, and partly I've changed.

MVL: I'd like to add a footnote to what Julian said. It's a fact I read not long ago and which pleased me enormously. It was about the number of critical works generated by French authors worldwide, and Flaubert came out third. After Victor Hugo and Montaigne, it was Flaubert who produced the most critical works, university theses, essays, scholarly tomes.

And on the personal front: I continue to reread, sometimes fragments, of Flaubert, and he is a writer who has never disappointed me and has always moved me. I even reread scenes that are already very clear in my mind, some of them for their literary intelligence.

The scene I always reread – and particularly when I'm

depressed – is *Madame Bovary*'s suicide. For a strange reason, which a psychoanalyst could no doubt explain to me one day. Why is it that that scene, which is so atrociously sad, the scene in which Madame Bovary swallows the arsenic, and there's that truly chilling description of what happens to her face, her mouth, her tongue . . . How is that a scene that draws me out of my own misery and demoralization, and makes me feel somehow reconciled to life?

I'm not joking. In periods of great depression in my life I've gone back to read the suicide scene in *Madame Bovary* – and the perfection, the mastery, the beauty with which that horror is described is so great that I feel an injection of enthusiasm, a justification for life itself. Life is worth living, if only to read the sort of skill to be found in those pages – the extraordinary lucidity, intelligence, dexterity, intuition with which he was able to bring to life a scene which, told straight, would produce a rejection of and a distaste for life. Julian, does that scene have the same emotional effect on you?

JB: Um, I don't go to it when I'm depressed. I think I'd turn to music rather than literature. But I think I'm a simpler and less perverse human being than you are.

But going back to what we were saying about how Flaubert has changed and how he's viewed. I've been thinking about how when you and I first read him, he was really rather unfashionable. I think he was a victim of political correctness from the Left, partly because he said harsh things about the Commune, and partly because he was after all a *rentier*. He didn't really live off his writing, he lived off the income from his family and property and so on, and he could be dismissed as a bourgeois – in fact he was resolutely anti-bourgeois. Fifty years ago he was read in schools, but afterwards you were sort of meant to forget him.

MVL: I remember that atrocious phrase of Sartre's against

Flaubert: 'I hold Flaubert responsible for the crimes committed against the Communards, because he never wrote a word condemning them.' Which reveals very well that rejection of Flaubert by the Left at a certain moment.

JB: Yes. It was political, and it was also aesthetic. In his auto-biography, *Les Mots*, Sartre writes of being 'poisoned by the old bile' of Flaubert and Edmond de Goncourt and Théophile Gautier. They were the enemy, who had to be wiped from the battlefield. I've only read the first of his three volumes about Flaubert, *L'Idiot de la famille*, and it's a kind of monstrous work. It's always struck me as an attempt to bury Flaubert. As if he said: I'm going to erect this enormous monument to Flaubert, which will be so vast, and so Sartrean, that everyone will forget who's buried underneath. But he failed.

MVL: Even Sartre recognized that Flaubert was the first modern novelist, in the sense that he gave rise to a certain model of novel that continues to this day. There were great novelists in the nineteenth century, but they didn't enrich the novels of the future in the way that Flaubert's teachings did. He created a whole technique for the invisibility of the narrator – a commitment to finding the exact word, so that the reader was not distracted either by excess or by absence. We have to rearrange our sense of realism when we read anything published earlier. The contemporary novel was born with Flaubert, and in that sense all novelists are Flaubertians now, whether we like Flaubert or not.

JB: Yes, I'd agree with all of that, and I'd add his clever and subtle use of irony, and his deployment of the *style indirect libre*, which he developed to a point of perfection that had not been there before. Also, he was, for me, the novelist who promoted the absolute importance of form in the novel. If we compare the Flaubertian method with what British novelists were doing at the time – Dickens, Thackeray, Trollope, George Eliot – there's one practical difference. Their novels mostly appeared first in monthly parts, and they would write them as they went along. They would be, essentially, brilliant episodes which were then bound up into a novel. I think a lot of novelists, pre- and post-Flaubert, have a very loose and fuzzy sense of what form is. Some think it's just telling a story, and going along until it ends – that structure is only important when writing a sonnet or something.

I remember the wonderful thing that Virginia Woolf said about Dickens. She compared a Dickens novel to a blazing fire, which sometimes seems to be dying down, whereupon Dickens suddenly creates a perfectly formed new character and chucks him or her on to the fire, which blazes up again and the novel takes off. Which is responding to the particular needs of writing weekly episodes.

Although *Madame Bovary* was published in the *Revue de Paris* in periodical form, Flaubert had already finished it, and he never published anything until it was formally complete. What I see increasingly as I understand more about novels, and write more novels, is the way in which things are held together. For example, there's a tiny character in *Madame Bovary* called Justin. He's the assistant to Monsieur Homais, the *pharmacien*. The main function of Justin in the book is to help Madame Bovary steal and swallow the arsenic. And when you read the book for the first time, that's probably the only time you properly take account of him. But Justin is there for three quarters of the novel in very tiny touches – often seen in doorways looking at scenes. All these touches, when out together, add up to a sort of parallel seduction, and parallel corruption, of Justin by Emma. At the end, he's the person who is seen weeping on her grave. His presence, and his subtle underlinings, are a way of stitching the novel together, which you can only do if you have a great sense of architecture. And great architects sometimes design the door handles as well as the walls.

MVL: I'd like to touch on another aspect of Flaubert, which is his attempt to achieve the impossible. I think that *Bouvard et Pécuchet* is a novel which proposes to do something unachievable, a novel that is born condemned to disaster. But it has aspired to so much, and gone so far, that even though it doesn't reach its goal, the work is extraordinary, unusual. Well, there's a thread in modern literature that is in some way encapsulated by that insane attempt of Flaubert's, to write a novel that synthesized all the knowledge of his time. Joyce – a great admirer of Flaubert, as were Proust and Kafka – wrote, after he finished *Ulysses*, *Finnegans Wake* – a novel that is almost impossible to read, and impossible to finish. In Spanish we have *Paradiso*, by Lezama Lima. I think that had never happened before Flaubert – a truly great, unfinished and frustrated masterpiece like *Bouvard et Pécuchet*. That too is a branch of his influence.

MP: I'd like to return to Madame Bovary, the character. She was a frivolous, vain . . .

MVL: No! I protest!

MP: . . . irresponsible, volatile woman . . .

MVL: That's a lie. Slander!

JB: Mario –

MVL: No, wait! I'm going to defend Madame Bovary! She was just a young girl who read romantic fiction. And she thought that life was as it was depicted in novels. And her tragedy, her drama, is that she wanted to turn that fiction into reality. Like Quixote – who read books about chivalry, thought life was as it was in those, and set out to transform reality into something resembling fiction. That's what Madame Bovary does. She wants life to be made of extraordinary passions that lead one to have great adventures, she wants life to be about pleasure – the pleasure of elegance, of extravagance, of sensuality; the pleasure of the sentimental excesses of passion. That's what she wants to bring about with her deeds, and what does she find all around her? Mediocrities – poor devils who are incapable of living at the level of sensitivity and imagination that she has been taught by fiction. That's the great symbolism of *Madame Bovary*, what makes it not just a little realist novel but a novel that expresses a fundamental element of the human condition: our inability, as human beings, to accept reality as it is. Our profound need to live in another way – not to have just this one life. It's why we read fiction. Throughout history there have been people like Don Quixote and Madame Bovary, and the world has changed, and progressed: we've come out of the caves and reached the moon, thanks to those crazy fools.

Madame Bovary wasn't frivolous. She was a great dreamer, a great rebel, an absolutely extraordinary and admirable woman.

JB: I had failed to inform our moderator that Mario has been in love with Emma Bovary for forty or fifty years.

MVL: It's true, absolutely.

JB: I too react – though not with quite such personal feeling as you do – when readers complain that Madame Bovary is a trivial person. She is the only person in the novel who attempts to extract herself from her circumstances. She's the only person who acts with boldness and courage, in difficult social circumstances for a woman. The men in *Madame Bovary* are all cowards. She is not a coward, either in love or in sex, and they don't measure up to her. People sometimes say: 'I don't like Madame Bovary.' Someone even complained to me that she was a 'bad mother'. And you think: What's that got to do with anything? You know, Hamlet: he couldn't make up his mind. King Lear: mad as a hatter. You don't go to great literature in order to like people, to find chums. This is the Oprah-fication of literature. But I yield to you, Mario, in your passion for Madame Bovary. I respect her, I admire her, I might even fancy her, but you can have her in that carriage.

Ian McEwan

with Peter Florence

Cartagena 2010

PETER FLORENCE: My name is Peter Florence, and it's a great honour to be here. My guest is an astonishingly successful and admired novelist, short-story writer, screenwriter, librettist. Ian, thank you for being here.

IAN MCEWAN: It's a great pleasure. And very exciting to be in this lovely town.

PF: You followed two collections of short stories, *First Love, Last Rites* and *In Between the Sheets*, with two extraordinarily powerful short novels, *The Comfort of Strangers* and *The Cement Garden*. What did you feel, at that stage, about scale and form for writing?

IM: I loved the short story. For me it represented a form of laboratory. The great thing about the short story is you can allow yourself to fail, and only lose two weeks of your life. You can write a terrible piece; if it doesn't work you can move on. I'm often giving this advice to young writers: don't start with the 800-page novel; start with fifteen pages. Let the short story be your crucible. Try on voices, like trying on clothes or disguises, keep moving, don't hang around, absorb the world into your life until you find the rhythm and voice that suits you.

So when I finally got round to writing a novel, it owed much of its structure to the short form. The first novel, *The Cement Garden*, ran from A to Z in a straight line. There was no subplot, it was highly structured, its setting was very contained: children, cut off from the rest of the world, their parents dead, enacting a set of difficult relationships within an isolated house that nobody visits. And in a way, it was a cover for my own nervousness. The second novel was rather the same. Again, I was still only taking my first faltering steps. But I thought, at that point: *Enough*. I've written myself into a corner: I've got to get cured of fictional claustrophobia; I've got to learn to be a larger writer. So I stopped writing fiction altogether for a few years, and wrote screenplays which pushed me out into a world of extended dialogue, social situations, history, politics. *The Child in Time* took me several years to write. It was more ambitious with regards to content, but formally it used all the resources of a traditional English novel. With this, my apprenticeship was over.

PF: Throughout the last thirty years, you've alternated contemporary novels with explorations of twentieth-century history. How do you find your subject matter, and how do you match it to contemporary or historical modes?

IM: Certainly not by thinking about it. Nabokov, in one of his Cornell lectures, gave some good advice to his first-year literature students. He said: forget for now the moonshine of *themes*; you're only just beginning to learn how to read a book. Think about detail in a novel, the details that please you, and learn to *fondle* these details. Although that was advice to readers, I think it's also a very good description of what *writers* do. We don't generally think: I'm now going to write a novel whose themes are the failure or growth of this or that, or human destiny. We generally start with something small, some particular little suggestion, some question, a sigh, a scrap of information, an overheard remark. Sometimes I doodle, I coax myself into a sentence or a paragraph. If I'm lucky it will have an allure that won't leave me alone.

When I started *Atonement*, for example, I didn't think: Now I'm going to write a novel about atonement. The title didn't come till much later. Nor did I think I was going to write a novel about redemption, or the Second World War, or what it means to dwell on a mistake. I was simply dawdling one day, my children were out playing, we were in a holiday camp, some horrifying place in Holland, and I was on my own for an hour or two. I wrote a paragraph about a young girl coming into a room, an eighteenth-century drawing room. She's holding a bunch of wild flowers that she's just picked. There's a young man out in the garden – the family's gardener in fact. She wants to talk to him, but she doesn't. She's confused, she's annoyed with him, she wants him – she's very confused indeed. Merely 600 words. I had no idea why they appealed to me. I didn't yet know who she was, I didn't know where this house was, I didn't even know which century I was in.

For a while I toyed with the idea that this was a science fiction novel, set in the twenty-third or twenty-fourth century, that the man outside – why am I telling you this? – it was a time when élites preferred to live like the gentry, the aristocracy, of the eighteenth century, and it was the proletarians, the working class, who had all the vulgar technology, including, in this young man's case, a little implant in his head which allowed him direct access to the Internet.

Now, this was going to be a terrible novel, as you can tell. I abandoned it with all the speed of a man leaving a bad party, making my excuses. I knew that I had started a novel, but I didn't know what it was. I started on the second chapter of what was to become *Expiación*. I gave the young woman a sister, and as the sister, young Briony, began to fill the page, I realized that she really was the protagonist, *not* her sister. Within a few months, I saw the whole thing. I had tricked myself into a large, complex story that I needed to tell. You don't begin with themes. You begin with the small things.

PF: You have an ability to conjure incredibly powerful physical images that are wonderful: as readers, we take pleasure in discovering them and thinking about them. But I wonder whether you feel, specifically with the incident of the balloon accident at the beginning of *Enduring Love,* whether it 'unbalanced' the novel, in that it is so powerful?

IM: One can think of novels as symphonies. They can start explosively. Novels can do that too. You don't always have to build to a climax; you can start with timpanis and a clash of symbols. After a year of writing I *still* didn't have the beginning of this novel. I wrote the middle first, but I didn't have an opening chapter that appealed. Then I was hiking with a friend, and he told me that he had read in a newspaper of a balloon accident in Germany. This was when the Internet was just coming into our lives, but not everybody had access to it. My wife was then working at the *Financial Times* and she had privileged access to a database. She typed 'balloon death Germany'. All that came back was 'balloon death'. She faxed me pages and pages of balloon deaths – do you remember fax machines? – at which point I decided I was never going up in a balloon. (Don't believe anyone who tells you they're safe. I have seventy closely typed pages of balloon fatalities from all over the world.) But I had my opening. I saw it clearly. We never traced that particular balloon death in Germany till much, much later.

I wrote that opening, I think, in two days, two insomniac days. I had a sense of being driven by a pulse, a drumbeat. There should be no problem with a novel that opens fast and then draws breath and begins to examine precisely what happened. *Enduring Love* explores how different characters have differing versions of the same event. Our memories are imperfect devices. We have not evolved to maintain a clear grip on everything that happens to us. Our memories are clouded, even completely falsified by belief or emotion, or by wish-fulfilment, or by plain inattention. We're great self-persuaders.

PF: When you talk about memory and recovery and retelling, I presume your interest in that, and your exploration of it, led to your interest in neurological science – the way in which our very rational minds can be played around with. And that must have led to *Saturday*.

IM: Well, one of the great mysteries is the fact that one kilo or so of soggy grey stuff contained within a knob of bone on our shoulders can produce a bright inward cinema of reality, of a self, of dreams and thoughts and deductions. I'd always had a secret wish to see a living brain. Once I started writing *Saturday* I found a friendly and highly distinguished neurosurgeon, Neil Kitchen. He took me under his wing. After talking to him over a period of six months, I started to attend brain operations. I became a familiar figure in my scrubs, I hung out in the coffee room as well as the theatre. I got to know the anaesthetists, the 'firm'.

Indeed, I was such a familiar item in there that, one day, I was standing to one side while the neurosurgeon was operating, when a couple of students came into the room, fifth-year medical students, and they said, 'Excuse us, doctor. Do you mind if we watch, and would you please explain to us what is going on?' I said, 'Certainly.' I took them over to the light box. 'We're clipping an aneurysm on the MCA – the middle cerebral artery – and we're taking this particular well-known route . . . ' I thought: I now know all this. If I can explain this, I can write this novel. At the end, they thanked me, and left. I've often wondered how they did in their exams . . . Those months were the most intense involvement with research I've ever had.

PF: What did you start *Saturday* with?

IM: Well, it started with this: endless notes going nowhere, and then suddenly I wrote a sentence about a man waking in the middle of the night and stepping out of his bed (his wife is asleep by his side), and just standing there. Here was my character, waiting to be dressed as it were – a naked figure. I liked the purity of this. He doesn't know why he's awake. He doesn't know what wakes him. He walks over to the window of his bedroom and looks out on to a wintry city scene. It's as if you were on a beach – as was once famously described by a great scientist – and you bend down and pick up a stone that appeals to you. Not that one, but *this* one. How to explain your choice. So there it was, a mere detail. I sat with it for a long time, thinking: Who is this man? What am I going to do with him?

PF: Your latest book to be published here, *On Chesil Beach*, takes, again, a very short time-frame for the great majority of it, certainly the central powerful scene, which is the portrayal of a truly excruciating and terrible wedding night.

IM: Chesil Beach is a rather extraordinary geological feature. It's a shingle beach, running for almost eighteen miles. It's a narrow strip bounded on one side by the English Channel – we're talking about southern England – and inland by a lagoon. The shingle, maybe 200 metres wide, runs parallel to the coast. Sometimes you see it from a plane. It's quite an exhilarating sight – it looks almost man-made. When I saw it last, before writing this novel, I thought what a wonderful place it would be to have some show-down, some emotional moment, some row, something to unfold and let loose from the heart, and then to have a character turn and walk away – a woman leaving a man and receding into the distance, someone he'll never see again. It was the geology that shaped the novel. The shingle shaped a love story.

PF: You're currently publishing in Britain, in the next month or so, a novel that is set among, shall we say, the big issues of climate change, but I presume is about individual identity in action?

IM: I went to the Arctic four or five years ago with a group of scientists and artists. We were on the eightieth parallel, it was minus thirty degrees. We were staying on a ship that was frozen into a fjord. What struck me – and this was really the beginning of a novel, although I didn't realize it at the time – was a particular comedy. We would be talking in the evenings, when the wine was flowing, about climate change, about politics, about what we must do, what governments must do, what the role of technology was, what individual responsibilities were. And next door was a room where we kept all our heavy Arctic gear – the suits, helmets, goggles, boots and thick gloves. As the week went by, this changing room became more and more chaotic. It became so chaotic and beyond our control that some people weren't even able to get out of the boat because they couldn't find their stuff. And I thought: How wonderful. We're dreaming of how to organize the entire planet, but we can't organize the changing room.

With this I saw my way into the subject of climate change, by way of human nature rather than facts or morals or virtue or blindness. For ten years I had been thinking that there was a novel to be written about climate change. But I couldn't think how to do it. Until I happened upon the comedy of the changing room. Even then, I went off and wrote *On Chesil Beach*, and then I wrote an opera. But I kept coming back to that chaotic little room and how we couldn't organize it. A tiny example of human frailty offered an entry into a massive subject.

Wangari Maathai

with Rosie Boycott

Hay-on-Wye 2007

ROSIE BOYCOTT: Hello, and thank you for that fantastic welcome to Wangari Maathai. Wangari Maathai was born in 1940 in a rural Kenyan village. She went through an extraordinary childhood, and so excelled at her studies that when she was in the United States, she took degrees – a master's and, indeed, a PhD. She became the first full professor of a Kenyan university, went into politics . . . That makes the story sound straightforward, it's anything but. She's also been, from childhood, a committed lover of the environment, and has an enormous understanding of the importance of the environment in Africa, and the importance of the role that women play in maintaining and nurturing it.

WANGARI MAATHAI: Thank you very much, Rosie Boycott, and thank you very much, audience at Hay Festival.

RB: I was very moved by your descriptions of your childhood in the 1940s in Kenya. You talk about a land where there's always a lot to eat. Everything grows; it's very, very vibrant and fertile. Tell us about your childhood and the impact of colonialism.

WM: Yes . . . well, for me I was not on the *White Mischief* side [audience laughter]. But it was a very exciting time; it was a time when the country was literally being opened up. We now read, sometimes very nostalgically, of how the first missionaries, when they arrived, they saw this beautiful land with mountains – right on the Equator, but nevertheless with snow and ice, with beautiful rivers, with very fertile soil. And they write, as they teach us how to read and write, about how we ought to be very grateful to God, because we have been given this land which is literally like the land of milk and honey.

Of course, at that time people are living a life of subsistence: they cultivate where they need, they cultivate enough food to eat, there is no export of crops, there is no machinery, everything is done by hand. And then suddenly we introduce machines, and we introduce cash crops such as coffee and tea and pyrethrum and sugar cane – we introduce really *commercial* agriculture, and we find ourselves being displaced from the land that is suitable for cultivation, and being moved to areas that are less productive, and our parents being moved to these plantations to start working as labourers.

RB: Your father did?

WM: My father was lucky, because he could just about read and write, and he had been taught some skills of a mechanic, and so when he went to work on a farm he finds himself privileged because he can drive and he can repair tractors, he can repair cars, so he gets a good job of about a dollar a month.

RB: How did you get to school, and how did you start to get on at school, because nobody cared much about educating a young Kenyan girl, did they?

WM: At that time, very few parents were thinking about education, but I think my father, because he had gone to school he had learnt how to read and write, he wanted his sons to go to school. The farm where he worked didn't have any schools; the children were used to pick pyrethrum, I don't know whether you know but pyrethrum looks more like daisies, I see a lot of them along the roads, beautiful daisies, it's that family and it produces a very potent insecticide. And at that time it was the insecticide of choice. Later it was replaced, and now because of environmental awareness we are going back to it. Many children were used to pick that flower because by the time you're about three feet you're almost as tall as the pyrethrum so you can pick the flowers very easily and we grew up knowing that's what we will do.

But my father wanted his sons to go to school, and so he decided to send his sons back to where he came from, to the land of our childhood, and my mother was supposed to go back and take care of the boys. But *I* went because I was required to help my mother, especially with my younger brothers and sisters. So I wasn't going back to go to school. It was my eldest brother who asked my mother why I didn't go to school with them, and my mother, bless her heart, she said, 'No reason, no good reason. She can go to school.' I really am forever grateful to my mother because she could have said, 'I need her, she has to fetch firewood for me, she should help with the little siblings. I need her.' Because that was the role of young girls. A young girl in that society was almost like the second woman in the home, and I used to take care even of my brothers: I used to wash their clothes, I used to cook for them and they were older than me. They never thought twice about telling me to cook.

RB: And once you got to school your teachers soon saw that you were really bright?

WM: Well, I don't know what my teachers thought, but they liked me. There was one teacher who actually liked me a lot and he encouraged me. And I loved school.

RB: You went on to specialize in sciences, in the natural sciences. Where did that early love come from? How did you start to understand the importance of the natural world in the bigger scheme of things?

WM: My mother was a peasant woman; she was growing her crops and so she took me wherever she went. I describe in the book how she gives me a piece of land, just about three feet by four feet, and she tells me: 'That's your farm, and you can plant whatever you want there.' So I would go there and cultivate a very small piece of land. I used to go and look at the seeds and see what was happening . . . I could see the roots going down, and I was fascinated, and then the shoots would come up, especially of the beans. The touch of the soil and the smell of the land and the beauty of the green countryside still fascinate me – when I come like now to Europe, it's beautiful – so for me, biology and nature study almost came as second nature.

RB: But when did you know you wanted to *use* it?

WM: When I came back to Kenya from America I was very enthusiastic, like most young people; they think they can fix all the problems of the world, and I thought I could at least fix the education system. I joined the University of Nairobi, and suddenly I found myself fighting for my rights because I was not getting the same terms of service as the men.

RB: Because you were a woman?

WM: Because I was a woman, and that was a shock, because I had never thought of myself as a 'woman'. I had thought of myself as a good scientist, and so when I was told, 'You are a woman', I said, 'Oh . . . wait a minute . . . I didn't know that!'
    I was teaching now, at the school of veterinary medicine. Even though I'm not a vet, my friends would come with their dog or cat and say: 'We know you are a vet: fix it.' And I would say, 'At your own risk' [audience laughter]. But I wanted to make a contribution, and I thought one way in which I can make a contribution is if I studied a disease which was very

prevalent, and which was making it very difficult for farmers to keep high-grade cattle: East Coast fever. We were trying to improve our indigenous cattle, and we would import either semen or bulls from Europe, but this disease, which is transmitted from one animal to the other by ticks, can have a one hundred per cent mortality rate. I decided I will make a contribution by studying the life-cycle of this parasite, so I would go and pick ticks from cattle to see how many of them were infected.

And while I was doing that, I got this understanding that there was massive soil erosion taking place in the countryside. Especially during the rainy seasons, the rivers would be *brown* with silt, and I could literally *see* the topsoil getting lost, and because I grew up in the countryside where rivers were clean, and there was no soil erosion, and river banks were protected, my mind was awakened to the fact that a much greater problem is taking place in my country, and is going to threaten, not only the livestock industry, but also the livelihoods of many communities. Therefore, I decided that soil erosion is a greater threat than the tick, so I left the tick alone, and . . . ah . . . somebody else can take care of the ticks [audience laughter], and I started looking critically at what was happening to the environment.

Now part of the reason we were having this massive soil erosion was because population had increased, and so people were cultivating in areas they had not cultivated before. We had introduced cash crops, and so we had pushed the agricultural land to the limit, and also we had introduced monocultures of trees in our forests especially to support the building industry, which was a new industry altogether. But it was really because the colony was being developed, and to develop the colony you needed fast-growing trees, and so in their wisdom, they cut some of those beautiful indigenous forests and you replace them especially with the eucalyptus and the pines that were coming from the southern and northern hemispheres.

They did very well because they were growing on virgin land, but they also have great environmental destruction, the capacity to destroy the local biodiversity especially. And they also do not absorb the rainwater. Rainwater tends to run off, and that's why there is soil erosion. So I started seeing what was happening to the land because of agricultural practices and forest management and, of course, the impact on the population. That's what took me completely away from the tick.

RB: And took you to the Green Belt Movement.

WM: It was close to 1973–1974, and those of you who may have been born by then, you may remember that in 1975 the United Nations decided to have the first United Nations Conference on Women, in Mexico, and that was the conference that declared the 'women's ticket', so, in the National Council of Women of Kenya, women are preparing, and I was raising awareness that in the universities, women were not being treated the same way as men. But we had come together as women from *all sectors*, and I started listening to the women of the countryside and they were saying that they don't have enough firewood – which is their main source of energy – and they don't have food, adequate nutritious food, because land was being used for export crops, like coffee and tea, and they were not having adequate clean drinking water.

RB: So it had changed? From the years that you were growing up in the forties when the countryside completely worked, in twenty years, thirty years, a total transformation had happened.

WM: There's change that I had experienced, because, you know, I had gone to America, and I came back and found my country had also changed a lot. That experience actually made me feel, during those preparations for Mexico, made me feel that what we needed to do was plant trees. And so I asked the women, 'Why don't we plant trees?' And that's what started it. We were going to plant indigenous trees. I knew they were not popular, because people want to plant trees they can *use*, and I also wanted to plant fruit trees. I knew we would have to do a lot of work to convince people that these exotic species – they are good, they grow fast, they have quick economic returns, but they are also damaging the environment. But that has turned out to be a marathon. To this day, we are still trying to convince people that we need to plant trees that are good for the environment.

RB: You didn't have much joy convincing men of this, did you?

WM: The men came much later, when they realized that if you plant trees, in five, ten, twenty years you can sell them, so they thought: Ah, this is a good economic return, so we can invest. So, whereas it was the women who looked for seeds, who established the tree nurseries, who nurtured those seedlings, and planted them on the land, the men wanted to just plant. Which was OK . . . Anything to make them work [audience laughter].

RB: At this time you also started to get very involved in Kenyan politics. It got very rough for you didn't it, your political life?

WM: Well, when I started I was a very innocent university lecturer. University lecturers are *benign* people . . . yes. I saw I could promote tree-planting, and planting trees is a very benign activity, you would think. Until we saw that it was necessary not just to tell people to plant trees but also to educate people on *why* we need to plant trees, why we need to protect the environment, and especially the forest.

The government was against us because we were trying to say *they* were part of the problem. You can't just do the work; you must also explain where the government is failing in providing the leadership. So we established a programme, which we called Civic and Environmental Education. That linkage is what put me into trouble, but that to me is the most important linkage. Because until people understand the linkage between the way they govern themselves, and the fact that if you do not govern yourselves responsibly and accountably, you do not protect the environment, you do not protect the resources that you have. And you also do not allow equitable distribution of those resources, so you end up with a society that may have very rich people, but very few by comparison, and a huge number of people who are poor. Now poor people get trapped in a vicious cycle where they keep destroying the environment. So you need government leadership and understanding, for the government to encourage citizens to be responsible towards the environment.

RB: But at first, when Daniel arap Moi was president of Kenya, this message fell on very deaf ears didn't it?

WM: Completely deaf. He didn't want to hear anything of the kind. He started saying something that we all hear when we are in developing countries and we are trying to address issues that are destructive to our societies: you are accused of having gone to university in the West, and therefore you have been indoctrinated, and you begin to be called a Westerner, a white woman in black skin – that's quite interesting.

RB: They really threw a lot at you. But you don't at any point say you were scared.

WM: There were some moments when I was scared – especially when I would be alone, because you can never know what they will do to you. When you are in jail it is scary, but somehow you also get this strong urge to continue because you know you are right, and you just hope that God will give you a few more years, a few more days, sometimes you say a few more hours, to do what you can do while you still can. The more they push you, the more they energize you, you can't give up. You don't have that choice. And you have so many people looking up to you, hoping that you'll hold on.

RB: After Moi left, you then became the deputy minister for the environment. Were you then able to put some of these plans into action?

WM: Well, when we finally were able to get rid of President Moi's administration and put in a new administration, it was an exciting administration because it comprised to a very large extent the pro-democracy movement that had been waging war against the dictatorship of President Moi for years. Unfortunately, the only way we could win, I guess, was if some of Moi's people split and joined us, so they came and we won and we made a very beautiful coalition called NAK [National Alliance Party of Kenya], and I actually believed that we would change, and we would do great things. But as soon as we were in government, we started fighting among ourselves.

RB: Was that depressing, after all that struggle?

WM: It was very depressing for me, because I could see that even though we had fought for so long, some people don't really believe in it. They take these opportunities to get power for themselves, and once they are in that power they almost act the same way as the power that you had tried to get rid of. After they had thrown some of the members of the coalition out of the government, I said: I'm not taking the oath, I want to be a middle person, I want to encourage these parties to come together, to work together for the benefit of the country. And I'm still trying.

RB: And now you face the problem of climate change. What actually is its impact in Kenya now?

WM: The climate in Kenya has changed. The droughts when they come are prolonged and when the rains come sometimes they come like a bucket has been let loose from the sky, not the drizzling rains that we were used to – it hits the ground, and runs off, with the soil, and causes a lot of floods downstream. So we see these changes, partly due to global climate change, partly due to mismanagement of the environment.

RB: Tell me about winning the Nobel Prize.

WM: That was an extraordinary thing, and I know for sure that when you're first informed it doesn't sink in. It takes a long time. It's still sinking in for me. It takes a long time to understand the power of the Nobel Peace Prize, the privilege and the honour that is bestowed on you, but also the responsibility that you have been given to be able to pass the message that you have been trying to give, but it's not passing. So, in a way, the Nobel Committee puts you in a grand stage and tells you: Now give your message. And then the world wants to hear your message and you travel constantly. I've been travelling ever since. And sometimes you feel . . . I say to my friends that I have now come to understand the English saying: *The spirit is willing.*

Robert Macfarlane

with Horatio Clare

Hay-on-Wye 2015

LAURENCE ROSE: Good afternoon. I've been invited to spend a few moments to set the context for why the Woodland Trust felt that this event was such an important one to sponsor. I work for the RSPB, and you'll have noticed, if you've been around the site here at Hay, that there are quite a few environmental NGOs here today and during this week. Many of us have worked together over the past years trying to rebuild the connection between people and nature. People are becoming less and less connected with nature, and we're aware of the effects of this in the way that children's lives, in particular, are changing.

Certain *words* appear to be in decline, and children are forgetting, or not learning, the exciting labels that characterized the childhoods that *we* had. The Woodland Trust wanted to sponsor an event that was a celebration of the words that connect us culturally to our natural environment, and Robert Macfarlane is the obvious person to help us to navigate that landscape of words, and the words of landscape. So may I hand you over now to Horatio Clare and Robert Macfarlane.

HORATIO CLARE: Well, ladies and gentlemen, hello. Thank you very much for coming to this event. I've been a little bit worried about it . . . Here's our guest . . . They said: 'Will you interview him?' I looked him up. Some chap from an ivory tower in the Fens. Spends half his time tramping around. Writes about footpaths, backwaters, the sticks. Rarely seen at festivals. Doesn't use Twitter: the only writer to live in such a hopeless mess. Publishes books about words *no one uses*. Not exactly Sephen Fry on a unicycle . . .

The multi-multi-award-winning author of *Mountains of the Mind*, *The Wild Places*, *Holloway*, *The Old Ways*, and now *Landmarks*. Robert Macfarlane, one of our most exciting authors . . .

ROBERT MACFARLANE: Thank you, and thank you all, as I always say at this point, for coming inside to hear me talk about the outside. This confusion of domains seems even truer today when I stand flanked by this double pseudo-grove of on-stage trees, and when, out at the back, I heard birdsong and had to ask Bridget, the stage manager, whether it was piped or real, and she said, 'No, no. That's the blackbird that nests here, and then all these tents turn up in its field, and it just keeps singing.' It is easy to confuse our categories, and I'm fascinated by the confusions and the need to keep certain kinds of category and certain kinds of language clear and precise in their meanings.

I thought I would just begin where the book began. Books always send their roots further and further backwards, and when you start following them you end up at birth, or before, but I'm going to go back just to 2007. That was the year I was up on the Outer Hebrides, as I am reasonably often, and I was with my friend up there, a Gaelic-speaker called Finlay MacLeod. If you've read *The Old Ways* you've met Finlay. He's an astonishing, generous, bilingual genius, a map-maker, a historian of cartography, and an archivist, a sort of memory of the island of Lewis.

Finlay, on that visit, gave me a typewritten document called, very modestly, 'Some Lewis Moorland Terms: A Peat Glossary'; he, and his friends Anne Campbell and Jon McLeod and others, had been gathering words for the peat and its aspects from just three townships on the west coast of Lewis, and these words had wonderfully run to 120 terms – just 'some', as the title said – and Finlay handed me these printed few pages and said, 'I think you'll like this.' And I did. I didn't then know what it would lead to in my own writing, and my own life.

Among these terms were '*bugha*' – a green, bow-shaped area of moor-grass or moss, enclosed by the winding of a stream. And there was this gorgeous phrase, which I can never get out of my head when I'm out and walking, '*rionnach maoim*', which is a wonderful compression: the shadows cast by cumulus clouds on the moorland on a sunny, windy day. And there was '*èit*', this three-letter word è-*i-t*, which means the practice of placing quartz stones in the gravel of a stream-bed so they sparkle in the moonlight and attract salmon. It's this fabulous condensation of meaning and vision.

I came back, and not long afterwards, in 2007, the *Oxford Junior Dictionary* issued its new edition. At the beginning of the next year, a sharp-eyed reader noticed that, as many of you here I think will know, certain words had vanished from that dictionary, and others had come in and taken their places in that dictionary. Among the words that were gone were acorn, buttercup, bluebell, catkin, conker, newt, otter – all the way through to willow: almost a perfect A to Z. What had come in? Attachment, block-graph, cut-and-paste, MP3 player, voice-mail. And I speak to you, I think, two days after Oxford University Press have declared that the children's word of the year is 'hashtag', based on the frequency that it appeared in 120,000 children's stories gathered through that fabulous 'Chris Evans's young people's writing initiative', *500 Words*. Now, this is not OUP's fault. They operate according to a lexi-cographical principle of *de*-scription rather than *pre*-scription. They record language as it is used, and they respond to those changes. They have a variety of dictionaries, of which the *Oxford Junior Dictionary* is only one. As one commentator said, getting angry at the OJD for losing these words is a bit like get-ting angry at a barometer for giving you the pressure-reading you don't want.

That said, these words *have* been pushed out, and this is a symptom, if not a cause, of a change in forms of life, and language use, that has become a sort of rallying point, or a provocation, to those of us who see that nature and language and landscape are intimately connected, and are there to be defended, celebrated and used. Oxford make their decisions about what to include in their dictionaries based on a 'corpus', as they call it: four million pages of text. Big data analysis gives you a frequency of the number of usages of words and, based on those frequencies, you make your decisions about what ends up in a dictionary that can only have a certain number of entries. So of course the response has to be: let's increase the way these words are used, let's bring them back into language and usage . . . and into children's mouths.

What it began for me was a project that eventually became *Landmarks*, a desire to gather language – as it is used, and has been used, and has been forgotten – from the dozens of languages and dialects and sub-dialects around our island group, to celebrate precision, diversity, acquaintance, love, intimacy, from Cumbria to Cornwall and from the Shetlands to the Scillies. And so I began gathering words, and they came, and they're still coming, they're coming in their hundreds, still, and so *Landmarks* became a celebration of strong style and single words and ways in which they could change the way we *see* the world a little, and the way we dream about it, and the way we care for it, I suppose.

HC: The book makes a passionate case for language, for place-words that you say will talk back to us. Can you explain what you mean, and give us some examples?

RM: How do words talk back to us? Well, we make do, I think increasingly, with an impoverished language for landscape. We speak of fields, we speak of woods, we speak of trees. These are fine, we need generics sometimes, but nature is made of specifics. Our landscapes are astonishingly complex, layered systems and to understand them, to appreciate them, and to some degree to be astonished by them, I think we need a rich language of precision that can respond to those. I also think that certain words, as I say somewhere in the book, they're like folded-up poems, they jack-in-the-box out of themselves when you speak them, when you open them.

Gerard Manley Hopkins, John Clare, these poets who, when they didn't have a word, would just make one up: John Clare's gorgeous verb 'to crizzle', which means for open water to freeze and you get that fantastic spiky, spicular, crystalline 'crizzle' going on; or Gerard Manley Hopkins's 'wolfsnow' for this particularly dangerous form of fast-moving blizzard. As I started looking, so they came: 'sun-scald' – the amazing gleam of light off open water that's so bright it can sear your eyes.

And you don't have to do much of this before you end up at *The Meaning of Liff*, by Douglas Adams and John Lloyd, which, for those of you who don't know it, is a comic catalogue of British place-names that are turned into the words for feelings and experiences that have had no name prior to this point . . . A lot of people grew up with it.

Actually I looked up some local ones . . . Symonds Yat . . . there's a few nods in the audience . . . 'symonds yat' is the little spoonful of egg left in the top of a boiled egg [audience laughter] once you've taken the top off. Aberystwyth: 'aberystwyth' is the feeling of nostalgic longing for a place or time that's actually far more pleasant than the place or time itself [audience laughter]. They're not my jokes, but they're just so good. And one more: Kimmeridge. A 'kimmeridge' is the light breeze that blows through your armpit hair, gently fibrillating it when you're sunbathing on the beach with your arms behind your head and you just think: Brilliant, I needed a word for that. So there are some wonderful words to laugh about as well as words that have this jack-in-the-box ability to force poetry into your mind's eye.

HC: How specific are they? If a 'windle' is, and it is, I now know, a snow-drift in East Anglia, is it only a snow-drift in East Anglia or do you get windles in the Hebrides? Do they travel?

RM: Do they travel? Sometimes there are a lot of synonymous words. So there's a Herefordshire word 'wurr', which sounds like it should have come from *The League of Gentlemen*, but this means hoar frost, that particular kind of gorgeous furry spiky hoar frost. There's this lovely Devon word 'ammil', which means the enamelled ice that cases leaves and twigs when a freeze follows a thaw. So I became interested in synonyms for similar phenomena, but also ultra-precise words, like *wurr* or *ammil*, where you're dealing with a very particular kind of phenomenon and a need to name it has arisen. Nature doesn't care what we call it, and I think if I rewrote this book I would say more about silence, because there's perhaps not enough in this book about our need *not* to name, as well as to name, and about the silent astonishment with which landscape can meet us.

HC: The whole area's become quite interesting recently, hasn't it? Because there's been a vast upsurge of 'nature writing'. You're a '*place*-writer', I believe.

RM: Well, without wanting to digress us into the meta-discussion, nature writing feels problematically *branded*, and also I'm more excited by the vast group-noun that is place or landscape, all the things that involve human relations – ethics, aesthetics, beauty, ecology, history, topography – everything folds in under that. So, yes. I also don't know very much about nature. No, it's true . . .

HC: Whatever you call it, what is it a symptom of? Are we sentimentalizing something while we destroy it? Is it redemption? Why are we reading it and writing it and mind-ing about it?

RM: It is . . . nostalgic, sentimental, defensive, celebratory, glorious, anxious, hopeful. It's vast in its implications. Some of it is terrible, some of it is dazzling and wonderful, and thrill-ing to encounter. Why is it happening? Because we are living through, and have internalized, a sense of global environ-mental damage – sixth great extinction pulse, climate change, these are contexts in which we live and, whether or not we're thinking about them all the time, whether or not we believe in them fully, we are conscious of loss and consequence in ways that we haven't ever been as acutely conscious, and inevitably that is expressing itself as forms of love and forms of loss: very broadly, loss giving rise to forms of love.

HC: It's eternal, isn't it: as long as we've been writing about landscape, we've been witnessing its destruction or its change.

RM: Yep.

HC: The centre of the book, it seems to me, is about percep-tion, and how language helps us to perceive, and how it gives us language to perceive with. Is your contention that however much we know, however wide our knowledge and experience, however many wonderful words we have, there is still more room for our perception to grow?

RM: Yes. The writers I'm drawn to are sure of their uncer-tainty, if I can say that. They are people who have studied their own landscapes so intensely, so microscopically, so binocularly, that the thing they have come to realize above all other things is that they will never know this place in its entirety, that it will always exceed their comprehension and their language.

I think I talk at one point about words being small tools for small place-making, and I love this idea of language as a tool, as a means of helping us achieve forms of proximity – connection, to use Lawrence's word. And ways of, I guess, coming to know – participate in – the other lives that aren't human, and the other forms of perception that we may not share but which language, words, can give us. Those little lenses, they slip over our eyes and suddenly we glimpse through a person from fifty years ago or a hundred years ago, or a farmer today who works but loves the landscape he or she works, and so, yes, I feel a pluralizing of our relations and 'the grace of accuracy', to borrow Lowell's gorgeous phrase, that words can give us in our perception. These seem to me uncomplicated goods.

HC: Can we understand in the way that a worker in the land-scape can understand, if we don't work it?

RM: It's a great question – and it's been thrilling to watch the success of *The Shepherd's Life* by James Rebanks, who wrote to me eight years ago now, I think. He'd read *The Wild Places* and it was a great, grappling letter saying: I know what you're writing about, but the landscape I live in is a really different one, and I feel that Romanticism in the form of Wordsworth has set the Lake District in aspic, and we're the caretakers, but we kind of get hidden.

It was a wonderful beginning of a conversation and it's amazing, years on, to see him writing about how love and labour can coexist, but also that slaughtering and ear-tagging and subsidies and stone walls, they're all part of the landscape too. So I'm fascinated by these things, and my books are full of time spent with people who know their places well.

Hilary Mantel

with Peter Florence

Hay-on-Wye 2012

PETER FLORENCE: Hilary Mantel is an extraordinary writer. She has written contemporary and historical novels, short stories, memoir, reviews and criticism. And she has embarked on this extraordinary project to explore a man who has been in sore need of a great deal of revision. She's done it so brilliantly she's already won the Booker Prize once. You wouldn't bet against it again [*Bring Up the Bodies*, the sequel to *Wolf Hall*, did indeed win the Booker Prize later in the year, making Hilary Mantel the first British author, and the first woman, to have won two Booker Prizes]. I would love to ask you to join me now in giving a very warm welcome to Hilary Mantel. I want to begin by asking: where does the novelist's line take off from the historian's?

HM: Well, it's interesting to see where the historians first have to start. Cromwell is a man who seems to have erased his own traces. He's an extremely well-documented man. He churned out reams and reams of paper in the course of his official career. But it's as if he leaves a long paper trail, and then, at the end of it, he vanishes. So, we start by looking at the *results* of his actions: that's where the historians start, with his work. He is so hidden, and I think deliberately. You have lots of books called 'Thomas Cromwell', but there isn't a man in there; they're all about aspects of his work for Henry – for whom he was really minister of everything. The man has gone missing, and he has to be found in those rare moments in official letters where something breaks through – black humour, or passion, or anger – just in little flashes, valuable because they are so rare.

PF: And what do you know when you've been through all those documents, all that paperwork? What were those flashes of black humour – where does the title of this novel, *Bring Up the Bodies*, come from?

HM: Oh, *Bring Up the Bodies* is simply the beginning of the writ for delivery of the accused to the court – it's like *habeas corpus* – 'you have the bodies: produce the bodies to the court'. So this is the writ sent by the court that's going to try Anne Boleyn's lovers to the Tower of London, where they're being held. Bring up the bodies for trial – this Latin word *corpus* is a rather chilling one when translated into English, because it gives you the idea that that 'body' – this man accused of treason – is in fact already dead.

PF: We have the great advantage of knowing the history when the characters don't. There is a wedding, and quite a few funerals [audience laughter]. But he – Cromwell – doesn't know that when we begin.

HM: The suspense is created in the gap between what we know and what they know . . . walking forward through their lives with no knowledge of the future, always negotiating their path in poor light, by the poor light of insufficient information – which is how we *all* live our lives, forwards. And I try to capture that. Hindsight is the greatest weapon in the historian's armoury. But for the novelist it can't be. You have to walk forward with your characters into their unknown future.

PF: And the whole project is riven with irony, the most sublime of which, which is the best joke ever played on primogeniture, is that this rough, irritating little girl who's running around because Henry can't get a son is going to turn out to be the greatest monarch of English history.

HM: Yes. Anne Boleyn, according to Henry, promised him a son. And of course, what did she deliver first but another useless girl? Who happened to be the future Elizabeth I, but no one knew it. So as far as Henry's concerned . . . he put a brave face on it. He just cancelled the jousts that were going to celebrate the baby's birth – he had been so sure of his prince that he had had official proclamations prepared, announcing the birth of a prince. And then, another girl.

PF: When you say that you're dealing in 'the present' . . . it's written often in the present tense. It's written in free indirect speech, and we are *with* Cromwell – your introduction already gives us this idea, and we've read *Wolf Hall* so we know that we kind of love him, and then we're made complicit in some of the more terrible things that he is going to do. Now, was it always going to be in the present tense?

HM: I didn't know how it was going to sound until – well, if I say 'I heard a voice', that will make me sound completely mad – but this first line, the first line of *Wolf Hall*, came to me: 'So now, get up.' And I had the instant picture of the fifteen-year-old Thomas Cromwell lying on the ground in his own blood; his father is kicking hell out of him, and this is the incident that's going to precipitate his running away. What I didn't realize was that the moment I sat down to write the line we were going to be behind his eyes. This was going to be the viewpoint, and it began to unroll like a cinema film. So *of course* it's the present tense, because we're living it second by second, as it happens. He can see in close focus the stitching on his father's boot and he's thinking: In a moment, he could kill me. And of course I had the chilling realization that this is where Cromwell begins, and it is where he will end – lying in his own blood, on the scaffold, with a voice in his ear saying, 'So now, get up.' And the whole project was book-ended. And so the decisions took themselves: the present tense, the viewpoint. They were taken in a second. What I didn't know was that it was going to be a trilogy. It's like Henry VIII, or me for that matter: it's always expanding [audience laughter].

PF: There's a wonderful bilateral relationship between Cromwell and Henry, where you get this man who has this wonderful patriarchal household: he has his son, he has all these male members of his family, it's a house *you* desperately want to join, *you* want to be in Cromwell's gang. And then you have this chaotic, capricious, terrible father-figure whose worst crime . . . you don't get to really hate Henry until the extraordinary hypocrisy, the beautiful line you have about him asking Cromwell what it means if a *woman* is sexually adventurous and imaginative – and it's at that moment where you lose all respect for him. Is that relationship with Cromwell a central one? Because his wife has died . . . Although he has his own retinue and his own staff, the primary relationship will always be with his king.

HM: Wolsey was the essential relationship, and Henry has destroyed Wolsey, but he's done it in such a way that he evades responsibility for it. But then Cromwell realizes that, the cardinal gone, or only reappearing occasionally as a voice in his ear, or a ghost, then Henry is the central relationship of his life, for better or worse. He has no friend but the king of England – quite a friend to have – but what happens if Henry dies?

And there's this fearful incident that's central to the book, which really occurred, when Henry took a fall: his horse came down on top of him, and he was unconscious for a couple of hours, and they thought he was dead. The Duke of Norfolk ran to tell Anne Boleyn: 'The king's dead!' We know the incident backwards, from Anne's relation of it, but I tried to take you there into the tent where the king's body is carried, and show you the scrapping that breaks out over this apparently inert corpse, the civil war that commences – immediately. They think Henry's stopped breathing, and the question is, where is Cromwell in all that, and can he take charge? In the end, he's the one that slaps his hand down on Henry's chest and announces: 'The King is breathing.' And off we go to the next phase in our lives.

PF: The words that come out of people's mouths are neither of Elizabethan or Tudor times, nor are they exceptionally contemporary. How did you craft, and how did you *nuance* the language you were going to use, that makes it feel both utterly present *and* historically authentic?

HM: I think it's something that people get really hung up about when they write historical fiction, and I think the rules are simple, really: that you have to privilege *clarity of commun-ication.* I couldn't be 'authentic', because none of you would know what my characters were talking about. Words have changed their meanings. And I hate pastiche. So my decision really was to opt for a fairly standard, 'modern-*ish*' idiom. But then there is something else I have to do, because where I *can* get real words, like the words of Anne Boleyn, I set myself to find a context for them, and to use the real words and then smooth my dialogue around them, so that hopefully you can't see the join. So this means that occasionally I am going to use words that are 'old', but maybe new to the modern reader, and I'm going to change the rhythm slightly, every so often, so you have a faint scent and flavour of Tudor England.

I didn't know how to do this when I began, but there's a wonderful book – it's really the first biography in English. It was written by George Cavendish who was a gentleman-servant to Cardinal Wolsey, and about fifteen years after these events, Cavendish sat down to write Wolsey's biography. But it was an intimate one, because he'd been there, he'd heard Wolsey talk, and George – like a novelist – didn't scruple to do dialogue; he has tension, he has all the devices a novelist would employ. And he knew Thomas Cromwell. He writes down Thomas Cromwell's words as best he can remember them, and so you get the flavour of people actually speaking to each other. So it was from the invaluable George that I learned to 'talk Tudor' [audience laughter].

PF: One of the things that struck me particularly forcefully was there are some ways in which it seems this book . . . the portrayal of Cromwell is as a secularist – religion is only as convenient as the politics or the class to him. Is that portrayal of him a particularly modern one?

HM: I think there are many schools of thought among historians on this. I think that he *was* a man of genuine religious feeling and religious commitment. After all, he committed a great part of his life to persuading Henry to permit the Bible in English to be placed in every church, and this is a landmark, not only in our religious history, but in our social history. It's part of the creation of 'English-ness'. There were no atheists in those days. Cromwell was a Protestant sympathizer, I think we can be sure of that; whether he was actually a Lutheran I don't know. I would dispute that. I think he thought the part the state would play, once Henry became supreme head of the church and so sort of merged with the state, was to stand between the warring factions, and enforce, if you like, a kind of tolerance, a middle way.

PF: Much of what we love about Thomas Cromwell is incredibly contemporary, is incredibly relevant. It's not just the desire to take down the posh boys . . . there's a wonderful line where he says, 'All these people are related to each other' . . . and he's the blacksmith's son. There's so much of it which, if you took out some of the details, would be a completely contemporary novel.

HM: He is a modern man because he was a great reformer; he was a revolutionary who had no recourse to a corpus of revolutionary doctrine, which is what makes him so extraordinary. But I do like to insist that the past be valued for its own terms, not as a rehearsal for the present. So when I'm writing about the economics of the 1530s, and the glint in Cromwell's eye that is a welfare state, I am actually writing about the *1530s*; I'm not just making a giant parable of events today. I think, you see, we have to honour and respect those people. They walked and talked just as we did. They're no less people because they happen to be dead. They were not a *rehearsal* for us, so we have to respect their stories in their own right.

David Mitchell

with John Mullan

Hay-on-Wye 2010

JOHN MULLAN: Welcome to David Mitchell, welcome to you all, to the Guardian Book Club at Hay. We're pulling David back down the years to what is probably his best-known novel, *Cloud Atlas*, because what we do in the Guardian Book Club is talk about a book, usually a novel, that readers have *already* come to enjoy, to know well, and have perhaps talked about in their own book clubs and reading groups, and try to catch the energy of that phenomenon.

One of the pleasures of *Cloud Atlas* is that it contains re-flections on its own form, on its own shape. Here's one of the several ways in which it describes itself: quite late on in the novel, one of its narrators, Robert Frobisher, is describing a piece of music that he's composed, and which he calls 'Cloud Atlas'. It's a sextet for six different instruments, each in its own language of key, scale and colour. In the first set, each solo is interrupted by its successor. In the second, each inter-ruption is re-continued in order. Revolutionary or gimmicky? Shan't know until it's finished. Six different narratives, each in a different period and genre and voice and each nested in the other. And yet this novel, as well as being short-listed for the Booker Prize, and which I would have once regarded as avant-garde, or experimental, or something, was the Richard and Judy Book Club 'best read of the year' in 2005 – as well as a sort of high-brow pleasure. And I remember, when it came out in paperback, everybody on the tube seemed to be read-ing it . . . yes, they were, they were . . .

David, when you adopted this ambitious, experimental

and quite testing structure for the novel, did you think: Well, I can do this, because there's a readership out there now of fiction-lovers who are used to tricks and devices and formal ambitions in their fiction? Or did you think you were doing it just for yourself and that it wouldn't be likely to get the wide readership that it's attracted?

DAVID MITCHELL: In a sense neither and both. I just like to write the things I like to read, and I've got enough faith that there are enough people out there who feel the same, who would also like to read the sorts of things that I like to read . . . Ooh [commenting on the echo] . . . this is getting quite Brian Eno . . . [audience laughter].

JM: I think the microphones are turned right up to maximum because it rained so hard and so noisily last night . . .

DM: I don't think about the readership when I write, because that's a dangerous road that leads you soon to the question: Which readership? *Guardian*-based readership or evangelical Mormons in the state of Utah? Or who? So that's no good but . . . in a way your question, John, is a very sophisticated variation on the highbrow/lowbrow question, and I don't believe in them. There's just a brow. There's a lot of brow, and the only question that matters really is: Is the book any good or not?

JM: When you were writing the different stories, they have such distinct voices and vocabularies, did you have to write them on their own and keep them in separate folders in your head?

DM: On my laptop, separate folders on my laptop, yes, of course I did. One world at a time is ample, thank you very much.

JM: And did you write them through to the finish?

DM: Yeah, yeah. Quite early on in each of the stories' life-times, I identified the cliff-hanger moment, and wrote them backwards and forwards from that cliff-hanger moment.

JM: So the sense of interruption had to be there from the beginning? You knew it was going to happen like that? I think you wrote once in an article in *The Guardian* that one of your inspirations for a particular structure was that wonderful book by Italo Calvino, *If On A Winter's Night A Traveller,* which also has lots of different, interrupted stories. But why was it important to you that they 'came back'?

DM: Because I really enjoyed *If On A Winter's Night A Traveller,* where they don't, and I felt slightly cheated, and so I wanted to 'un-cheat' my readers with *Cloud Atlas.* Even with what we now call postmodern novels, experimental novels, if they last and if we like them, it's not the jiggery-pokery we really like; it's actually old-fashioned meat and potatoes – plot and character development – in all of them. I think this al-ways has to be true of a novel – very simple. Character is cre-ated and the writer taunts the reader with the fear that bad things will soon start happening to him or her. I think that's it. From *Beowulf* to Stephen King. But it's not just me. Novels that neglect that, they might be admirable in other areas, and they may be magnificent formalistic experiments, but really are you going to run into a burning building to save the man-uscripts? Probably not. It's meat and potatoes, it's plot and character that you run into a burning building for.

JM: Each story has a central character to whom you fear bad things are going to happen in some way, and on the other hand, thematically I suppose, the book is about human beings who prey upon each other.

DM: Yeah, some writers do almost start with the 'meaning' and the theme, and that's in the manifesto right at the beginning. For me it never works like that. I think about plot and character first, and meanings and themes, they hopefully rise up slowly to the surface where I can see them and then start working with them.

JM: Are you risking doing something with the novel-reader, then, by adopting this structure, which is to play with that very thing that you've described: caring about the character, what happens to them, worrying about them, perhaps? You get us involved, you get the reader involved, if it works. But then you say: I'm going to stop that . . . That seems like a risk, an undoing of the very spell you've cast.

DM: I wanted to interrupt you about four times just then! I knew I had about three or four pages to re-engage the reader really quickly – and that's something Calvino *does* do. I don't have any time for a nice, slow, elegiac introduction. Immediately, I've got to get the reader: Don't go away – this is really good too.

That was one interruption. Another interruption was the answer to your actual question. I've got two answers to that question, and I was thinking about them while you were speaking, which is why I might have had a zoned-out look at one point. My two answers are contradictory, but I think they're both true. Yes, it was a worry, and it is a risk. I felt that I could do it, and I felt this could be something I'd really want to read if someone else had done it. It was the weird pretence – that this is a book being written by someone else that I'd love to read if it's only done well – that dispelled my sense of *Jesus*! This could be the end of my career. Which I think whenever I hand a book in, as my wife could testify. I'm impossible to live with for the four or five days until my editor phones up with, so far, the good news that they're not going to send the boys round to get their advance back – which *is* good news, because it's always spent by then.

Then there's something to do with youth. I'm able now to talk about 'my writing career'. When you're young, you just don't worry about this stuff, the voice saying: *What?* Are you *sure?* Now I'll spend days agonizing over a scene . . . it's more: No, no, no, no . . . that's no good, start again. That fluency that you once had sort of goes the more you learn about writing, in a kind of trade-off between the artisan-level craft that you acquire only through experience – that's good, but what goes is the sort of . . . Yeah! I'll have a go at that. In my *Cloud Atlas* days, I was much more *yeah!* I'll have a go at that than I am now. It's the process of . . . *maturation* . . . nice word.

JM: Did each of those voices, or those six stories, the fluency of just going for it, did each of them come equally easily? Was each of them written with equal relish?

DM: I think . . . thinking back . . . the first story in the novel was tough, because it was the first time I'd written any kind of historical novel, and I didn't know how to avoid long-windedness . . . I was duplicating Melville – which is good: if you duplicate anyone in the nineteenth-century seafaring world, then Melville's a good guy to go for. But I hadn't yet learnt how to, in the words of James Ellroy, skip the bit that the reader tends to skip. So that caused me some trouble, and I ended up rewriting that quite extensively. The other really tough one was the fifth one.

JM: The dystopia . . .

DM: Yes. One price you have to pay for multiple narratives is that it's not only a world you need to invent; it's also the vocabulary and the language, each time. So I had to distinguish this later one from the earlier ones, where Latin verbs are still in vogue. The drift of English is away from Latin-based vocabulary through to now, when high-register vocabulary – words like *maturation* – has almost replaced what obscenity was just a generation ago. They're the words you say sheepishly and apologetically, slip under the radar: Sorry, I'm using this naughty word. So I was purging the language of that in the stories set in the future, but where's the *texture* of that language? If you're not really careful then you end up with everyone sounding like the computer on the *Enterprise*, this metallic, odourless, flavourless way of speaking. That one was certainly the hardest.

Whatever language characters use, and whatever their relationship with language is (are they confident users, are they sheepish users, are they frustrated-because-they-can-never-find-the-right-word users?), you need to get that sorted at quite an early stage. Write letters to yourself from them, is my advice to aspiring writers in the audience. It's schizophrenia-inducing, but it's helpful and useful, and it's a good way to attack the blank page right at the beginning. So the Cavendish section, relatively, was a breeze. I wrote it on one flight, really.

JM: Poor old Timothy Cavendish goes to a sort of gulag-like old people's home outside Hull, but other stories, except Frobisher's, take us around the Pacific rim in some way or another. Why the particular places? Are the locations important? You went to the Pacific, didn't you?

DM: Yeah, I went to the Chatham Islands themselves. I had fewer responsibilities in those days, John. I read about them in *Germs, Guns and Steel*, that multi-disciplinary book by Jared Diamond and, yeah, sometimes you come across something and you think: If I can't do something with that, then I'm not much of a writer.

JM: And he writes about the confrontation between . . . ?

DM: Well, that book arose from a very simple question he'd been asked at a campus one time: Why was it that it happened to be a bunch of Europeans who went all over the world and imposed their way of life and eradicated populations, why was it the British who exterminated the Tasmanians, and not the Tasmanians who came to England, why, how come? He spent about 700 pages brilliantly and lucidly answering that question. And in that I read about a branch of the Māori, who presumably were blown off course, or blown on to what, at the end of the eighteenth century, became called the Chatham Islands. So, 400 to 500 years before they were called that, these people would first have arrived and, it would seem, pretty quickly 'forgot' tribally that there was ever anything but these islands, and it was a world of water, except for this little scrap of land . . . the idea that technology goes backwards instead of forwards, and that there's nothing automatic about 'progress'.

JM: But their fate as described in the novel, which perhaps explains some of the reasons why the locations matter to you, is quite a terrible one, and seems to be a story that runs through all six narratives. They become the defenceless victims, don't they?

DM: This was an example of what I said about meaning 'floating up'. I sort of found these locations and these back stories, and wrote the first two, and began thinking: What's happening here? What are the common denominators between these and these other ideas of stories that I've yet to write? And around about that point, 'predacity', the other noun is 'predation', had just begun to emerge as a dominant theme, and there was one tribe preying on and really exterminating another tribe, and this can be done on an individual level as well. Sometimes you get predatory relationships where one is devoured by another. Cannibalism literally, but it can happen at a level of the will, and then, next, it's about the predacity of corporations. Then the young devouring the old, the elderly, and then, in the future, the genetic devouring that perhaps can occur, perhaps will occur. And this future: I strongly believe the future looks disturbingly like the past. So the theme emerged, and I tried to make each world, each plot, a variation on that theme. Six variations . . . the 'enigma variations' . . .

Toni Morrison

Hay-on-Wye 2014

Toni Morrison was interviewed by Peter Florence on 27 May and by Razia Iqbal on 28 May. These are extracts from those two conversations.

27 May

PF: Welcome back to Hay. We're here today to talk about *Beloved*. Can we start with a bit of context, both for you and for the book? When you came to write this book, you had written *Sula*, *The Bluest Eye*, *Tar Baby*, *Song of Solomon*. You were fifteen years into writing, you'd been editing for twenty years . . . You are at the top of your game, confident in your voice and mastery of form . . . and you have this story. Had you been waiting to explore it? Or did it come to you at a particular time, just when you were ready for it?

TM: I think two things happened. One, I lost my job at Random House as an editor. 'Lost' – with quotes. I edited all these brilliant books, and everyone loved them and no one bought them. So before I looked for another job, there was this moment when I was sitting out front on my pier, and feeling very nervous and sort of jittery. It was a strange feeling, I hadn't had ever, and I couldn't figure out what it was, until I thought carefully . . . What is this thing I'm feeling? The feeling I learned was happiness. I'd felt content and even successful in certain areas, but not just sheer happiness. Freedom too. So that was a new state for me.

I go back in the house, and I remember a book I did while at Random House called *The Black Book*, and it was a sort of catalogue-type book of the history of Africans and

African-Americans, especially in the United States: newspaper clippings, photographs, advertisements, all sorts of stuff
– good stuff, terrible stuff, things that made you feel good,
things that made you feel bad, and so on. But one of those
items was a newspaper article about a woman, named
Margaret Garner, who had killed her baby, tried to kill her
other two children, and was put on trial. The journalist's question was: Why was she so calm? She wasn't crazy, she wasn't
wild, there was no vengeance involved. So he was very surprised at her tranquillity, and the other thing he noted was
the conflict between the Abolitionists, who were fighting to
get rid of slavery and wanted her tried for murder, and the
slave-holders who wanted her tried for theft, the theft of the
infant, the theft of herself, and so on. Murder they couldn't
support, because that would mean that she was *responsible* for
her child, which, if she's an animal, like a sheep or a cow, if she
has a calf . . . she's not responsible *morally* for its life. So that
was a major, major question in this little article. And I didn't
read much else because I didn't want to know any more. It
was just the setting-up of a question. So I invented a situation
in which a woman commits infanticide, a slave woman, and I
try to explain why.

But the problem was, I couldn't make up my mind either.
Not about whether she should be tried for theft, but whether
she should kill her child, and I talked to a friend of mine about
it because I remember the mother-in-law in the case had said:
'I couldn't condemn her, and I couldn't praise her.' So I talked
to somebody, and he said: 'It was the right thing to do to keep
her child from being enslaved, but she had no right to do it.'
I thought: That's perfect. And I thought: Who could answer
that question? And the only person who could answer it,
legitimately could answer it, would be the dead child.

I happened to be looking out the window – sorry, it sounds
so stupid – and I saw this woman – I live right by the Hudson
river, and my house is about thirty feet from the shore, and I

was looking away toward the trees, the river's over *here*, and I saw this woman crawl up out of the water, fully dressed, with a hat on, and sit down on a stone out there. Well, of course that's a hallucination, or whatever, but it was a solution as well as a hallucination . . . or whatever . . . Ghosts . . . You know, whatever writers do, they see stuff . . . and so I thought, yeah . . . That's how I got that scene. She just appears.

But I wanted to make it so she could be the return of the dead daughter – the dead daughter's mother Sethe thinks she is, everybody thinks she is – but she could also be a person that had been held in slavery since she was an infant, and the master dies, and she finds her way from there, but having been on the ship among others who were dying, and having seen her own mother leap into the sea – to be abandoned by her mother that way – her relationship with Sethe would be real, whether she was the dead daughter, or the living, escaped, abandoned slave.

PF: How did you find the language?

TM: Always difficult . . . if you can only get that first sentence. But I have to say, what was in my mind was the end of the book, because I sort of know the beginnings, I know how to get a reader into it. But the real point of *Beloved* was memory. Generations after major terror don't talk about it. It's like coming home from a war, you can't get veterans to talk. Holocaust survivors, the first generation, never spoke of it, and it took several generations to begin. Same thing with enslaved people in the United States. My great grandfather never spoke about it, didn't want to talk about it. So memory was the most important thing for me. The book could have begun with the last two pages, which is where I really sort of started . . . I had the question at the beginning, and then, I knew the ending. How to get there is sometimes problematic. But the ending of *Beloved* is about footsteps . . . sometimes you see a photograph and if you look at it too long, it seems to move . . . footsteps on a beach . . . and they go away . . . and they come back . . . it was that kind of feeling I was trying to engender in the whole enterprise.

PF: In so far as slavery is addressed in American literature before this, it's by white men largely. The reports of it that are handed down, even in newspaper cuttings, are by white men. There's little *understanding* of the stories that could come from these official, published sources. So how do the stories come down to you? Apart from finding this document about Margaret Garner, what else did you know, and how did you know it?

TM: There were stories, and there were books written by former slaves, like Fredrick Douglass and people like that. But it was very clear to me that Douglass was not writing to *me*, he was writing to Abolitionists and white people who could help his cause, so he wasn't going to disturb those people, because he was pleading: This is a horrible life, and I did this . . . this is bad, but . . . the wicked slave-owner is *over there*. So there was an absence of relationship in his book. He knew that his readership was not Black. Even when some of the slave writers, like Equiano, who sees a bit in a slave woman's mouth in the kitchen, and he asks, 'What's that?', and someone says, 'Oh, that's a bit', and he says 'Aha', and he goes on working. He doesn't say: *'What?'*

On the other hand, there were the stories – my grandfather was a little boy in 1865, and his daughter, my mother, remembered people in the family older than *he* was – and they had stories but they were very – how can I put it? – metaphorical. They were kind of ghost stories. Not really about *it*; it was translated – it was in code. You hear African-American spirituals that aren't even about God; they're about how to escape: 'Gonna lay down my burden, down by the riverside, down by the riverside.' It's something else they're telling one another. I learned – this stunned me – my father was born in Georgia. He described his life in Georgia as being *horrifying*. I mean he just . . . just nothing good would come from Georgia, OK? And yet he went back every year to visit relatives . . .

I go to Georgia to the town where my father was born. He said white people were incorrigible; they would never, ever be *reasonable*, let alone good. He wouldn't let white people in our house – when they would come to collect the rent, he'd just stand outside. He was unbelievably hostile. My mother, she judged everybody one at a time, how they were as people, whether white or black. So, one day I go to Cartersville, Georgia, where my father was born. My maiden name is Wofford, and there's Wofford College, Wofford Plantation, Wofford this, Wofford that. Obviously, that's the name of the family that owned them. There's a Wofford preacher, and a church. I go and find the house where my father lived – the preacher knows of the family. There were two Black men, right down the street, who owned little businesses, who were lynched on my father's street. And he was twelve, no, fourteen years old, and he saw that. And left. Went to California, San Diego.

So, there were two things . . . as a child he saw the lynching. But he also was part of a family that he went to see every year. There was that part of 'slavery' that was there after the Emancipation Proclamation that was unspeakable, literally 'unspeakable'. But there were also the vestiges of it that he could see down the street, from his house. So that's very complicated . . . 'They're bad, we're good' . . . that's not it. It's very complicated. It's as bad as you can think of, and then there's some respite in it. For me it was the *resistance*. I don't mean running away or fighting. It was imaginative resistance – the language that came out, the stories that came out, the songs that came out. And it changed over time . . . that there was such movement towards art and beauty even though it was despised then, it nevertheless kept whole communities together.

PF: You mention the bit, which is a shocking image that is not immediately recognized. And you had to 'find' that, 'make it', along with other images ... the milking ... Rendering those in language that lets those images work must be incredibly difficult.

TM: The bit: you couldn't buy them, you had to *make* them ... the mouth bit. It's for an animal ... that symbol, which is *handmade*, personally made, you had to think about it, for punishment, control, violence – some of them were very *carefully* crafted. There is something so personal, so intimate, *so intimate*, about the relationships within slavery, and at the same time, so distant ... these are not human beings, but they cook my food, they wash my body. It was that combination of intimacy and separation, non-human and excessively intimate ...

28 May

RAZIA IQBAL: *The Bluest Eye* was your first novel, written when you were an editor at Random House in the 1970s. The impulse was not just the historical context but a particular incident, an anecdote, a friend of yours who wanted blue eyes, an African-American girl who wanted blue eyes.

TM: Her name was Eunice, we were very close, schoolgirls – ten or eleven, I think – and we were discussing whether God existed, and I said he did, of course, and she said, 'No, no. There's no God.' And I asked her how she knew, and she said, 'I've been praying for blue eyes for two years, and I don't have them.' What I remember is looking at her – she was very dark, high cheekbones, big beautiful eyes . . . I don't know . . . The point is, I was young enough to be in the same category . . . when you're ten, people are cute or not cute. But when I looked at her, I thought two things: If God had answered her prayers, it would be grotesque, she would look awful. And also, I recognized beauty for the first time. That she was really *beautiful*, and that was not a ten-, twelve-year-old's word in connection with your best friend or anything. And so when I began *The Bluest Eye*, I used that anecdote, what she must have been thinking, how desperate she was to be other, to be white, or to have some characteristic that would set her apart.

RI: Was there also a sense that you wanted to write a story that didn't exist, that there was a silence of that perspective?

TM: Oh yes. I wanted to read that book, and I couldn't find it. I thought maybe if I looked hard enough, somebody would have written a story about those things. To put a young Black child in centre-stage without making fun of her – she's not Topsy, she's not any of these other cliché things – and I thought somebody was probably writing that book, or would write it. No one did, and I was eager to read it, and I didn't think I could read it unless I wrote it. And all my books have been like that, *reading* experiences for me, as well as writing.

RI: Your first three books, *The Bluest Eye*, *Sula*, *The Song of Solomon*, none of them have any white characters in them at all. The White world is there, it's a presence that is an oppression, if you like. I wonder if I can take you back to your childhood to try and understand where that perspective comes from. Where did your sense of your identity as an African-American girl come from? Did it come more from your father, your mother, your grandparents? Because all of them had different perspectives on the White world, didn't they?

TM: That's true. I didn't experience a Black neighbourhood or segregation at all when I was a child. I lived in Lorain, Ohio, which was a steel town and it was full of immigrants, people from Poland and Mexico, there were Black people who came down from Canada, so it was very racially mixed. There was no segregation because there was only one high school, and everybody was pretty poor. It was really very different in the 1930s and in that northern part of Ohio, but on Sunday you did see the divisions. There were four Black churches, nine Catholic churches – Polish, Czech, Italian, Irish, etcetera . . . and then there were the Protestant ones – Episcopalian, Baptist, Methodist, Lutheran. Only on Sundays would we do our specific ethnic things.

But to really answer the question about the *feeling* . . . it was family oriented because ours was a family of storytelling and singing. It was inescapable and it was participatory. That is to say, as a child, I had to retell those stories to other adults. Same story over and over again, but I was allowed to edit it – me and my sister; you could change it, a little bit, you could recite it a little bit. But you were very much involved in that process of telling these stories, that were pretty much horror stories, about life as an African-American.

RI: I want to ask you about a short story you wrote called 'Recitatif', in which two girls meet in an orphanage, and then encounter one another again throughout their lives. In the story, one is white and one is black, but the way you write the story the reader never knows which one is white and which one is black. It occurs to me that that's something that has informed all of your writing, that you want people to see the characters that you have written about as people first, and not as the colour of their skin.

TM: That was very important to me. In 'Recitatif' I had all the cultural clues, who worked where, but nothing about which one was black because it was . . . it's a language problem in writing. There's an interesting line in one of the Hemingway books . . . which one is it? Anyway, doesn't matter, I'm old . . . but I remember the line: he says, 'Two men' – the story takes place in Cuba – 'two men came toward him, one was Cuban, one was black'. Maybe they were both Cuban . . . but to Hemingway the Black man has no home, he doesn't belong in Cuba, he's outside of it.

So I find this in so much classical White literature, this use to which Black people are put, as different, as separate, and so I began carefully to try to figure out . . . Faulkner was the best example of *not* doing that, which is why he impressed me so much when I was a student, but my idea was to de-race the language. And it's hard, because I don't describe people very much in my books, and most readers don't know what they look like. But I try to really make it clear who they are, what's inside them, how they think, what their emotions are, and where they come from. Anything but *that*, anything but *race*, and so I get it out of the language completely.

RI: I want to talk for a moment about that 'epitaph' at the beginning of *Beloved*, 'Sixty Million and more', and whether you feel that that has been confronted by American society.

TM: No . . . a little bit . . . Why did you need three million people to cut cane in Jamaica, a tiny little island? And then you realize that they died. They came over at twelve, and they were dead by the time they were fourteen. So you need some more, and you need some more, and you need some more. And then there were the ones no one speaks of . . . the ones who didn't survive, who threw themselves into the water, who refused to get on the ship, or who died on those ships.

Two-hundred-fifty years of slavery could easily produce sixty million slaves. So that's part of what I was hoping for in the construction of *Beloved*, because she, Beloved, might be the returned dead child – a ghost, but she also might be a survivor from a slave ship and she's looking for the mother who jumped into the sea and left her alone.

So I wanted all of those things to mingle there, because . . . we were talking yesterday about the ending of *Beloved*. I was trying to write about these women who become everything, except themselves; they become mothers, and *that* was a mother, right? – Sethe. Or they become lovers, or they become workers, or labourers, or preachers, but they're not individuals, so that at the end of *Beloved*, when Sethe says, 'She was my best thing', and Paul D says '*You* are your best thing', and she says, 'Me?' as though the word is foreign to her – as the beginning of recognizing herself as an individual – not an individual in the twentieth-century way, but as a complete human being. *That's* the difficulty in the slave society.

RI: Next year is the 150th anniversary of the end of the Civil War . . .

TM: The heartbeat of the Civil War is *wealth*. I know it was about freeing the slaves, but it was really about *land*, and it was about ownership, and it was about labour: who is going to cut that cane, cotton, who's going to work those mills? You're going to get a whole bunch of people from another country that you *own*, that you can *trade*, that you can *barter*. This is about *mon-ey*, whether it's North or South. So the South decides to split, and the North says: No, no, no. We're not doing that.

And so it's that way that I like for the history of the country to be told. America got into the industrial revolution in the shortest possible time. This was an agrarian country, with some Native Americans, you know, and buffalo, and how did they move from that to trains and cotton and weaving . . . that fast? And it's because not only of African-Americans, there were others, Chinese people as well, working that way . . . But I want to get away from the idea that it was always and only about slavery . . . the heart of it now is less about race, which doesn't exist anyway, and everyone knows that. The 'real' thing – like war, and most other things – is about *money*. It's about wealth, and I don't know if it was precisely sixty million they needed, including the dead because we haven't counted them, but I just wanted not to leave anybody out.

When I was young, we were American 'citizens'; African-Americans were second-class citizens, but nevertheless citizens. Then after the Second World War they forgot about all that, and we became consumers, so we said OK, and we bought stuff, and we're still buying stuff – the consumer was king. Not any more . . . what we are now are taxpayers. That's a whole different thing. If you feel like you're a citizen, there's something you belong to, a community; if you're a consumer, OK, you buy stuff, and you feel better because you have *more*. But if you're a taxpayer, you resent everybody who's using your money. So they always mention that: We're not taking taxpayers' money – my money – to pay someone who's on welfare, my money to pay for somebody who's ill, my money . . .

RI: Do you think Americans have become meaner?

TM: The language is meaner, and I think it sifts down. And now we have the other thing . . . which is guns. Guns . . . The coward's solution to life. And if everybody has a gun, and everybody is mean, and you think you're a taxpayer, and then somebody insulted you . . . I don't want to go on in this direction . . .

RI: This project you have set yourself, even if it wasn't a self-conscious project, this chronicling of African-American history, most obviously in the trilogy *Beloved*, *Jazz* and *Paradise*. At what level was that a project that required sustained thinking about? Because you didn't write *Beloved* for years. The idea of chronicling the history of a people through fiction, I'm not sure has ever been done in quite this way, not least with a novel like *Jazz*, in which the form is as important as the story.

TM: I didn't think of it in those large terms. There's *Home*, but before that, *A Mercy*, and that was the one where I wanted to move outside America as a race-based country, to a time *before*. *Before* . . . when white indentured servants and black slaves worked in the field together, *before* it was useful to separate them. And then the white people figured out something, that if you take poor blacks and poor whites, and make them hate one another, they will never attack *you*. You could manipulate *that*, and it has been working brilliantly for a long, long time. And the language is just full of it.

So when I was doing *A Mercy*, I did a lot of research about where those immigrants came from, what were they coming over here for. Well, land. They couldn't get it in England, the poor ones, it was all owned by the lords and so on, so they wanted land.

And as I am always able to tell people, my understanding is that, when the Declaration of Independence was written, Jefferson said inalienable right to 'Life, Liberty and the pursuit of Property'. Then he changed it – for which I am glad, because I would have been that property they could pursue – and he changed it to happiness, 'Life, Liberty and the pursuit of Happiness', which I thought was a little silly. Pursuit of happiness – who does that? Especially in the eighteenth century. Nobody's thinking about being happy. Saved, maybe, or secure, or comfortable. But that happiness thing has taken hold of Americans and they are very upset if they're not *happy*. I tell graduate students: It's not good enough. I want you to be happy when you graduate, but you have to be better than that. This world is interesting, and it's difficult . . . and happiness? . . . Don't settle for that. There's much, much more to work for.

Orhan Pamuk

with Peter Florence

Alhambra 2009

PETER FLORENCE: In the Nobel citation for Orhan Pamuk, the Swedish Academy likened his relationship with Istanbul to Dostoyevsky's with St Petersburg, Proust's with Paris and Joyce's with Dublin. Yes, the geographical references are acute, and also that is great company to live in. It's an astonishing honour to have a man many of you, and I, consider to be one of the greatest living novelists here as our guest tonight. Orhan, thank you for being here.

Let me start with a question that, as an anglophone who reads your books with great pleasure, I am slightly fascinated by. What is the Turkish language like to write in? How is it made, and what does it sound like for you?

ORHAN PAMUK: Before we go into the Turkish language let me be a 'politician' for the first and last time tonight. What a sweet beginning you just introduced. Thanks for the sweet words; it's a great pleasure to be here.

What was the question? Turkish language. Look, just before we came in, I said, 'Peter, are you going to ask me tough questions?' Just five minutes ago. And he said, 'I'm going to ask you about Turkish language first.' And I thought: My God, I'm in this forest, living in this forest, and only identifying the trees one by one . . . but I never noticed *the forest*, being *in* the forest. I'm a writer; I am *in* the Turkish language, I will be *buried* in the Turkish language. I am a part of it. It made me. But I cannot make, and I don't want to make, general statements about it. It is like my *body*, it is like my dreams, it is my secret poems, everything for me. It is my relationship with the world, the rest of the world. There is . . . our inner being, the sounds and sights and things we see and hear, then the rest of the world. The only way to communicate to the rest of the world, if you do not count pictures, images, is *this language*. I am in it, I am thinking of it all the time, but not as 'Turkish language', something else. So scholars, linguists, can make judgements on it. I'd rather not 'know' it. That I can *live* with it, that I'm happy in it, that it's like part of my body.

What I can say, is it works with suffixes, and the verb is at the end, and you add and you add, and eventually you will get there. It comes from Central Asia; in our history, over 2,000 years, everything has changed, but the language structure has stayed the same.

PF: What is your relationship with the Turkish literature which preceded your generation?

OP: The previous generation of authors, I thought, were more socially committed, more realist, and their examples were not the examples that I really cared about. That previous generation of Turkish writers was more interested in rural conditions in Turkey – poverty, hardship, hard life – what we today call 'village novels'. And there are writers who were influenced by more experimental techniques or focused more on individuals, on problems of being, existential problems. But they were always marginalized, and they were not at the centre of fiction, not at the centre of what the Turkish readership paid attention to.

PF: Your memoir *Istanbul*, which engages your childhood and your development completely with the city, continues your absolute, intense immersion of your own life into literature. Though you are often cited as a political writer, and you have been embroiled in large contentious issues, it seems to me that you are actually the most literary and the most *engaged* literary writer that exists.

Now, there are all sorts of dualities, of copies, of siblings, of twins – not literally twins but twinned characters – in your books. You wrote in your Nobel lecture of the writer's patient search for the second self. Could you just explain what the second self means to you, and your search for it?

OP: The joy of reading books is that you discover that, well, I think *I'm* like that, like *this person*, but I didn't know it. I think this is the essential joy of reading a good book, a fresh book – if you're not going to read the same detective book *again* – that revelation, that immense pleasure of reading good books, is that you sense that a part of humanity that exists, and that you identify is also within you but you did not *know* is within you, is now crystallized in front of you, and you think: I am also like that, but I did not know it. This person is very similar to me, but then the interesting thing is that he knew how to tell this simple fact. The concept of world literature is coined by Goethe: if you're going to talk about 'world literature', it is essentially based on the idea that the familiarity of another person's fictions moves our hearts and in fact seems so familiar – that is the magic of literature.

PF: Now allied, and running beautifully parallel, to that second self, is a constant source within your work of exploration of a divided or twinned self which seems to recognize the Eastern and Western meeting place in Istanbul.

OP: Let me continue with this, that in my books also, including in my Nobel lecture, I argue that sitting at a table, writing books, we discover that second self within ourselves, and that second self is richer. We all have our potential, but we explore it through literature. Literature – just as I refer to language – is a way of communicating that we know there is an endless self within ourselves. We know this through our dreams, through our angers, through our moments of loneliness. But only through an attempt to express it do we understand there is such a richer person in ourselves. We need patience, and a strong belief in literature, which also signifies that communication in depth, communication in all its richness, is possible. Once we have that, we begin, as we write, to explore another person in ourselves. Literature is possible because we *believe* that communication is possible with other persons, that, more or less – whatever the language, whatever the literature we believe in – more or less, humanity is the same.

The other self – that was a fantasy that I developed as I wrote in my Istanbul book. That is the essential truth about the desire to *belong* through literature. World literature is possible because everyone's spirit is more or less alike. That other worlds are possible, that this world that I am in may not be adequate, but that there is another Ohan some place, I will join him: this is a childish fantasy which I developed, perhaps because it also was harmonious with the Turkish culture, with being influenced by essentially two cultures, which was the Turkish situation.

PF: Tell me about *My Name is Red*, because, just as you can say that there is humanity that is recognizable across the globe, there is also humanity that is recognizable across the ages, and I'm fascinated by your engagement with historical fiction.

OP: First, historical fiction is a limited genre, I think. Readers who read historical books to gain information about past times or, more dramatically, to identify with people and see the world from their point of view and go back to, say, the sixteenth century, I think are misled. I don't think we can invent *that* much. Daily speech was not recorded before the novel was invented: inventing a fiction that took place in those periods is definitely inventing lies, but, on the other hand, there *is* a desire to see those ages through fiction, and I think such fiction is possible only the way Calvino did it. That is, open a parenthesis and say: this is fiction, this is my guess, and this is my playfulness of, say, the sixteenth century, fifteenth century.

PF: The essential issue of the book, which is informed by your early training as a visual artist, is about Eastern and Western representation, isn't it?

OP: I wanted to be a painter between the ages of seven and twenty-two. Then this or that happened, it's a complicated process, I stopped painting. I managed to establish myself as a fiction-writer, say at the age of thirty-five, in Turkey. I said: I will write a novel about painters. Then I began a novel that took place in contemporary Turkey, but I immediately realized that the problems of the *contemporary* Turkish painter will be the problems of originality, imitation, being derivative, being at the margins. I didn't want that. I wanted to write about the essential facts and joys of painting, how my hand waved and my mind was coming behind later, and looking at what my hand did with the brush and admiring it. This was actually my subject.

There is what we can call today Islamic painting, very similar to Western painting before the Renaissance – miniatures, no perspective, no representation of reality, illustrative – there is first text, then an illustration of it, most of the time ornamental. Western painting then and, say, Islamic painting are very similar. An immense change came after the Renaissance – the consequences, or ways of seeing the world, of what was invented in, say, Florence and Venice in the fourteenth and fifteenth centuries. The globalization of post-Renaissance painting, its philosophical consequences, were so important that, when I began writing about this subject, I realized I wanted to set my novel about painters, not in contemporary

Turkey, but in the past. I just didn't want identity-issues of contemporary Turkey to intervene in my philosophical story. I didn't want to write a philosophical story, but a story going towards a philosophy of ways of seeing.

PF: And at what point did you decide upon the unusual structure of having so many narrators for your story?

OP: It's not that unusual . . .

PF: I mean unusual for you.

OP: I wanted to tell my story through the points of view of many, many narrators, and consistently unreliable narrators, also through the point of view of a horse, a tree, a dead man; even the colour red speaks, saying: My name is Red; I want to tell my story. It's a joy to do that. I have a childish ease, an ability to identify with another person's point of view, and I think this capacity of humanity is what lies at the heart of the *novel*. We human beings have a strong power; we can also be moved by other people's pain, jealousy, desire; we can put ourselves in other people's point of view and identify with their spirituality, and our hearts can be moved by that. That's a very humane thing. The art of the novel is based on this very distinct human power, to understand others, to make a mental effort to see the world through another person's point of view. This lies at the heart of the novel. So why not go one further step, already done by William Faulkner? So I continued it and told my story, not in an artificial voice of first person singular, third person singular, a person who knows everything, but various narrators who don't know the whole truth; I like that.

PF: Can I move on to *Snow*? If you choose as your protagonist someone who is called 'Ka', you are, to anybody who has lived after Kafka, inviting a very particular resonance.

OP: I am a literary, bookish writer, but I know my readers will also know I'm a literary bookish writer, so that's the beginning. When I say: One day Ka was doing this, it's obvious, in the third page, to identify Kafka – so the reader thinks: Let's see what he will do with Kafka.

I wanted to write a political novel in the late 1970s, when I was in my twenties. But then I began writing a political novel, not a propaganda novel . . . we have to make this distinction too: there are very many political novels, most of them are propaganda novels with angers and agendas, but most of them end up only being propaganda novels. But there are some political novels which are about deeper issues. I had a hope of doing something like that in my youth. I began writing a political novel. It was, in a way, nostalgically, romantically, about my youthful friends – they were politically engaged, I was not. I was reading my Virginia Woolf or William Faulkner while they were reading their Karl Marx and this and that, but they were my good friends. I wanted to write a sort of generation novel, but then there was a military coup in 1980 in Turkey and I realized, although this is *not* a propaganda novel, the political authority would not allow me to publish it, and I would be banned. So I left it aside.

Almost some twenty years passed, but the desire to write political fiction stayed with me; this time the subject was not Communists or Marxists, but sons of rich bourgeois who were leftists, so this time the interesting subject was political Islam in Turkey. The influence of the Iranian Revolution was felt in Turkey, so I decided to venture into this very hard subject. I'm not a very religious person, but I began to read, I began to get engaged. I remember reading most of the small political Islamist magazines, newspapers, buying them every day, getting addicted to them, reading them, having fun, and I had a story. Then I decided to set this story in the most impoverished part of the country, tormented by all these problems that Turkey had: lots of poverty, and ethnic problems and issues of nationality, and military coups as well.

So I went to this north-eastern town of Kars, and imposed myself there just like Ka in the book, and began to get in touch with people. I had a video recorder; I was walking around the town. Most of the things that happen to my hero in the first 200 pages of the book happened to me – an upper middle-class boy from Istanbul who wants to understand.

PF: I picture you sitting in the flat in Istanbul writing, in long-hand on graph paper, the minutely and perfectly constructed and plotted novels. And then, from that outsider status, you become the Nobel laureate, and now you are a global superstar. You live part of the time in New York, you teach at Columbia, you have *millions* of readers rather than the hundreds of thousands that you had in Turkey, and for many people around the world their first access to Turkey is through you. How much of a problem is that for you?

OP: It is a problem . . . but to say, 'Well, I'm so famous – what a problem!' is so dishonest, because an author also *wants* that problem. But then, does the author want fame in that shape? is the question. Of course, I enjoy all the things you say, they are true – and I wanted them. To say that I just wanted to write books, to say that I'm so famous now that writing books is not easy, all that is partly true, but not a major problem. I hope *all* authors enjoy that problem [audience laughter]. In the end, you *can* unplug the phone, you just don't check your email, and this happens so easily, and you can continue writing your fiction.

I strongly believe that for me fiction has, thank God, this medicinal quality too. I have to be alone in a room every day, write fiction, imagine, believe in what I write, be attached to what I write, thinking: All my other novels were nonsense; *this* is the only thing I should pursue. That is such a joy. Then, yes, there are problems of being famous, or, more so, problems of living in a country where there are not many internationally recognizable cultural figures; these are problems, I know. When I talk to you, I am not at ease. One part of my mind is already checking it – will it be picked up by some bad-meaning Turkish tabloid in a headline? But then, it is now I develop that muscle. I think whatever the constraints are, we are free in the end. The joy of writing fiction, the joy of being creative – writing, doing any sort of art – is recognizing the constraints, hardships, limitations, and finding a way out of them.

Salman Rushdie

with Peter Florence

Hay-on-Wye 2012

PETER FLORENCE: This is the British Council lecture. It's the British Council lecture for two reasons. Firstly, because of what happened to Salman in Jaipur: the issue of censorship is not something we have to suffer here in Britain, for which we are deeply thankful, and we wanted to make clear that this is a platform, a platform that we share with our friends in Jaipur and our friends all around the world. Secondly, because twenty years ago Salman Rushdie made one of his very first public appearances after the *fatwā*, in Hay-on-Wye at this festival. It was wonderful to see him then, and it will be wonderful to see him now.

A quick word about the British Council. They are our Global Strategic Partner. They are in the business of cultural diplomacy, and they talk to the world in a way the British government sometimes doesn't, but in the way British art and British business and British enterprise hopes to. It's wonderful to have them on board, and on their behalf I would like to say good evening, Delhi, good morning, Bogotá, good morning, Mexico City. And good afternoon, Hay-on-Wye.

My guest is an extraordinary writer. He is an essayist; he is now a playwright, a movie writer . . . but fundamentally, and heroically, he is a novelist. Please give a very warm welcome to Salman Rushdie. Salman, good afternoon. It's very good to see you.

SALMAN RUSHDIE: It's always nice to be here, being dripped on . . . Hay-on-Wye, the Venice of the West.

PF: I feel with you, my cinematic friend, of all people, that we might perhaps start with the greatest question ever asked of a writer in public, which was asked in Graham Greene's pen to Mr Holly Martin's: Now, Mr James Joyce. Where would you put him?

SR: I read *Ulysses* when I was a kid, when I was twenty, I suppose, and had fantasies of being a writer. And, when I read it, I almost changed my mind, because I thought: What is there left to do? I think, in some ways, those of us who want to be writers have to recover from the scale of the achievement of Joyce, and begin to understand that there *might* still be small territories left for us to carve out for ourselves. But I was overwhelmed by that novel, and I've read it probably at least once a decade since then, and it never fails to inspire and challenge, and it's funny. It's one of the things . . . everyone thinks Joyce is so difficult, and so on, but it's not really – at least *Ulysses* I don't think of as a very difficult book. I think it's a very funny book. I have difficulties with writers with no sense of humour.

PF: Let's start with *Midnight's Children* . . .

SR: Well, I was born on 19 June 1947, exactly eight weeks to the day before the end of the British Empire, and my father used to tell a joke, which I never thought to be very funny: 'Salman was born. Eight weeks later the British ran away.' And that was not funny the first time, really, but the one-thousand-and-first time it grew a little old. But in some ways it helped me, that joke, because it made me wonder what would happen if there wasn't that eight-week differential. How about if the boy was born at *exactly* that moment? And I suppose that was the germ of the book.

PF: I think that the question that I *ought* to have asked is:

What was the tradition that you were both moving into, and working against?

SR: I was very lucky when I was at Cambridge that I over-lapped briefly with E M Forster. We were at the same college, King's, and I met him a few times, and he was interested in my Indian background and I was interested in his Indian back-ground, and I was a great admirer of *A Passage to India*. And I feel very lucky to have briefly been able to meet him. But actually, when I started to write *Midnight's Children*, in some ways I wrote it *against* the Forster project. That very cool, controlled, Forsterian English, which I admired in the book, felt to me to be not like the sound of India. India's not cool, it's hot. And I began to wonder what a *language* might sound like that was not cool but hot, that was noisy, and crowded, and vulgar, and sensual, in a way that it seemed to me that the Indian reality is. And that, in a way, is not represented by that Forsterian language.

And so, certainly, the language project of *Midnight's Children* was, in some degree, a conscious piece of writing against the language in which English people have written about India, most notably in *A Passage to India*, which I think is a master-piece, so it's not that I want to criticize the book. Sometimes you find out your voice imitatively, and sometimes you find your voice by direct influence and by trying to write like other people, and sometimes you find it by trying to write *unlike* people, and, for me, trying to write unlike Forster was a way in which I found out how to write.

PF: Can I ask about the second part of that extraordinary golden decade you had, and the novel that followed *Midnight's Children*? *Shame* was an angrier and more authorially dynamic book, in that you thrust yourself into it. What was it about the subject of 'not-Pakistan' that made you want to participate in it so much? Even though your language is present in every line of *Midnight's Children*, you don't get *Salman Rushdie's* voice coming in so commandingly.

SR: *Shame* came out in 1983 – it was the novel after *Midnight's Children* and before *The Satanic Verses*, and it tended to get squeezed a little bit because of that. Now, I find more and more people seem to be pointing to that novel as one of the books of mine that they like best; because the subject of Pakistan, I suppose, is in people's minds now around the world, in a way that perhaps it wasn't then, the book somehow seems more relevant or more apposite now.

PF: You were presumably buoyed up by confidence with *Shame*; it was extraordinarily well received. When you then embarked upon your next project, which was *The Satanic Verses*, what did you intend?

SR: I intended to write pretty much the book I wrote, which is primarily a novel about migration. I felt that I'd written these two novels, one of which was substantially about India, although some part of it takes place in Pakistan, and another novel which was substantially about Pakistan although some part of it takes place in India, and that I should now address the thing that had happened to *me*, which is migration into the West.

That was to me the very interesting phenomenon of the age in which we live, which I began to think of as the age of migration. The age in which we live is the age in which more people have moved across the world than in the whole of human history: there are more people now living in countries in which they were not born than in the rest of human history combined. And what that has done to our cities, to our cultures, is very profound. Walk down the street of any big city in the world now, and you see a pluralistic culture, you see a hybridized culture. And since I myself am a migrant – I'm a first-generation migrant to this country – it was something I wanted to write about.

A thing that happens to migrants is that they lose many of the traditional things which root identity, which root the self. The roots of the self you could say are place, the place that you know, the people that you come from, the community that you come from, the language that you speak, and the cultural assumptions inside which you grow up. Let's say those would be the four great roots of the self, and, very often, what happens for migrants is they lose all four of them: they're in an alien place, they speak an alien language, they're amongst people who don't know them, and the cultural assumptions are very different. And then the question that both individuals and communities of migrants have to ask themselves is the question of adaptation: what do you absorb from the world to which you come, what do you retain of the world from which you came, and how do you make that transaction in your new reality? Where do you root yourself? It's an act of radical questioning; everything you think you know about the world has to be questioned and re-examined and reconstructed. And so I thought: If that's what I'm writing about, if that's the phenomenon I'm writing about, then the novel itself should be, or should try to be something like, that act of radical questioning. It should question all those things about individuals, their beliefs, their behaviour, their assumptions, their morals. So that's the book I thought I was writing.

One aspect of that was to question the subject of belief systems, and that's the bit that some people didn't like. Other people, by the way, did like it, and I would just say the reason why books endure is not that people *dislike* them or that there's a *controversy* around them; the reason that books endure is that there are enough people who *like* them. It's the only reason why books last; it is the people who love books that make them last, not the people who attack them. So my hope for that book, as for all my books, is that they will survive because people like them enough and not because some people dislike them.

PF: You followed it with an exquisite novel for children, *Haroun and the Sea of Stories*, which is an argument for story-telling and for freedom, but is also a parental act of love.

SR: There was a moment after *The Satanic Verses* when it really wasn't that easy to get back to writing. Partly because of the daily circumstances in my life, but also psychologically, and I had made a promise to my son that I would write a book that he would perhaps enjoy reading, and I thought I'd better try and keep the promise. It was a way of getting back to work. It had its origins in stories I'd told as a father, but obviously it expanded into much more than that.

PF: Did the discipline of writing for the eleven-year-old child bring out anything in your writing that you think you've treasured as a result of that?

SR: I'd always been really interested in the form of the fable. I think some of the great literature of the world has used the convention of the fable: Kafka, for example – *The Metamorphosis* is a fable, there are the fables of Italo Calvino. One of the great things about the form is that it usually uses very simple language. It's formally and linguistically quite simple. But what it talks about is very often *not* simple, and it's that ability to say complicated, very difficult things in very simple language that the fable gives you. What's always been wrong with the fable, in my mind, is that it often leads to a simple moral: Aesop's fables all end with a simple moral. I thought if you remove that moralizing aspect from the fable and just use the manner of it, then it really allows you to write in a way where you don't have to make too many decisions about whether you're writing for children or grown-ups. You just write this very clear, simple, hopefully limpid prose, and through it you can say very difficult things, and it can be read by anyone who wants to pick it up. That was for me the key to that book, and a key that I held on to, and I might have used a bit later on.

PF: What contract do you think you make with the reader?

SR: Well, I think the thing that readers really want is a world that they enjoy inhabiting, and a guide through that world that they trust. By which I don't mean a character in the book, I mean the author. You want to feel: Here's an interesting place to be, and I'm in good hands as I make my way through it. Speaking as a reader, that's what I want, and I think it's a good idea to try and provide that if you can. If you do that, people will essentially follow you anywhere.

One of the things I've become more and more interested in is exactly in what sequence you tell people things, because the idea that linear narrative is the best way to write is one I've always rejected. It seems to me, as the King of Hearts says to the White Rabbit in the courtroom scene in *Alice* – the White Rabbit is a bit flustered having to give evidence and doesn't know what to do, and the King of Hearts says to him: 'Begin at the beginning, go on until you come to the end: then stop.' This is what we understand by classical form, and I've always thought it was nonsense. No reason to start at the beginning or to end at the end; you can start at the end and finish at the beginning, if you know what you're doing. You can have stories within stories within stories, if you know how to do it without confusing your readers. So I've always thought that that playfulness of form was more interesting than linearity. But I think, to make that work, you have to develop a very clear sense of how to tell the story in a way that doesn't con-fuse the reader, that doesn't put them off, that doesn't make them think: Why am I hearing about this now?' You have to bring them with you.

Owen Sheers

with Gaby Wood

Cartagena 2011

GABY WOOD: My name is Gaby Wood. I'm the literary editor of *The Daily Telegraph* in London, which is now the proud sponsor of Hay Festival. I'm more than delighted to introduce Owen Sheers. Perhaps it's not even an introduction, because I know many of you will already be familiar with his work. He has been a protégé of Hay Festival since the age of thirteen? . . . fourteen?

OWEN SHEERS: Fourteen.

GW: He was discovered as a teenage poet, much the best poet in any selection, and he's since gone on to write two volumes of poetry, an award-winning work of non-fiction about Zimbabwe, a novel, which he's going to talk to us about today, a novella, an anthology of poetry, TV series, radio programmes. And he's a great champion of, among other things, poetry in our country, and his poems are studied in our schools. So he's an important man, and also he's a great friend of mine. A few years ago we shared an office in New York, and I'm incredibly pleased to see him, and I know you will be too. Please welcome Owen Sheers.

OS: Thank you very much.

GW: So *Resistance*, a wonderful novel, has been turned into a film. Will you tell us first how the novel came about?

os: I always find that's a difficult question, because to travel back through time to that moment when a book starts to form in your head . . . I'm not sure how you find it, but you can quite often tell yourself *stories* about how a book or a certain project happened. So I always have to be careful to be as truthful as I can. And I think this novel, like many books, has three or four starting points. One was actually the landscape of Wales, the part of Wales where I was brought up. The prose book that I had previously written was set in Zimbabwe, and one of the biggest challenges of that book was to come back to Cardiff, where I was then living, and to bring the Zimbabwean veld off the page in a way that truly lived – quite difficult when you had Cardiff outside your window. So I was aware that, after writing *The Dust Diaries*, I wanted to try to write a story set in a landscape I knew very, very deep in the bone, because I think if you write from a landscape you know so well, you're writing with an incredible head start.

And then really a few things happened at once, and they were the sort of intersections of ideas that writers hope for. One was that I began to hear stories about the network of secret units, called the Auxiliary Units, which would have been the British civilian insurgency in the event of a German occupation during the Second World War. The existence of these units had been kept more or less completely secret, for fifty-five, sixty years, but around 2000 or 2001 some very old people were starting to talk about how they were recruited into this organization, really when they were children – sixteen, seventeen, eighteen years old. And then I became aware of another aspect of all this: there was a farmer whom I had known all my life, and when I went to talk to him, he explained to me how he was recruited, but most importantly, about what would have been expected of him in the event of an invasion: a young man – seventeen years old – from a very, very small village, who would have been suddenly thrust into these incredibly complex moral conflicts, one being that he was given a sniper rifle and told: this is not to be used against the occupying forces, not against the Germans; this is to be used against anyone who helps them in any way and could be accused of being a collaborator. And he said, 'There was no way, if I had had to use that rifle, that it *wouldn't* have been against someone that I knew, and at seventeen I would have been expected to make those choices.' The Auxiliary Units, I should say, were completely illegal, against all international conventions – a civilian insurgency, trained and funded by the government; but it was Churchill's baby and he was very keen on it.

Another of the fascinating things is that husbands, wives, parents, brothers, sisters, knew absolutely nothing about these people's involvement, so if they had actually had to go into action, which would have involved going into one of the 350 underground bunkers that were built all over Britain, in theory, wives and parents would have woken up one morning, and someone from their family would have just gone. And it was that fact that also began to fascinate me. And I realized then that, if I wanted to write about this, I could set it in the Black Mountains, which have a very specific historical pattern that I think really lends itself to this kind of story. And I realized that I wanted it to centre not on the people who leave, but on the people who are left.

So the book opens with six women who wake up in a very isolated valley one morning, and find that their husbands have gone, have left. And a few weeks later, a patrol of mostly very young German soldiers moves into this valley during what is a very harsh winter. I took the real winter of 1947, and just transposed it to 1944, because it's a novel and you can do that. Over the course of this winter, these two disparate groups, the occupiers and the occupied, are forced into a situation of, I suppose, mutual dependency, and when the spring comes some very serious questions have to be asked about what borderlines have been crossed and blurred.

GW: It's interesting that much of it is from the point of view of a woman, Sarah, who's been left. It's very vivid, your writing, not in the voice of the woman, but in the *mind* of the woman. How did you do that?

OS: I've got a very strong Welsh mam.

GW: [Addressing the audience] So it's all about his mother.

OS: Well, that's partly true . . . And I have some very good friends who are women, some very good readers who are women. But actually it's a question that I'm occasionally asked, and the most honest answer is that in the writing of the book it never really crossed my mind that I was writing in the voice, from the perspective, of a different gender, and I suppose I do believe that when it comes to fear and hope and expectation, deep down we are essentially the same . . . it never appeared as a serious obstacle for me, and it's interesting, the novella *White Ravens* that you mentioned is also partly written from the point of view of a woman as well. Maybe I should ask that question of myself more often. But . . . do people ask women novelists about writing in the voice of men?

GW: Maybe. I don't know. OK, fair enough, you're allowed. I'm not criticizing.

OS: I'm just in touch with my feminine side . . .

GW: And so when the idea of the film came about, you were the co-screenwriter. How did that process of reconfiguring the novel as a screenplay alter your view of it?

OS: I ended up co-writing the script with the film-maker Amit Gupta, and everyone told him: 'Never write a script with the original novelist. They'll be a pain; they'll be too attached to the novel.' And everyone told me: 'Just walk away. Just give the book over and walk away. You'll hate it.' I'm very pleased to say that we both ignored all that advice.

Amit is quite an experienced screenwriter, so he really held my hand through the early stages of the process and, to be honest, writing novels and poetry is an incredibly lonely business. It's thousands of hours of silence, and without those thousands of hours of silence you have no engine for your writing. So to actually go into a situation where I was writing *with* someone – I was anxious about that, but it felt like a real privilege. We spent a month working out the real architecture of the story, and that's when all the weak hinges become apparent, and there were many. And then Amit came over to New York where I was living and we sat in an apartment for a week, and we wrote the first seventy pages, and it was suddenly like being a married couple because co-writing is a prolonged process of gentle mutual criticism.

GW: Did you feel that the film still had your voice? Or did it not matter if it was yours?

OS: It's a really interesting question. The only way I was able to go into this process, which is a huge process of compromise, was to really accept the idea that in many ways I was the more fortunate person, because the novel was *there*, it was safe. In theory, they couldn't do anything to my novel. So once I knew that, I saw the whole process as a chance for experimentation, and really a process of translation. But you're quite right. The most interesting aspect of translating something from the page to the screen isn't so much what happens, or the dialogue; it is that *voice*. And to be honest, on the page, I wasn't sure how much that voice was there.

What was important was that Amit as the director had of course read the novel. As we went through the process, I kept being surprised by how influential the voice of the novel – in lots and lots of pages which aren't in the film – was for the cameraman, even for the composer, and now the film editor has the story, and I think actually this is where a film lives or dies. The film editor is the 'poet' in the whole process, I think, and I was very relieved to meet him and hear him speak very powerfully about the voice of the novel, and he said, 'That's what I'm going to try and do, find the filmic equivalent.'

But it is all about *equivalent*, and you do lose a lot of that in translation, but you also gain so much. I've got a huge appreciation now for film actors, who have to 'turn it on', out of sequence, when there's something that looks like a building site around them, and at their best these actors were doing, with a look or word, what I was doing in many pages.

GW: One of the things I wanted to ask you was whether the *core* of the book became transformed. I know you were trying to render the voice, and portray it accurately, but did you in fact have a complete new idea of what the book was about?

OS: I think one of the most interesting parts of the process of adapting my work was that the translation on to the screen really sent me back to my own novel. And it asked a very important question that every writer should ask of their own work, which is: what is this book actually about at its deep heart? I think once you have located that core, that heart, then that part of the book has to be kept safe; you have to make sure that core, that heart, stays true. And once you know what it is, you can change so much else. You could set this book in a different country, on a different planet, but for me what was important was identifying the heart of the novel and making sure that, each time we came up against a big compromise – if we'd lost some of our budget, or an actor couldn't come on a certain day, and we did have to deal with those practical problems, or if I had to rewrite – that is the question I would ask myself: is this rewriting in some way affecting the heart of this novel?

GW: And what *is* the heart of it?

OS: The heart of this novel ... it's about two people, Albrecht and Sarah, two people in a particular situation who have a very real connection on a very deep level. The situation that they're in could be anything, but for me the heart of the novel was about this concept of resistance, how much we are willing to sacrifice, what will be the nature of our sacrifice, and how the nature of that sacrifice alters depending on our idea of what resistance is. So it was about the relationship between those two people and what they both had to sacrifice, what they both had to lose. But, in losing, they became more themselves than they had ever been before.

Andrew Solomon

with Stephen Fry

Hay-on-Wye 2015

STEPHEN FRY: Welcome to what I'm reliably informed is 'Event 82', an event in association with the Wellcome Book Prize, which is a prize awarded annually by the Wellcome Institute, that really remarkable organization, for work that engages with science and medicine. In 2014 they awarded the prize to our hero here, Andrew Solomon. Andrew Solomon is an extraordinary writer and academic. Andrew, you have a position at Columbia University in psychology, and the other 'C' you attended was Cambridge University, where you got your PhD.

Andrew is a very academically respected worker in the fields of psychology, particularly, in the past, with his opening salvo in the field, *The Noonday Demon*, a magnificent book; I would call it one of the top five books ever to read on the subject of depression. His latest book is what we're here to discuss and celebrate. I think it's one of the most fascinating books on culture, society, and the mind that I've read. It's called *Far From the Tree*, and is about so many different things that I don't want to try and sum it up.

ANDREW SOLOMON: I must say, ordinarily when I speak about *Far From the Tree*, I am quite far from the tree, and so to have this podium on which I'm surrounded by appropriate foliage is an unusual delight.

> Even in purely non-religious terms, homosexuality represents a misuse of the sexual faculty. It is a pathetic little second-rate substitute for reality, a pitiable flight

from life. As such it deserves no glamorization, no rationalization and, above all, no pretence that it is anything but a pernicious sickness.

That's *Time* magazine in 1966, voice of the mainstream. And yesterday, as most of you probably know, Ireland approved the right to gay marriage by an enormous majority. And I set out to write my book determined to understand how we got from there to here. How something that, when I was a child, was universally understood to be an illness came, instead, to be understood as an identity, and how, if that shift had taken place, other 'illnesses' might be considered as identities.

When I was perhaps six years old, I went with my mother and my brother to a shoe-store on Madison Avenue in New York. After fitting our shoes, the salesman said each of us could have a balloon to take home, and my brother wanted a red balloon – and I wanted a pink balloon. My mother said that she thought I'd really rather have a blue balloon. And I said, 'No, no.' And she reminded me that my favourite colour was *blue*. The fact that my favourite colour now is blue, but I'm still gay, will give you some sense of a mother's influence, and its limits [audience laughter and applause].

When I was growing up, my mother used to say all the time: 'The love for your children is like no other feeling in the world, and until you have children, you don't know what it feels like.' And when I was very little I took that as the greatest possible compliment. It meant that bringing up my brother and me had been among the primary joys of her life. Then, when I was an adolescent, I began thinking: I'm gay, and if I'm gay I probably can't have children, and so when she said it, it made me anxious. And after I came out, in my early twenties, when she said it it made me angry. I said: 'You know that's not the path I'm on, and I want you to stop saying that.' But she never did. *The love for your children is like no other feeling in the world, and until you have children, you don't know what it feels like.*

About twenty years ago, my editors at *The New York Times*

asked me to write an article about Deaf culture, and I was taken aback at the time, really for two reasons. First, because I had thought of deafness entirely as a disability: these poor people couldn't hear … what could we do for them? And then, beyond that, because I'd been doing mostly foreign reporting. But my editor said to me, 'This *is* a foreign culture, in our own midst.' I went out into the deaf world, and I went to deaf theatre, and I went to deaf clubs, and I went into households where the alarm clock flashed lights instead of making a sound, and I even went to the Miss Deaf America contest in Nashville, Tennessee … where everyone complained about that 'slurry southern signing' [audience laughter].

And, as I immersed myself in that world, I came to understand more and more clearly that Deafness was a *culture*, a culture united by the shared use of sign language. I remember arriving at a meeting of the National Association of the Deaf, and thinking: I wish I were Deaf. Which is not to say I wished that I couldn't hear, because I make great use of my hearing and am very reliant on it, but I wished, in that instant, that I were part of the culture I was arriving at, because there were so many people, conversations flying off the ends of their hands, all engaged with one another, and while I could have spent years trying to learn sign language, I was never going to be a part of that unless I were actually deaf. So I saw it was not only a culture, but also a beautiful culture.

And then I learned that most deaf children are born to hearing parents, that those parents have, by and large, wanted to try to integrate them into the hearing world, and that many of them discover Deaf culture in adolescence, or thereafter, when it comes as a great *liberation* to them. And I thought how similar that was to the experience of gay kids who are born to straight parents, who often pressure them in one way or another to conform to what they see as the mainstream world, until those children discover gay identity in adolescence, or thereafter, when they find a great *liberation* in it. And then a friend of a friend of mine had a daughter who was a dwarf, and it turns out most dwarfs are born to parents of average height, and suddenly Lisa was saying: 'Do I bring her up to think she's like everyone else but short, or do I have to get involved with one of the Little People's organizations and construct some kind of a sense of dwarf identity?' As she narrated these concerns, I thought: Here it is again, here it is again – a family that perceives itself to be normal, with a child whom they perceive to be in some way abnormal, trying to figure out what to do.

It was at that point that I really came to the idea that there are two kinds of identities. There are what I have called 'vertical identities', passed down generationally from parent to child – so, one's ethnicity, one's nationality, usually one's language, frequently one's religion. Those are all things that a parent and a child often have in common. Now, we can say many of those identities are difficult, that it's still probably easier in the UK, as it's currently aligned, to be a white person and to be a Christian than it is to have dark skin and be Muslim. But nobody has proposed 'treating' that by getting medical advances that will allow us to ensure the next generation of children born to South Asian or African parents come out with blond hair and blue eyes. What we say is that we need to get to a more accepting place in society. But then there are what I call 'horizontal identities', horizontal because they're actually learned from a peer group rather than from your parents, and are therefore things that are often incomprehensible and bewildering to your parents. Those are identities like being gay or deaf or a dwarf, like being autistic or having Down's syndrome, like being transgender, like being a criminal, like being a prodigy – all these situations in which the child is not what the parents imagined *at all* when they set out to have children. And as I looked at these, I came to a distinction I had never before understood, which is the distinction between love, and acceptance.

My experience is that most parents love their children, but acceptance is a process and it takes time. It always takes time, even when the child is not exceptional in these extraordinary ways. When I understood that, it was a great liberation for me, because when my parents had seemed less than pleased about my being gay I had experienced it as a lack of love. As I interviewed the people for this book, I realized that my parents had always loved me, but took a while to *accept* me, and that everyone takes a while to arrive at acceptance, and, all things considered, they hadn't taken such a very long time.

Now I'm going to tell you the stories of some of the people I interviewed as I worked on the book, and I'll start with Clinton Brown, who is a dwarf friend of mine. He was born with something called diastrophic dwarfism, and his parents were told when he was born that he would never really learn to walk or to talk, that he would never recognize them, that he would never interact with them in any meaningful fashion, and that it would possibly be easiest if they just left him at the hospital, because he wouldn't live long, and he could die there quietly. His mother thought about it, and after three days she said, 'That's my baby, and I want to take him home, and I want to try.' And so she took this child home with her. Every doctor she saw told her about the complications she could expect, about everything that was likely to go wrong.

Then, even though she didn't have vast economic or educational resources, she managed to find her way to Dr Steven Kopits, the best doctor for dealing with skeletal dysplasias and dwarfing conditions in the United States. She described taking Clinton there when he was nearly a year old, after so many doctors had told her all of these bleak things. She said that she walked into his office, and he picked Clinton up in his hands, and he said: 'Let me tell you, that's going to be a handsome young man one day.' And she said that it was an extraordinary moment of revelation for her. In the course of his childhood, Clinton had thirty significant surgeries with Dr Kopits, as a result of which he is, in fact, now able to walk. And since he was stuck in hospital for long periods of time for

those surgeries, some of which were spinal surgeries and involved his being completely immobilized for months on end,
he thought there was nothing else much to do, so he might as
well do his school work. And he turned out to be better at it
than anyone in his family had ever dreamed possible, and was
the first person in his family to go to university.

He went to university not very far from where his parents
lived, and he joined a fraternity where he lived with his so-
called brothers, and he had a specially fitted car that could
accommodate his tiny physique. And one day I got a call
from Clinton's mother, and she said: 'I was driving home
from shopping, and I went past a *bar*, and there was Clinton's
car, parked *outside a bar*. And I thought to myself: He's three
feet tall, they're six feet tall; two beers for them is four beers
for him. And I wanted to go in there and interrupt him,
but I knew I couldn't do that, so . . . I left eleven messages
on his voicemail [audience laughter], and then I thought: If
someone had told me when he was just born that my future
worry would be that he would go drinking and driving with his
college buddies, I'd have been so *thrilled* to have that problem.'
I said to her: 'What do you think you did that allowed this to
happen, that allowed someone for whom the prognosis was
so dire, to emerge as a person who's popular, and successful,
and happy, and accomplished?' And she said, 'What did we
do? We loved him, that's all. Clinton just always had that light
in him, and we were fortunate enough to be the first to see it
there.'

There's another dwarf I know, a young woman whose
mother developed breast cancer, and the mother described
to me how, when she found out, she told her children about
it, and her daughter, Kiki Peck, who was nine years old, said,
'What happens now?' Her mother said, 'Well, I think I'm
going to be fine, but I have to shave my head because I'm
going to have chemotherapy.' Her daughter said, 'Well, I'll
help you shave it.' And her mother said, 'OK.' So they shaved

her head together, and then her daughter said, 'Now I'll shave my head.' And her mother said, 'What are you talking about? Why would you do that?' And her daughter said, 'I've spent a lot of time being different all by myself, and I know how lonely it can be, and I would like for you to have someone else who's different in the same way you are, at the same time.' Clinton and Kiki had not achieved a lot *despite* their dwarfism; they had become remarkable people in large part *because* of their disabilities and the ways they negotiated them.

Now I'm going to quote from one other magazine from the 1960s. It's an American magazine, but it was a view widely held at the time; it was written by an ostensibly liberal ethicist who said about children with Down's syndrome:

> There is no reason to feel guilty about putting a Down's syndrome child away, whether it is put away in the sense of hidden in a sanatarium or in a more responsible, lethal sense. It is sad, yes, dreadful, but it carries no guilt. True guilt arises only from an offence against a person, and a Down's is not a person.

Now, there's been a lot of ink given to the progress of gay rights; you've all seen reports of it in the paper – virtually daily. There's been much less coverage given to the *larger* social shift in our attitude towards difference altogether, a change in our understanding of what it means to have a society that embraces some measure of diversity. I spent a lot of time with families of children with Down's syndrome, even of grown children with Down's syndrome. There was one person I talked to who's worked in that community for many years, who described going out to lunch in Los Angeles with the actress with Down's syndrome who appeared in the television series *Glee*, and she said people were coming up and asking her for her autograph. 'She was a celebrity first, and a person with a disability second,' the social worker explained. 'I never thought I'd live to see such a day.'

People with Down's syndrome now live nearly twice as long as they lived when that article was published. They have educational attainments that were considered unimaginable. Their lives are utterly changed. Many of them are able to live semi-independently, and some have meaningful careers. I talked to a family who have a child with Down's syndrome, who would be, I guess, coming up to thirty, about what their experience had been; they were hard-charging Wall Street types when they found out that their son had this disability; they became involved in trying to advocate for change, with a group of other parents, because the educational options were so unsatisfactory. They hired a teacher and managed to con-vert a disused public lavatory, owned by the Archdiocese of New York, into a classroom, in which their teacher could teach those few children. That endeavour has since grown into the Cooke Center, where untold tens of thousands of people with intellectual disabilities have now been educated, and where some of the changes that have altered the lives of people with Down's syndrome have taken place.

I said to the parents of this child, now an adult: 'Do you wish your son didn't have it? Do you wish you could make it go away? This has been so much of your life.' His father said, 'Well, for our son David, I wish that I could make it go away, because for David it's a difficult way to be in the world, and I would like for him to have an easier life. But I believe that if all the people with Down's syndrome disappeared from the planet, it would be a real loss. So the social and personal wishes are not fully aligned.' And his mother said, 'Well, I'm the same, in that I think if I could cure it for David, I would, to give him an easier life; but speaking for myself, while I would never have believed when he was born all those years ago that I could come to this point, I have. For him, I would change it, but speaking for myself, it's given me so much more purposeful, so much more engaged, and in so many ways so much richer a life than I would ever have had without it, that

I wouldn't exchange these experiences for anything in the world.'

Now, we have a moment of extraordinary social progress, in which all these forms of difference are valued in ways that they used not to be. But we also live in a time of enormous medical progress. The cochlear implant, a device that can be surgically implanted and connected to a transmitter allowing sound information to bypass the ear and go directly to the sound centres in the brain: that has meant that many deaf children grow up effectively part of the hearing world. There's a compound called BMN-111; it blocks the action of the gene that causes achondroplasia, the most common form of dwarfism. Mice with the achondroplasia gene that are given BMN-111 grow to full size, and the drug is now being tested in human beings. Blood tests allow people earlier and earlier in their pregnancies to pick up Down's syndrome and other genetic anomalies, making it ever easier to terminate these pregnancies.

I'm a great believer in medical progress, and I'm a great believer in social progress. But sometimes they seem to be on a bizarre collision course, and I think, when I see these extraordinary triumphs of social acceptance, that some of the time it's like witnessing what happens in the last act of so many operas, when the hero realizes he loves the heroine at the moment she lies dying on a sofa.

I'm going to quote you from one other activist about the question of *cure*. This is Jim Sinclair, who has written about autism, and what he writes can be very powerfully argued.

> When parents say, I wish my child did not have autism, what they're really saying is, I wish the autistic child I have did not exist, and I had a different (non-autistic) child instead. Read that again. This is what we hear when you mourn over our existence. This is what we hear when you pray for a cure. This is what we know, when you tell us of your fondest hopes and dreams for

us: that your greatest wish is that one day we will cease to be, and strangers you can love will move in behind our faces.

Now that's a very strong way of articulating that position. And, because autism is a spectrum condition, the question of how one autistic individual speaks for the entire community is a very troubled and a very complicated one. But if you look at any of the conditions that I have examined, each contains a certain measure of what I think of as 'inherent pain'. I, for example, as Stephen mentioned, have written about depression. We can take all the stigma in the world away from depression, and it's still going to be a very disagreeable experience. Being depressed is very painful, it's inherently painful, it will always be inherently painful. The other part, though, is the social pain, and so I look at being gay. And the reason that being gay presents so much difficulty in the lives of so many people, and has even more so historically, is because of social intolerance. So it seems to me that we should aspire medically to treat the *inherent pain* of conditions, and that we should aspire socially to treat the *socially determined pain*, and that a distinction should be drawn between the two.

There are some aspects of autism that some autistic people find incredibly painful and difficult; there's a lot of prejudice against people who've got autism, and that's really a social problem, and the juxtaposition is sometimes very dramatic. I think, for example, of a woman who described having a daughter who, at the age of twenty-five, has spoken only three times in her life. She talked about the frustration of trying to figure out: Why those three times? There were three sentences, each of them situationally appropriate. Finally, she said, 'My daughter is the Zen lesson. Why does Cece have autism? Because Cece has autism. And what is it like to be Cece? Being Cece. Because no one else is, and we'll never know what it's like. It is what it is. It isn't anything else. And maybe you'll never change it. And maybe you should stop trying.' And that comes back to my theme of acceptance. Sometimes, it's helpful to cure a condition, sometimes it's helpful to accept it. And much of the time, you can't tell which you should do.

You have to, as a parent, change your children: not to is neglect. You educate them, you teach them moral values, you instil in them a sense of how to conduct themselves, you try to instil in them some manners. Not to do that is neglect. But you also need to make your children feel valorized, accepted, adored. Some things clearly need to be accepted, some to be changed, and many lie in a confusing middle.

Now, if some glorious angel dropped through the ceiling of this tent at Hay Festival, and offered to take all of your children away, and exchange them for other, better children, you'd cling to the children you have – at least *most* of you would cling to the children you have. And so it goes with these families and their extraordinary circumstances.

When I was working on this book I decided to have children myself. And people kept saying: 'How can you be doing that in the midst of a book about everything that can go wrong?' And I said, time and again: 'But it's not really a book about everything that can go wrong; it's a book about how much joy there can be even when everything *seems* to be going wrong.'

I will now describe my family in the most condensed way I can, by saying that my husband is the biological father of two children with some lesbian friends in Minneapolis. One of my closest friends from university in America asked me, after she got divorced, whether I would consider being the father of her child, and so we have a daughter, who lives with her mother, and now her mother's male partner, in Texas. And then John and I wanted to have a child to bring up full time, so we have George, of whom I'm the biological father; John is the adoptive father; we had an egg donor; and the surrogate was the lesbian mother of my husband's two biological children [audience applause]. So my shorthand is six parents of four children in three states. And there seem to be people who think that the existence of families such as mine undermines the integrity of families such as theirs, and I don't accept those subtractive models of love. Only the additive ones. And I think that, in the same way that we need species diversity to sustain the planet, so we need diversity of affection to sustain the ecosphere of kindness.

The day after our son George was born, the paediatrician came and told us that he wasn't extending his legs correctly, and that she thought that he might have neurological damage; then she said insofar as he was extending them he was doing so asymmetrically, and that indicated the possibility of a tumour or mass in his brain; and she added that he had a very large head and should be tested for hydrocephalus. And I remember feeling the whole of my being pouring out on to the floor, and thinking to myself: Here I am, in the midst of this book about how much value people have found in these lives with their disabled children: I don't want to join their number. We went off for an MRI and a CAT scan and X-rays, and an arterial blood draw (had I ever heard of *that*?). We went from thing to thing to thing, and I felt so helpless to protect this child less than a day old, and I felt such despair about what *my* life would be like and what *his* life would be like, and I realized that like all parents since the beginning of time, I wanted to protect my child from harm, for his sake and for my own. And yet even as we went through those experiences, I recognized that, if any of the things we were testing for turned out to be wrong with him, they would become his identity, and if they became his identity, they would become my identity too. And suddenly I heard a voice in the back of my mind saying: *The love for your children is like no other feeling in the world, and until you have children, you don't know what it feels like.*

At the end of four hours of this we were called into the consultant's office and she told us with some fanfare that the scans were all clear, and that George was now extending his legs correctly. And when I asked what she thought had been going on in the morning, she said that George had probably had a cramp.

I think children had ensnared me the minute I connected fatherhood with loss, but I'm sure I wouldn't have noticed that if I hadn't been immersed in this particular body of research. I had encountered so much bewildering love, and I was quite shocked by how easy it was to fall into its exquisite patterns. A lot of the time, for all the admiration in my prose, I had thought the parents I was writing about were ridiculous, trying to breed identity out of disaster and setting off on a lifetime's journey with their miserable children guided only by love. That day in the hospital I suddenly understood that my research had built a plank, and that I was ready to join them in their ship.

SF: Fantastic. Well, you can tell it's a remarkable book, and a remarkable series of people that Andrew found in the course of his long and detailed research. It's profoundly moving and raises extraordinary social, political, ethical questions ... We're having discussions now that are quite unlike any we had twenty years ago at Hay. The world has moved on quite extraordinarily in its acceptance, in its understanding of how diverse the human race is – it's not about ticking quota boxes, it's not about that at all. It's about understanding and embracing the full nature of humanity, and I think this book goes a long way towards that without being in any way po-faced. It's a magnificent, serious science book, scrupulous in its research, a long time in the writing, beautifully written, so accessible, charming and funny as the author is, so I can't recommend it more highly. And now, just before you go, I ought to tell you here about the collection, which is for the NSPCC, which seems appropriate enough, supporting every child's right to a childhood. I hope you'll support that.

Desmond Tutu

with Peter Florence

Hay-on-Wye 28 May 2009

PETER FLORENCE: Thank you very much for being here. It's a particular pleasure to welcome you to the Hamlin Lecture, which is graced by one of the world's great men. We are deeply honoured this year to welcome Desmond Tutu [huge applause].

DESMOND TUTU: Thank you . . . thank you . . .

PF: It's wonderful to see you. May I start in the deep end and ask you how, in South Africa, the Truth and Reconciliation Commission was such a success?

DT: Yes. I've got to say 'Good evening' first. Why are we sitting like . . . the last time I sat in this way was in the Oval Office [huge applause and laughter].

PF: Did you get what you wanted?

DT: [Laughing] I have to tell you this story of Jack, who was an even more inveterate name-dropper than I. Someone asked him, 'Jack, but man, why are you so fond of name-dropping?' And he said, 'Oh, that's strange, you know. Yesterday when I was in Buckingham Palace, the Queen asked me the same question' [audience laughter].
 Yes . . . I think we got to be able to do many more things than people had expected, but we had an enormous advantage. How many people have got a Nelson Mandela? I mean

we trumped everybody when he said to people: 'Let's try the path of reconciliation and forgiveness.' No one could say to him, 'You're just being glib. What do you know about suffering?' He would say, 'Twenty-seven years.' Twenty-seven years in jail. So he had incredible *credibility*. But I also believe that we've been the beneficiaries of incredible, *incredible* support from the international community. I mean, do you know of any cause, now, that has the same universal appeal? You could go anywhere virtually in the world, and you would find a group who said they are part of the anti-apartheid movement. We are the beneficiaries of incredible support and prayer. I think we weren't a scintillating success, but we did enough taking account of our past to be able to begin to move together into the future.

PF: You very graciously credit Nelson Mandela for this, but surely there is a wide partnership, an essential part of which is *you*, and I'm intrigued by the way in which you and Mandela worked together on this, and I would like to ask to what degree the entire process was informed by your *Christian* faith and his *political* activism?

DT: [Laughing]I have to tell you that I was a very, very good captain . . . You know, the successful captain is a captain who captains a winning side [audience laughter]. And this is not just being sort of falsely modest. We had, in the Commission, some incredible human beings – we had to hit the ground running, and it was just one of the most wonderful gifts from God that we had Alex Boraine, the deputy chair of the Commission, who was superb as an administrator. In next to no time he had got us offices all over the place, staff . . .

But your question is what my faith did. Perhaps we should say the faith of *all* of those people, you know, because I suggested that this was really far more a spiritual exercise, as it were, than a political. It was quasi-political and legal, but fundamentally, I mean . . . politicians don't *usually* have in their discourse reconciliation, forgiveness. That's not a normal discourse; it's something that you usually expect from *clerics* [audience laughter] . . . we had Jews, Muslims, Christians . . .

And when I wrote to the secretary general of the Anglican Consultative Council, which operates with the archbishop of Canterbury, I said: 'Please, on our behalf, can you write to all the religious communities and the monks and nuns of our Communion and let them soak this process in their praying.' And I also suggested to my colleagues that we ought to start our work with a retreat, a quiet day, and my spiritual counsellor, who was a very, very sensitive human being, was the person who accompanied us. So we went off to a retreat house and spent a time of quiet, together, before we even ventured into all the nitty gritty of the Commission. And they also agreed that, whenever we had a meeting of the Commission, at midday we would stop our proceedings and invoke the transcendent. I would ask, after a moment's silence, I would ask perhaps a Muslim, to collect our thoughts, prayers, in a summing-up prayer. And if you saw any television images of what we called victim hearings, we always began – I mean it was a ritual – we began with hymns, and we lit a candle in memory of all of the people who had died, as part of the proceedings. And that was an element that was quite crucial.

And when we finished the Truth and Reconciliation Commission, we went to Robben Island and said, 'Now we are having a closure, for ourselves, and for everybody.' And we had another retreat, this time at Robben Island. We went the into cells and sort of offered all of that up . . .

PF: I'm intrigued by the process by which you gathered different faiths into that process. How applicable is that interfaith togetherness to other conflicts that you now advise on through the Council of Elders?

DT: Well, I would certainly hope that . . . people have sometimes glibly said, because of September 11, that Islam is a violent faith. And one has to keep saying: Christians are the *last*
people to say that. I mean . . . we burned witches, we burned
those we said were heretics at the stake . . . I mean just *think*
of all of the wars, and then, more recently, the Holocaust –
it wasn't pagans, it was Christians. The people who were the
perpetrators of apartheid were not heathens. They said they
had the support of the Bible . . . The Crusades! . . . [laugh-
ing]. So we ought to be a great deal more modest, and actually
tread *very carefully*.

We were a diverse group. It was an incredible spread. Can
you believe that we actually produced a unanimous report?
And Kofi Annan summed it up in this way: 'The trouble is not
the *faiths*. The trouble is the faith-*ful*.' There are good Christians, and there are *very bad* Christians. There are good Muslims, there are *very bad* Muslims. I mean . . . have you ever met
the Dalai Lama?

PF: No –

DT: No, no, no [applause and laughter]. Well, I think he's one
of the holiest people I've ever met. He's been in exile over fifty
years. He's one of the most serene people you could ever imagine, and *bubbling* with joy – actually mischievous, and you
know sometimes when we are together I think: Oi, oi! The
cameras are on us; try to behave like a holy man [applause].
But, you know, there are some of us who imagine that when
the Dalai Lama appears before God, God will say: 'Oh, Dalai
Lama! Oh, you're such a fantastic guy, man. You really are a
wonderful chap. What a shame you're not a Christian.' What,
crazy! Most of us actually think God is a Christian. God is not
a Christian [laughing].

Yes, when we were struggling against apartheid it was
fantastic – we would walk arm in arm with a Muslim imam,

with a Jewish rabbi, because there is no faith that I know that propagates violence. There is no faith that I know that says it is a good thing to *murder*, it is a good thing to be *cruel*, and so yes, we were fortunate that we had this manifestation of different faiths represented in the Commission, and we worked together. We worked together because, I think, on the fundamentals, most faiths speak about a 'transcendent one'. Most faiths speak about the *absolute value* of a human person. Most faiths speak about the fact that this is not the end of the story. This life that we know, there is a better life in the hereafter.

PF: Can I ask you how, when the apartheid government were kidnapping and torturing and assassinating people, how, through the death of Steve Biko, through the death of Chris Hani, you maintained the conviction and the hope that good would prevail?

DT: Well, yes . . . My own life experiences, I believe, helped a great deal. I worked for the World Council of Churches; for about three-and-a-half years, I was working for something called the Theological Education Fund and our offices were in Bromley, in Kent. We were a very diverse team: there was somebody from Malaysia, who was born on mainland China, there was somebody from Brazil . . . we were a very great team, and our boss-man came from Taiwan. And I was exposed for the first time to liberation theology, and very soon thereafter I went to the United States and encountered Black theology, and realized then, much more than I had previously, just how explosive, how revolutionary our faith is, how revolutionary, like dynamite, our Bible is.

And then I also was very blessed to have met people like Trevor Huddleston, who was a major influence on my life, and then being trained for the priesthood by a religious community who made it quite clear that, for them, the priority was always the spiritual. But it was a spiritual that did not quarantine you from life. It was *precisely* because you had this encounter with God in prayer, in the Eucharist, in retreats and quiet days, in meditation, that you returned to have a concern especially for those who are God's favourites – the marginalized, the vulnerable, the weak, the poor. And it is a fantastic thing actually. In the midst of all of that darkness that we had, to be able to tell people that we were worshipping a God who was the God of this Exodus, who said, 'I have seen, I have heard, and I know. And I will come down.' I mean, it was almost as if the scriptures had been written directly and especially for us, you know. When you want to oppress people, the last thing you should give them is the Bible. If you want to succeed, don't, *don't* give them that, because where you had people saying, in their ideology, that the thing that invests people with worth is a biological irrelevance – skin colour, the Bible comes along, and it says: No, no, no, no, no. Not everybody is Black . . . but most are . . .

It is the fact that you are made in the image of God. And that is a fantastic assertion: I, little I, am God's representative. I am a God-carrier. When I was general secretary of the South African Council of Churches, I was also a rector of a little parish in Soweto. Most of my congregation were not very important people, and I was saying to them: 'Mama, when you walk down the street and they ask you, "Hey! Who are you?" you say, "Me? I am God's partner. I am God's representative."' And you could actually see the people in the congregation sit up a little more, and getting their shoulders a little squarer, and going out of church carrying their heads a little higher, because we had this incredible faith, this faith that said: Our God is not blind, our God is not deaf, our God is not stupid. Our God knows, and this God is going to come down. And when we still had Nelson Mandela and the other people in jail, it sometimes seemed like a pipe-dream. And then God came down, and God opened the prison doors.

PF: How is God going to come down to the people of Zimbabwe?

PF: As God always does, through others. The situation there has been a dire, a horrendous situation, and it is, in many ways, unbelievable that a country with so much potential, a beautiful country, could in a few short years be changed into a hell on earth. But now we've got what may be the best chance of salvaging and helping Zimbabwe return to her former glory, in this Government of National Unity. As you know, I have on many occasions said that perhaps we ought to dangle a carrot in front of President Mugabe, and suggest to him: step down. It doesn't seem like it's going to happen soon . . . because, I think, the generals are scared that if he does step down, then they are for the high jump.

PF: Do you talk to him?

DT: [Laughing] *Me*? Well, I used to. He seemed a wonderful person, and one has been shattered by this transformation. No, I don't think he would want to hear from me . . . I'm that little, bitter bishop . . . I'm sad for his country, but I am hopeful. And one of things that perhaps you very caring people might be able to do is to pressure donor countries, yours included, to increase humanitarian assistance, and even give a tiny bit more. The schools are a *shambles*; the sewerage systems are awful – you know, they had cholera as a result of the water being polluted. And I hope where you can, you can help Morgan Tsvangirai, because I think that if the electorate notices that things became better for them as a result of Morgan's being involved, it just might be that at the next election the result would be far more clear-cut than previously, and that there will be no doubt about who should be the president.

PF: In terms of God moving through other people, what is

your relationship with your own new president, and do you have his ear to guide him in dealing with Zimbabwe?

DT: Oh, I couldn't be so presumptuous – he's a very warm person, and he's a people's person, and engages people much more. He's very attractive, he's very, very popular . . . Thabo Mbeki spent too much time in England . . . [audience laughter].

PF: It's all right: we're in Wales [audience laughter].

DT: Yes, I think he imbibed a bit of . . . I mean, you're scared of carrying your heart on your sleeves, and so he was very reserved and . . . well, Jacob Zuma isn't, and what I hope is that we can all say: Let us give him the opportunity of having a go.

PF: You don't feel, from your churchman's position, any need or desire now to criticize his behaviour? You've accepted a pragmatic view?

DT: I've said my piece. And, remember: I am *em-e-ri-tus* . . . We have a wonderful young man who's archbishop of Cape Town now, and he's young, and he's handsome . . . I'm not jealous . . . no – but he's actually remarkable; he's in his forties or so, and already he has made his mark . . .

PF: I completely accept that you are emeritus, and that you are in some way slowing down, but not much. You are an advert for global travel; you are a world statesman; you don't seem to be in any way stepping back. Now, I know you've said you love, or are partial to, the limelight, but your position as a Nobel laureate conveys extraordinary power.

DT: Yes. I have said, I think that the Nobel Peace Prize does seem to impose an obligation on the laureate, and as you know there is this fairly new group called The Elders. Peter Gabriel and Sir Richard Branson are really the people responsible for thinking this up. They said: 'Ours is now a global village. In a traditional village, you used to have elders who were looked on as repositories of wisdom and experience. They are not any longer looking for kudos, they are not running for office; they should have an independence, be able to speak boldly in situations, and be able to act behind closed doors as well.'

So they took this idea to Nelson Mandela, and in 2007, on Nelson's birthday, it was launched. Yes. There are some quite remarkable people there who put their heads together and try to influence, sometimes very publicly, sometimes – maybe most times – by picking up the phone. If Jimmy Carter picks up the phone and says, 'This is Jimmy Carter', the person on the other side does not usually drop the phone. Or Kofi Annan or Mary Robinson. It is an interesting group of people.

PF: Your country gained immeasurable prestige and won many more friends even than it had before when it hosted the Rugby World Cup, and the abiding image of your president wearing the Springbok shirt is one that is iconic for our times. What is your dearest hope for the 2010 World Cup?

DT: Soccer?

PF: Yes. Beyond you winning it of course.

DT: Ah yes. You spoke about 1995; you've forgotten that we won the World Cup a second time.

PF: Yes. It's good of you to rub it in [applause]. It's hard for the Welsh, go easy on us.

DT: Sorry, sorry. I should behave more like a Nobel laureate [audience laughter]. Well, I don't think we are likely to win it. But short of that, I'm hoping that it will be something that demonstrates to all of us in the world that we're basically meant to be community, to be family. Enjoying competing with each other, but more than anything else knowing that despite the many things that distinguish us from one another, we are fundamentally one. You've discovered that science is saying you are all Africans . . .

*

AUDIENCE QUESTION: I want to thank you for talking about what is happening in Zimbabwe, my country. *Nothing* goes to my country. I believe personally, on behalf of Zimbabweans, our problems in Zimbabwe have partly been caused by South African leaders believing that Mugabe is a great hero for Zimbabwe, and this has not changed. My question to you, Desmond: is there a way you can use your undeniable influence to help the world to realize that we Zimbabweans are *there*, and also to persuade the South African leaders to understand that Mugabe is no longer the same person as he was before. He has changed. *What can we do for Zimbabwe?*

DT: Yes . . . I obviously feel very deeply with you in your anguish. And I have to say that some of the leaders in the southern region have been as you describe. But there are others who have been more straightforward: the president of Botswana, particularly, has been quite consistent; he said long ago that Mr Mugabe should step down, and he has been a lone voice. I believe that our new president is probably going to take a tougher line, but as you heard, I'm appealing, certainly, to you, our sisters and brothers, to try and persuade your own country, and where you have the influence to persuade other donor countries, to increase the support that they are giving to Zimbabwe.

But I don't think that we are going to see radical change until they have the next election, and we South Africans walk about feeling a deep shame, because we were – *awful*; I mean, last year we saw an explosion of xenophobia in our country that was just abysmal. It was one of the most awful moments in our lives. And The Elders, to whom I have referred, have written appeals to various leaders of donor countries asking them to step up their support. Clearly, though, they don't want to do that if the money is going to be syphoned off and go to the cronies of ZANU–PF; they do face a real dilemma. Do you send funds to the Reserve Bank of Zimbabwe when you know that the governor of the Reserve Bank is a very close buddy of the president? Very many in the world are with you, and we certainly would want to see the change happen.

PF: But can I ask . . . there is a lack of senior African leaders condemning Mugabe, and there is an argument to say that some form of physical intervention from a combined *force* of southern African states might not only be welcomed by the great majority of the people of Zimbabwe, but would establish a great international power within Africa that would be recognized universally.

DT: Yes, yes, yes.

PF: And that is something you might be in a position to encourage?

PF: You know, quite early on in this business, I said that all of us – political leaders, religious leaders, all of us – needed to hang our heads in shame for the way we had responded to such an awful crisis. And I have also said in the past that I would myself think that we might advocate a military intervention, invoke the principle of this new responsibility to *protect* – that if a country does not have the ability or the willingness to protect its own people, as has happened in Zimbabwe, then the international community is under an obligation to intervene.

PF: Do you think they are in this case?

DT: No . . . I've said, since we've had the formation of the Government of National Unity, that we ought to give that a fair chance, because it is probably the best chance just now of pulling it off. It doesn't mean you scrap all of the other possibilities, but you say: Let's try to make as sure as we can that this thing succeeds.

AUDIENCE QUESTION: Was the situation in South Africa forty years ago similar to the situation now in Gaza, and, if so, should peace come through similar means, that is, integration?

DT: I was in Gaza fairly recently . . . I was part of a fact-finding mission for the United Nations Human Rights Council . . . and it was one of the most eerie things I have experienced. We came into Gaza from Egypt, and we were in a UN convoy. Now, almost anywhere in the world, when children see a line of cars or vehicles, they will almost always, universally, rush out on to the street, to wave, or whatever. We must have travelled something like fifty miles or so – not a single child appeared, and Gaza City, which used to be the hub of economic activity, had very few cars on the road because they are not able to get petrol. Those who have cars use cooking oil. There are far more donkey carts . . . And we were supposed to go and make a finding on what had happened in Beit Hanoun when nineteen people were killed, and we went to the house where they were killed. And one of the mothers said: 'I picked up my baby as the shells were bombarding, and I had to scoop his brains from the floor.'

There are some incredible people in Israel; you might have heard of something called the Parents Circle Families Forum, which was started by a Jewish woman whose son was killed by a sniper and who said: 'I want to talk to the parents of the sniper' – from that encounter she knew the son of those parents was vulnerable now. From all of that they formed the Parents Circle, which is parents from both sides who have lost children as a result of the conflict. There have been very many who have refused to serve in the army because they have found that it was contrary to the best in their faith. And then there are the women who stand by the checkpoints and try to shame the soldiers into good behaviour.

I have sometimes said that I can't quite understand how people with their history could be doing this. But we human beings do in fact have short memories, because at home, we, *we* who have been suffering under apartheid – you go into some of our public offices now, and you find that Black clerks are behaving in exactly the same way as the Afrikaaners . . .

But . . . I believe that one of the reasons why God put the South African example as a small success was to give the world some tangible notice of the fact that there is no situation that is ultimately totally intractable, that the world could say: If they could do it in South Africa, then they can do it anywhere. I have a Jewish friend who's very good at aphorisms, and she says: 'Anything that has happened is possible.'

I actually think, you know, that the West feels a deep, deep shame for what it did or didn't do during the Holocaust. And that is right; we ought to feel that shame. But then, the penalty, the penance, is being paid not by the West. It's being paid by the Palestinians. When we were preparing and being briefed for this Beit Hanoun mission, we met with a number of ambassadors, and you know, the German ambassador said to us: 'Germany is responsible for two awful instances of suffering. Germany was responsible for the Holocaust, and Germany is responsible for the suffering of the Palestinians.'

I still myself believe that the two-state solution can be viable; a solution that says Israel is a sovereign state, that there will be a sovereign Palestinian state, and that Israel's existence will be guaranteed. And, as you know, the Arab nations have taken a resolution that cancels what they used to say in the past – that they would not recognize Israel. They now say they recognize Israel as a sovereign state. And so, if that is the case, it is possible. It is possible. But if we don't solve that problem, you can give up on all other problems. You can give up on nuclear disarmament, you can give up on ever winning a 'war against terror' . . . You can give it up. You can give up any hope of our faiths ever working really amicably and in a friendly way together. This, this, this is *the* problem, and it is in our hands.

Jeanette Winterson
Shakespeare in Space
Hay-on-Wye 2016

SHAKESPEARE IN HIS SPACE

Imagine him: he's twenty-three, the year is 1587, and Will is on his way to London. The journey took three days by horse, coming into the city via a night's lodgings at Oxford, then on to High Wycombe for a second night, and at last along what is now the A40, past the sleepy, sheepy hamlet (sorry about the pun) of Shepherd's Bush, past the gravel pits of Kensington, and towards Tyburn, where the hanging tree stood. Here the road parted – towards Westminster, or along the Oxford Road, now Oxford Street, to the city itself.

London was a medieval city, with its walls and gatehouses, London was a continuous city – it had been inhabited for 1,500 years when Shakespeare arrived. But London was something else too – a young and energetic city whose population had quadrupled in eighty years, from 50,000 to 200,000. And half of that population was under twenty. London was a loud, rude, intense, in-your-face, violent, raucous city. Everyone carried a weapon, including women – a rapier, a knife, a set of long pins concealed in skirts or hair.

And the city stank – of dung, of offal, of animals being slaughtered, of wood and turds burned on fires and of pigs and sheep roasted over the top, of tanneries and breweries, of smelting and tarring, of fish fresh and rotting, of the long dank smell of the Thames, of pie shops, of sweat, of breath, of sex. London was crammed with brothels. Prostitutes dyed their clothes with blue starch – the origin of the blue movie.

Brothels and theatres . . . The Rose – built over a brothel – held 2,400 people, bigger than the present-day opera house at Covent Garden. When the Globe was built on Bankside, it held 3,300 people. And the plays changed every day – in each of the four main theatres. Like London itself, the theatre was fast, restless, opportunist, often terrible – some plays only lasted a week because they were booed off the stage. But some plays were pretty good. Christopher Marlowe and Thomas Kyd were already in London writing for the stage, and, like Shakespeare, they were both in their early twenties. Shakespeare saw Kyd's *The Spanish Tragedy* soon after he arrived. Later he harvested its body-parts and called it *Hamlet*.

The playhouses were like echo chambers. If one had a hit, others would copy it – and writers worked in teams, like they do now on soap operas or long-running TV shows. Shakespeare wasn't a lone genius. He was a collaborator from start to finish. Forget the idea of here's a play, get a director, find a star and a cast. Theatre companies worked as a team. If you had a great clown you wrote more clown scenes. If you had a beautiful boy who could play a girl – women weren't allowed on stage – then write him/her better lines. If you had a powerful older male, give him a tragedy.

Shakespeare ripped off – or to be more accurate, riffed off – everything and everybody. Don't blame him. There was no time to wait for an idea. Life was now. If you didn't get stabbed or die of the French Pox – syphilis – the plague would be back any day soon. Life expectancy was short. Fifty-something if you were lucky. Shakespeare had seven siblings, none of whom lived out their forties, and Shakespeare himself was dead at fifty-two. Theatre was a way of cramming in more life to your short span, experiencing what you couldn't experience, loving where you hadn't loved, killing where you hadn't killed.

But there was more to it than time. There was eternity.

For those who have forgotten their *Horrible Histories*, remember it was Henry VIII who triggered the first Brexit

– the break with Rome and the Pope, that at its simplest allowed Henry to divorce Catherine of Aragon, and at its most complex changed the psyche of England. Shakespeare's grandparents – everybody's grandparents – were Catholic. You don't wipe that out with an Act of Supremacy. The old ways take a long time to be killed off. England was a Catholic country. Catholicism was, and in some countries still is, a flamboyant religion. Think about all the costumes, the ritual, the processions, paintings, frescoes, stained glass, statues, incense, music, pageant, drama, candles, saints' days, effigies. Like theatre, Catholicism had offered spectacle as well as story, and it had been completely successful at co-opting and rebranding every bit of paganism, from Christmas-tide to St George and his dragon.

When Shakespeare was seven he must have witnessed a strange sight. On the summer solstice, the longest day of the year, the church in Stratford upon Avon had all its stained glass smashed out. The lit-up saints and Bible stories – gone. The puritans in charge put in clear glass instead. The town stood in silent mourning. The stained-glass window that Shakespeare liked best was of St George slaying the dragon. Shakespeare loved that St George – and he was born, and died, on 23 April, St George's Day. Later, when he was rich and famous, Shakespeare bought New Place, the big house right opposite the church.

But first the little boy who had lost his dragon had to find a way in his head to put the window back. Put the colour back. Put the story back. Put the hero back. Put the monster back. Put the magic back.

And theatre offered all of that. Theatre was the best of church without the boring bits. It was a place to stand and stare. It was a place outside of the normal round. No wonder the puritans were always trying to shut it down.

When the Globe theatre was built – and Shakespeare was an investor in that – the name itself tells us how the Elizabethans understood theatre as a world in little, but also how they understood life – shadows, strutting players, brief candles. There was a sign outside the Globe that said *Totus mundus agit histrionem* – All the world is a playhouse.

This reading of yourself as fiction as well as a fact, as an actor playing a part, turns the stage into the play within the play. Every day is a play, and a part to play, and inside that, we go to the theatre to make sense of the parts we play.

And what does the play allow? There's a non-rational, non-linear capacity in art, and especially in drama where time itself is so compressed. The visions unfolding before us on the stage have a dream-like quality where events don't have to happen in the right order for the story or the stage-craft to work. But events and characters have to have *an* order that satisfies some deeper sense in us. Life isn't a how-to manual or a Seven-Step Programme or even something that can be learned. Shake-speare's theatre was not afraid of mystery, of non-logic, of the cruelty of chance, but it had faith too in the patterns we make out of chaos. Creativity is, above all, a shape made out of chaos.

Elizabethan theatre had very few sets or props. We think of the bare stage as something modern; it's not. Shakespeare's theatre used painted cloths to set a scene, but that's about it. Play companies were also travelling companies, and when everything you need has to go in a cart and be dragged to Stoke-on-Trent, you can't manage a fancy set. A list of props at the Rose Theatre included a cave, a bear's head, swords, stools, a well, a tree, a wooden leg.

In any case, with the play changing every day, there can be no such thing as a set. Theatre's beginnings were in strolling players, the village green, the town square, mummers, Morris dancers, the maypole, the Christmas and Easter street-pageants carrying the saint or the shrine through the streets. The spectacle lay in the energy of the actors, in singing, dancing – and language. Shakespeare's language was always a challenge. He invented words – torrents of words – faster than anyone. That's why *reading* Shakespeare can be so daunting. Plays are first and foremost to be seen as well as heard.

Shakespeare's writing life crossed the turn of the century and the turn of the monarch. Elizabeth, mysterious as a unicorn, died in 1603 and James VI of Scotland took the throne. James was obsessed with two things: uniting England and Scotland into what became known, for the first time, as Great Britain, and witchcraft. He had already written his own book on it – *Daemonologie*, and his first bit of business as king was to pass the Witchcraft Act in 1604: 'It is an offence punishable by death to conjure a spirit'. Unsurprisingly, Shakespeare soon wrote *Macbeth* for the king – with its three witches. *Macbeth* is the shortest of Shakespeare's plays, probably because James didn't like the theatre and had a short attention span. Shakespeare the showman just worked with what was there.

But he was working for himself too. He had enough money by now and he was in the last few years of his life. The late plays, as they are known by scholars, are a kind of code, as well as a coda. He revisits his own earlier plays and shows them to himself again. *The Winter's Tale* (1611) is *Othello* on speed. Everything that happens in the whole of *Othello* happens in the first part of *The Winter's Tale*. But this time the action turns out differently. At the end of the play, three women, three generations of women, are left alive on stage. Each of these women has worked separately, and together, to defeat the usual tragic consequences of male rage.

In the real world, of course, the most infamous witch trial in history was about to begin in Lancashire in 1612. It would be a long time before what Shakespeare understood about women, wisdom, and power, would find a place in the real world.

SHAKESPEARE IN OUR SPACE

We don't go to Shakespeare to find out about life in Elizabethan and Jacobean England – in the most basic sense, his
is not 'period drama'. We go to Shakespeare to find out about
ourselves now. As a woman, I find Shakespeare essential reading – his unfolding of the female was ahead of its time back
then, and it's unsettling now.

Women in Shakespeare are not there to make the guys look
good. In fact, it's the opposite. Think about inspired Helena
and swinish Bertram in *Measure for Measure*, truth-telling
Cordelia and vain Lear, loving Hermione and jealous Leon-
tes in *The Winter's Tale*, Viola versus Duke Orsiino in *Twelfth
Night*, Portia in *The Merchant of Venice*, or Kate in *The Taming of the Shrew*, Shakespeare's most troubling play if you are a
woman. Does Petruchio come out of it well? No, he doesn't.

In the creative industries men don't write parts for women
– we know that when we look at what's available to women on
stage and screen. Men are interested in each other and they
expect, without even thinking about it, that women are interested in them too. Women in the movies and on stage, with or
without guns, still work within a narrow stereotype of sexual
interest, kook, or Queen of Hell.

Shakespeare wrote parts for women who really are women,
not sidekicks or line-feeders or just pretty faces. Shakespeare
can do the Queens of Hell like Lady Macbeth, or Goneril and
Regan. He can do boy meets girl: he wrote the most famous
love story of them all, *Romeo and Juliet*.

But the girl, Juliet, speaks in poetry while Romeo speaks
in clichés. If you don't believe me, read it for yourself. Shakespeare knows that some women, like Desdemona or Imogen
or Helena or Hermione, will be fearfully wronged by their
husbands, that women are duped, beaten, raped, murdered.
If the men are forgiven it can only be by their women: Shakespeare's men are not let off because they are men. Shakespeare
brims with inadequate, tyrannical fathers – he was obsessed

with the relationship between fathers and daughters, again beginning with *Romeo and Juliet*, where Juliet is to be forced into marriage. Lear is the enraged father gone mad. We have to wait until Shakespeare's last play – *The Tempest* – before a daughter, Miranda, gets a father worth being born for.

Women – as daughters, mothers, wives, lovers, friends – he's lovely on female friendship – can find themselves in Shakespeare. Older women are here. Powerful women are here. Women who are unafraid of sexual desire. Women who must win the day by their wits. Shakespeare's women are not only the narrow consequences of their lives – though that is always present. They are the catalyst of the lives of others, and the emotional crucible of the men around them.

The women in Shakespeare invariably get the worst of the marriage bargains, in the sense that their men are not their equals. In the comedies, where everyone is supposed to have a merry dance and live happily ever after by Act V, the future – that is, the married future – is left open to speculation. We must decide how things will work out according to the evidence offered by the play we have just seen. In the most pessimistic comedy, *All's Well That Ends Well*, the devoted Helena ends up with a shallow cad whose own mother can't stand him. In *Twelfth Night*, the Duke counsels:

> *Then let thy love be younger than thyself,*
> *Or thy affection cannot hold the bent*

But this is a man who can't tell the difference between a boy and a girl, a man who never searches for an original line when a cliché will do.

Shakespeare – a good feminist – sings to women across time.

> *Sigh no more, ladies, sigh no more!*
> *Men were deceivers ever,*
> *One foot in sea, and one on shore;*
> *To one thing constant never.*
> *Then sigh not so,*

But let them go,
And be you blithe and bonny,
Converting all your sounds of woe
Into Hey, nonny nonny.

(*Much Ado About Nothing*)

Shakespeare, the national playwright, mentioned in the same breath as the Bible, was no poster-boy for marriage. At eighteen he had a shotgun wedding to the pregnant Anne Hathaway. She was twenty-six. They soon had a daughter, followed by twins. Four years later Shakespeare left Stratford. He returned once a year, and bought substantial property there, but he didn't live with his wife again for nearly thirty years. What was that all about? We'll never know. With Shakespeare, we can't use the life to explain the work. He thwarts our confessional reality-TV fixation with biography as truth. He stands against the current notion that autobiography explains imagination. It doesn't. It never did.

All we can say for sure is that the atom smasher of a writer's mind is where autobiography and imagination collide – in unexpected ways.

Four hundred years after his death, millions of performances and interpretations later, Shakespeare is still unexpected, still a surprise, still has that quality of extraordinariness that marks out the best writers. And, four hundred years after his death, we are in a world Shakespeare would recognize very well. Brexit.

Shakespeare grew up in an England still wounded, as well as bullish, about the decisive break with Europe. Shakespeare's last decade under James I was a decade politically obsessed with the unification – or not – of the kingdoms of Scotland, England, and Wales into a united kingdom. And faith wars. What is the Gunpowder Plot of 1606 if not religious terrorism?

James didn't succeed politically – there was no united

kingdom in his day. What James did leave behind was a huge cultural force – the King James Bible. We talk about the Bible and Shakespeare in the same breath because they *are* in the same breath. They are the same language. I can never forget, because I was part of it, that any working-class man or woman who could read at all had no difficulty reading Shakespeare. Why not? We were brought up on the King James Bible. Once the middle-class do-gooders modernized the Bible, they broke for ever a simple everyday connection with the English language and its power.

It's not that we go back to Shakespeare. It's that we have never left him. His world isn't doublet and hose and horse-back. It's nationhood, national identity, religious extremism, conscience versus authority. They knew how to deal with whistle-blowers back then; that's what the Tower of London was for. And James forbade any direct reference, in drama, to political events, and any insult to his person was punishable by a prison sentence or a slitting – nose or ears. Trump, Erdoğan . . . the vicious personal attacks from the right-wing press on anyone who speaks out . . . Look what happens to Falstaff when Prince Hal becomes Henry v. Falstaff, drunk, fat, loving, loyal, cleverer than anyone and addicted to words, can have no place in the regime-machine that will rewrite history. The Henry plays look like nation-building and jingoism – and they are. But there's a troubled current underneath about power and the price it pays – and the price we pay – for the strong man.

How are we to make sense of the human condition?

Shakespeare, skilfully political, the mirror of this world, dramatist of conflict, was also the poet of the inner world, the man whose great theme was the fate of love.

For this reason, when we leave earth behind one day, in triumph or in ruin, Shakespeare will be coming too.

SHAKESPEARE IN OUTER SPACE

Shakespeare's own time was the discovery of new worlds, the vast opening up of the planet, unimaginably big as it seemed then, the global village it has become now. Technology suggests that in another hundred years all humans will be engineered in some way – genetically screened for diseases, enhanced for performance and longevity, and wired permanently to a computing network.

Our world, like Shakespeare's, is changing rapidly. He was at the beginning of the modern world. We are at the end of that world, cusping into something as unknown to us as America was to them. Artificial intelligence and robotics. The end of work. Perhaps the end of money. Certainly the end of politics as it has been for a long time. Probably Google and Facebook and Amazon will offer to run the world officially, instead of unofficially.

If we are moving away from objects and towards experiences, then art in all its forms will become much more, not much less, important. The inner life is, by definition, invisible and portable. It comes with us. We will be our own streamed content.

If we are going to protect what is uniquely human in a future which is moving away from the uniqueness of the human, we need to protect two things: Love and Language.

Love is more than sex and self-interest. Love is more than an arrangement: in Shakespeare's day the question of marrying for love was just hitting the stands. Unrequited, wild, risky, all-consuming love had always been around, of course, but usually placed outside of the marriage bond. Marriage was pragmatic, commonsensical, about children and inheritance. Now we want it to be something different – we want friendship, a soulmate, as well as sex and passion.

Capacity for love means accepting that love might take us further than we want to go. Shakespeare, in *As You Like It* and *Twelfth Night*, with his boys dressed as girls dressed as boys, unsettles certainties of gender and therefore of erotic attraction. This unsettlement stretches across species, and is at its most playful in *A Midsummer Night's Dream* with Titania's drug-fuelled enchantment with Bottom as an ass. It's funny, but don't we pause for a minute to wonder about our own brief encounters, one-night stands, unlikely crushes, sudden desires and . . . the laughter of our friends?

Love is irrational, says Shakespeare. We try to civilize it, codify it, cheat it, explain it, contain it, but it remains the glory, terror and saving grace of the world.

Capacity for love and capacity for language have this in common – we can't do it alone. We learn a language easily when we hear it spoken. We learn to love in the presence of another.

Shakespeare believed – really believed – that if he could render the world into words, then we could hear it talking back to us. We could listen to ourselves as larger human beings. We can see our actions, follies, chances, lost chances, second chances. We could see our own cruelty and vanity. We're eavesdroppers on someone else's lives – except that those lives happen to be our own.

Language was never developed so that we could ask directions to the river or the cave. Language allows us to communicate at the deepest levels, with each other, and across time. Our ideas. Our vision. Our hearts.

Coleridge said of Shakespeare that he wrote 'exactly as if of another planet'.

Perhaps that's because that's where he's going next.

[Jeanette Winterson's lecture 'Shakespeare in Space' has been edited for publication by the author. The reference to Brexit is therefore one of happened rather than happening.]

NOTES ON CONTRIBUTORS

DAVID AARONOVITCH is a journalist, broadcaster and author. He is a regular columnist for *The Times* and a past winner of the Orwell Prize for political journalism.

GEORGE ALAGIAH is a BBC news anchor and journalist. He is the author of *A Passage to Africa* and *A Home From Home: From Immigrant Boy to English Man*.

NIMKO ALI is a social activist and co-founder and director of the Daughters of Eve, a non-profit organization that works to protect girls and young women who are at risk from female genital mutilation.

TAHMIMA ANAM's Bengal Trilogy chronicles three generations of the Haque family, from the Bangladesh war of independence to the present day: *A Golden Age* (awarded the Commonwealth Writers' Prize for Best First Book), *The Good Muslim* and *The Bones of Grace*. She was a founder director of Hay Festival Dhaka.

ANITA ANAND is a broadcaster and journalist and chair of BBC Radio 4's *Any Answers?* She is the author of *Sophia: Princess, Suffragette, Revolutionary*, about the Indian princess Sophia Duleep Singh, and co-author, with William Dalrymple, of *Koh-i-Noor*.

MARGARET ATWOOD writes novels, poetry, short stories, critical studies, screenplays, radio scripts and books for children. Her latest novel is *The Heart Goes First* (2015).

JOAN BAKEWELL is a journalist, television presenter and member of the House of Lords. She is President of Birkbeck, University of London. Her most recent book is *Stop the Clocks: Thoughts on What I Leave Behind*.

JULIAN BARNES's first novel, *Flaubert's Parrot*, was awarded the Prix Médicis (France). His novel *The Sense of an Ending* won the 2011 Booker Prize. His latest is *The Noise of Time*.

LAURA BATES is the founder of the Everyday Sexism Project,

a collection of more than 80,000 women's daily experiences of gender inequality. Her latest book is *Girl Up*.

ROSIE BOYCOTT is a journalist, publisher and author. She founded the feminist magazine *Spare Rib* and was a co-director of Virago Press when it launched in 1973. She has edited three daily papers and *Esquire* magazine. Since October 2008 she has led the development of a new London Food Strategy. She is a trustee of Hay Festival Foundation.

JIMMY CARTER served as US president from 1977 to 1981. He has championed human rights throughout the world and is the author of twenty-nine books, including *Talking Peace: A Vision for the Next Generation*. Since 2007 he has served as a member of The Elders, a group of independent global leaders.

JUNG CHANG is the author of *Wild Swans: Three Daughters of China, Mao: The Unknown Story* and *Empress Dowager Cixi: The Concubine Who Launched Modern China*. During the Cultural Revolution (1966–76) she worked as a peasant, a 'barefoot' doctor, a steelworker and an electrician before becoming an English-language student at Sichuan University.

HORATIO CLARE is the writer of two memoirs, *Truant* and *Running for the Hills,* which won the Somerset Maugham Award. *Down to the Sea in Ships: Of Ageless Oceans and Modern Men* won the Dolman Stamford Travel Book of the Year. He has recently written two children's books: *Aubrey and the Terrible Yoot* and *Aubrey and the Terrible Ladybirds.*

GILLIAN CLARKE was National Poet of Wales from 2008 to 2016. Her collection, *Ice,* was shortlisted for the T S Eliot Award and *Zoology* is due in August 2017. Her work has been studied for GCSE and A Level exams for thirty years. She has published books for children (*The Animal Wall and Other Poems* and *One Moonlit Night*) and has written for stage, television and radio. She was the first writer invited to the first Hay Festival in 1988.

HANNAH CRITCHLOW is a neuroscientist and teacher. In 2013 she was named as one of Cambridge University's 'inspirational and successful women in science' and the following year was named as a TOP 100 UK SCIENTIST by the Science Council for her work in science communication.

SONIA FALEIRO is the author of *Beautiful Thing: Inside the Secret World of Bombay's Dance Bars* and *13 Men*. She was awarded the Karmaveer Puraskaar award for Citizen Social Justice 'for drawing attention to India's most vulnerable and writing about them with sensitivity, humanity and integrity'.

NIALL FERGUSON is a historian, broadcaster and teacher whose books include *The Pity of War, The Ascent of Money, Colossus, The Cash Nexus* and a biography of Henry Kissinger.

CHRISTIANA FIGUERES is an internationally recognized leader on global climate change. She served as Executive Secretary of the UN Framework Convention on Climate Change until 2016 and directed the successful Conferences of the Parties in Cancún 2010, Durban 2011, Doha 2012, Warsaw 2013, and Lima 2014, culminating in the Paris Agreement of 2015.

PETER FLORENCE is Director of Hay Festival.

STEPHEN FRY is an actor, writer, comedian, director, librettist, quiz show host and compère extraordinaire. He has written five novels: *The Liar, The Hippopotamus, Making History, The Stars' Tennis Balls* and *Revenge: A Novel*. His autobiographies and memoirs are *Moab Is My Washpot, The Fry Chronicles* and *More Fool Me: A Memoir*. He is President of Hay Festival.

GERMAINE GREER is a scholar and teacher. She has taught English Literature at the University of Warwick and Newnham College, Cambridge. Recent books include *The Whole Woman* (1999), *Shakespeare's Wife* and *White Beech: The Rainforest Years*.

DAVID GROSSMAN has written about his native Israel in *The Yellow Wind, Sleeping on the Wire, The Book of Intimate Grammar* and *To the End of the Land*. His latest novel is *A Horse Walks into a Bar*.

YUVAL NOAH HARARI is professor in the Department of History at the Hebrew University of Jerusalem. He is the author of the international bestsellers *Sapiens: A Brief History of Humankind* and *Homo Deus: A Brief History of Tomorrow*.

SEAMUS HEANEY wrote more than twenty volumes of poetry and criticism, and edited several widely-used anthologies. He won the Nobel Prize in Literature in 1995 'for works of lyrical beauty and ethical depth, which exalt everyday miracles and the living past'. Heaney taught at Harvard University and served as the Oxford Professor of Poetry. He died in 2013.

CHRISTOPHER HITCHENS was the godfather of Hay Festival, a mesmerizing speaker and the author of many books including *Letters to a Young Contrarian*, *Hitch 22*, *Arguably* and *God Is Not Great: How Religion Poisons Everything*. He died in 2011.

ERIC HOBSBAWM was a historian of the rise of industrial capitalism, socialism and nationalism. His best-known works are the trilogy *The Age of Revolution: Europe 1789–1848*, *The Age of Capital: 1848–1875* and *The Age of Empire: 1875–1914*. He was President of Hay Festival. He died in 2012.

BETTANY HUGHES is a historian, author and broadcaster. She is the author of *Istanbul: A Tale of Three Cities*, *Helen of Troy: Goddess, Princess, Whore* and *The Hemlock Cup: Socrates, Athens and the Search for the Good Life*.

RAZIA IQBAL is a special correspondent for the BBC presenting *Newshour* on the BBC World Service and *Talking Books* on the BBC News Channel.

KAZUO ISHIGURO was nominated by *Granta* magazine as one of the twenty 'Best of Young British Writers' after publication of his first novel, *A Pale View of Hills*. *The Remains of the Day* was awarded the Booker Prize. His latest novel is *The Buried Giant*.

JUDITH KERR left her native Germany for Britain with her family in 1933 to escape the Nazis. She is best known for her self-illustrated children's books, the seventeen-strong *Mog* series and *The Tiger Who Came To Tea*, and the novels *When Hitler Stole Pink Rabbit* and *The Other Way Round*, which tells the story of the rise of the Nazis in 1930s Germany from a child's perspective.

GWYNETH LEWIS was the first National Poet of Wales. She has published eight books of poetry in Welsh and English, including *Chaotic Angels*, *Parables & Faxes*, *Zero Gravity* and *Sparrow Tree*. Her first non-fiction book, *Sunbathing in the Rain: A Cheerful*

Book about Depression, was short-listed for the MIND Book of the Year.

MARIO VARGAS LLOSA won the 2010 Nobel Prize in Literature. His early novel, *The Time of the Hero*, initiated a boom period in Latin American literature. His most recent works are *The Discreet Hero* and *Five Corners*.

IAN MCEWAN has written seventeen books including *The Cement Garden, The Child in Time, Enduring Love, Amsterdam,* which won the Booker Prize, *On Chesil Beach, Saturday* and *Atonement*. His most recent novel is *Nutshell*.

WANGARI MAATHAI founded the Green Belt Movement, an environmental organization that empowers communities, particularly women, to conserve the environment and improve livelihoods. She won the Nobel Peace Prize in 2004. Maathai was the author of four books: *The Green Belt Movement' Unbowed: A Memoir, The Challenge for Africa* and *Replenishing the Earth*. She died in 2011.

ROBERT MACFARLANE, a writer on nature and landscape, is a Fellow in English at Emmanuel College, Cambridge. He is the author of *Mountains of the Mind, The Wild Places* and *The Old Ways: A Journey on Foot*. His most recent book, *Landmarks* is 'a field guide to the literature of nature', collecting a glossary of terms used in different British dialects to describe terrain.

HILARY MANTEL is the author of thirteen books including *A Place of Greater Safety* and *Ink in the Blood: A Hospital Diary*. Her novels *Wolf Hall* and *Bring Up the Bodies* both won the Booker Prize for Fiction. She is currently working on the third novel of the series.

DAVID MITCHELL is the author of *number9dream, Cloud Atlas, The Bone Clocks, The Thousand Autumns of Jacob de Zoet* and *Slade House*. He has co-translated Naoki Higashida's *The Reason I Jump*.

MICHAEL MORPURGO's books for children include *Why the Whales Came, King of the Cloud Forests, My Friend Walter* and *Out of the Ashes. Private Peaceful* and *War Horse* are both set during the First World War. In 2003 he became the Children's Laureate. *An Eagle in the Snow* and *The Fox and The Ghost King* are his most recent works.

TONI MORRISON is novelist, editor, teacher, and Professor Emeritus at Princeton University. Her best known novels are *The Bluest Eye, Sula, Song of Solomon* and *Beloved*. In 2012, President Obama presented her with the Presidential Medal of Freedom. She was awarded the Nobel Prize in Literature in 1993.

JOHN MULLAN is Professor of English at University College London. He specializes in eighteenth-century literature and is the author of *Sentiment and Sociability: The Language of Feeling in the Eighteenth Century, How Novels Work* and *Anonymity: A Secret History of English Literature*. His latest book is *What Matters in Jane Austen? Twenty Crucial Puzzles Solved*.

ORHAN PAMUK is a novelist, screenwriter, academic and recipient of the 2006 Nobel Prize in Literature, the first Turkish writer to have been honoured in this way. He is the author of *The White Castle, The Black Book, The New Life, My Name Is Red, Snow, The Museum of Innocence* and *Istanbul*. He is the Robert Yik-Fong Tam Professor of the Humanities at Columbia University, where he teaches writing and comparative literature.

SALMAN RUSHDIE's novels include *Shame, The Satanic Verses, Shalimar the Clown, The Ground Beneath Her Feet, The Moor's Last Sigh* and the children's book *Haroun and the Sea of Stories*. *Midnight's Children* won the Booker Prize for Fiction in 1993. His latest work is *The Golden House,* to be published in autumn 2017.

PHILIPPE SANDS QC is Professor of Law and Director of the Centre on International Courts and Tribunals at University College London. He is the author of sixteen books including *Lawless World* and *Torture Team*. His latest, *East West Street: On the Origins of Genocide and Crimes against Humanity,* was awarded the 2016 Baillie Gifford Prize for Non-Fiction. He is Vice-President of Hay Festival.

OWEN SHEERS is a poet, playwright and novelist whose work includes *Skirrid Hill, The Blue Book, Pink Mist, The Dust Diaries,*

Resistance, I Saw a Man, the National Theatre of Wales plays *Mametz* and *The Passion,* and the BBC film-poem *The Green Hollow.*

ANDREW SOLOMON is President of PEN America. His award-winning books include *Far From the Tree: Parents, Children, and the Search for Identity,* and *The Noonday Demon: An Atlas of Depression.*

NICHOLAS STERN is President of the British Academy and was Chief Economist and Senior Vice President at the World Bank, 2000–03. His ground-breaking *Stern Review on the Economics of Climate Change* was published in 2006. He has published more than fifteen books, his most recent being *Why are We Waiting? The Logic, Urgency and Promise of Tackling Climate Change.*

FRANCINE STOCK presents *The Film Programme* on Radio 4. She has published two books: *In Glorious Technicolor: A Century of Film and How it has Shaped Us* and a novel, *A Foreign Country.* She is on the board of Hay Festival.

DESMOND TUTU is a South African social rights activist and retired Anglican Archbishop who rose to worldwide fame during the 1980s as an opponent of apartheid. He chaired the Truth and Reconciliation Commission and has continued to draw attention to social injustice. He has published several books of his speeches and sayings. He received the Nobel Peace Prize in 1984.

JEANETTE WINTERSON is a playwright, screenwriter and novelist, author of *Oranges Are not the Only Fruit, The Passion, Sexing the Cherry* and *The Gap of Time.* She has written the children's books *The Battle of the Sun, The King of Capri, Tanglewreck* and *The Lion, The Unicorn and Me,* and a memoir *Why Be Happy When You Could Be Normal?*

GABY WOOD is literary director of the Booker Prize Foundation, and was formerly literary editor at *The Telegraph.*